CW00607316

A Tribute to Caroline Benn:
Education and Democracy

A Tribute to Caroline Benn: Education and Democracy

EDITED BY
MELISSA BENN AND CLYDE CHITTY

continuum
LONDON • NEW YORK

Continuum International Publishing Group

The Tower Building,   15 East 26th Street,
11 York Road,   New York, NY 10010
London
SE1 7NX

British Library Cataloguing-in-Publication Data
A catalogue record for this book is available from the British Library.

ISBN: 08264 7493 4 (hardback)

Library of Congress Cataloguing-in-Publication Data
A catalogue record for this book is available from the Library of Congress.

Typeset by Tradespools, Frome, Somerset
Printed and bound in Great Britain

Contents

Foreword

Caroline Benn made an immense contribution to public life through her work on educational politics and as one of the leaders of the Comprehensive Movement.

She was a committed democrat, Socialist and internationalist and this book of essays dedicated to her life and work was the idea of Professor Clyde Chitty, her friend and colleague over many years, as a labour of love and to recognize her achievements.

The fact that so many people in her field have contributed chapters is evidence of the influence she had on those who knew her and worked with her.

Being an American she brought an international perspective to her work and made a special point of studying the educational systems whenever she went abroad, drawing parallels and noting the weaknesses and strengths that might contribute to improvements here.

For her the purpose of education was to strengthen democracy by giving confidence to everyone as part of providing access to the full range of knowledge in a fully comprehensive system throughout life.

She also came to understand very clearly that the British Establishment was deeply opposed to comprehensive education for exactly that reason, fearing that their power might be successfully challenged by a confident electorate.

She always took a genuine interest in everyone she met, listening and encouraging them in such a way as to give them confidence in their own ability.

She also had a great sense of history as revealed in her book on Keir Hardie which is the story of how the Labour Party came to be founded and her next book – unfinished when she died – was to have been about Socialism in America which interested her deeply.

Although a cautious and realistic person she was sustained by the belief that improvement was possible if the necessary effort was put in and in making that effort she did not spare herself, right up to the very end when she knew she was dying.

This book puts her life and work on record and I hope and believe it will encourage those who take up the same challenge in the years ahead.

Tony Benn

Notes on Contributors

Patrick Ainley is Professor of Education and Training at the University of Greenwich School of Education and Training. His research interests are the interface between further and higher education and training, flexible employment, privatization and the new market state. His many publications include: *Degrees of Difference: Higher Education in the 1990s* (1994); *Learning Policy: Towards the Certified Society* (1999).

Melissa Benn, daughter of Caroline and Tony Benn, is a writer and journalist who contributes regularly to *The Guardian* and *The Independent*. Her books include: *Public Lives* (a novel) and *Madonna and Child: Towards a New Politics of Motherhood*.

Tony Benn – a Cabinet minister in the Wilson and Callaghan Governments and one of the most influential socialists in Europe – famously 'retired' in 2001 after fifty years in the House of Commons to 'devote more time to politics'. He is a prolific author (his published diaries cover the period 1940 to 2001), broadcaster and public speaker. He was married to Caroline Benn for over fifty years: from June 1949 until her death in November 2000.

Clyde Chitty is Professor of Policy and Management in Education and joint Head of the Department of Educational Studies at Goldsmiths College, University of London. He taught English and history in a number of London comprehensive schools from 1966 to 1977 and was then Vice Principal and later Principal of a pioneering community college in Leicestershire from 1977 to 1985. He is the author, co-author or editor of over thirty books and reports on education, including *Thirty Years On* (with Caroline Benn) (1996); *Understanding Schools and Schooling* (2002); *Education Policy in Britain* (2004).

John Clay works in an Inner London borough as a Senior Inspector with responsibility for promoting Ethnic Minority Achievement. Previously he worked as a Senior Lecturer in Science Education at Greenwich and then Brighton Universities. He has written extensively in the areas of 'race', ethnicity and educational policy and is currently a Visiting Research Fellow at the University of Brighton.

Mike Cole is Senior Lecturer in Education at the University of Brighton. He has written extensively on issues of education and equality. Recent publications include: *Red Chalk: On Schooling, Capitalism and Politics* (2001); *Marxism against Postmodernism in Educational Theory* (2002); *Education Equality and Human Rights* (2nd edition, 2004). He is also the author of *Marxism, Postmodernism and Education: Pasts, Presents and Futures* (forthcoming 2005).

Rosalyn George is a Senior Lecturer in Education in the Department of Educational Studies at Goldsmiths College, University of London. Her teaching and research interests focus on issues of social justice and equity. She is an active member of the Anti-Racist Teacher Education Network (ARTEN) and has written collaboratively with members of the Hillcole Group of which Caroline Benn was a prominent member in the 1990s.

Andy Green is Professor of Comparative Education at the Institute of Education, University of London. His major publications include: *Education and State Formation* (1990); *Education, Globalisation and the Nation State* (1997); *Convergences and Divergences in European Education and Training Systems* (1999); *High Skills, Globalisation, Competitiveness and Skills Formation* (2001).

Roy Hattersley is a politician turned writer. He was elected to Parliament in 1964 and served in each of Harold Wilson's Governments and in Jim Callaghan's 1976–79 Cabinet. In 1983 he became Deputy Leader of the Labour Party. He has written 'Endpiece', his column for the *Guardian*, for twenty years, and before that was a columnist for *Punch* and *The Listener*. As well as contributing to the *Daily Mail,* the *Observer* and *The Times*, he has written fifteen books. He has been Visiting Fellow of Harvard University's Institute of Politics and of Nuffield College, Oxford. In 2003, he was elected a Fellow of the Royal Society of Literature.

Janet Holland is Professor of Social Research and Co-Director of the Families and Social Capital ESRC Research Group at London South Bank University. She worked closely with Caroline Benn as a long-standing member of the Hillcole Group. Her research interests centre on education, youth, gender, sexuality and family life. She is also interested in feminist theory and methodology and has published widely in all of these areas.

Max Morris is proud to have been one of the group of left-wing teachers who created and developed the idea of comprehensive education in the 1950s and 1960s. He has spent his life in education – as a teacher, teacher-trainer, head teacher and campaigner. Outside school, his life has been dominated by activity in the National Union of Teachers of which he was President in 1973 and is now a Trustee. His recreations are described in *Who's Who* as baiting the Department of Education, ridiculing Blairism and tasting malt whisky.

Maurice Plaskow was an active campaigner for comprehensive education from the 1960s onwards, working closely with Caroline Benn in the Campaign for Comprehensive Education (CCE), chairing CASE (Campaign for State Education) and STEP (Stop the Eleven Plus) in Surrey. He was Schools Council Curriculum Officer from 1970 to 1984 and in 1985 edited an important collection of essays, *Life and Death of the Schools Council*. He is currently Chairperson of the UK Education Forum and a Trustee of RISE (Research and Information on State Education).

Chris Searle, born in Romford, Essex in 1944, is a teacher, ex-comprehensive school headteacher and the author or editor of over thirty books. He has taught in East London, Sheffield, the Caribbean and Mozambique. In 1973 he won the Martin Luther King prize for his book *The Forsaken Lover: White Words and Black People*. At present, he is a Visiting Professor at the University of York in Toronto.

Jane Shallice has been active in socialist politics since the 1960s. She has been involved for the last six years with *Red Pepper*, both writing for the journal and chairing the Editorial Advisory Committee. Since September 2001, she has played an active role in building the anti-war movement and is the National Treasurer of the Stop the War Coalition.

Brian Simon, who died in January 2002, taught at the University of Leicester for thirty years, from 1950 to 1980. He will be best remembered for two things: his lifelong advocacy of equal secondary opportunities for all through comprehensive schooling and his four-volume history of the English education system covering the years from 1780 to 1990. His study of the emerging comprehensive school, *Half Way There* (co-authored with Caroline Benn), was first published in 1970. His history is a standard text and among the most translated of the forty of so books he wrote.

Sally Tomlinson is Emeritus Professor of Education Policy at Goldsmiths College, University of London and a Senior Research Associate in the Department of Educational Studies, University of Oxford. She has taught, researched and written for thirty years in the areas of education policy, race and education and special education. Her recent publications include: *Education in a Post-Welfare Society* (2001) and *Selection Isn't Working: Diversity, Standards and Inequality in Secondary Education* (with Tony Edwards) (2002).

Colin Waugh taught formerly at Brixton, Tottenham and then Barnsley College and is now a Lecturer in the School of Basic and Key Skills at the College of North West London. He is an editor of the magazine *Post-16 Educator*.

Geoff Whitty, a former comprehensive school teacher, is the Director of the Institute of Education, University of London. His main areas of teaching and research are the sociology of education, education policy and teacher education. His latest book is *Education and the Middle Class* (with Sally Power, Tony Edwards and Valerie Wigfall) (2003). His recent research has been concerned with the effects of marketization in education.

Susanne Wiborg works at the Danish University of Education in Copenhagen and is currently completing her comparative PhD thesis on the development of comprehensive education in Scandinavia. She has published a number of articles in English and Danish on comprehensive education in Scandinavia.

Introduction

Melissa Benn and Clyde Chitty

By any reckoning, Caroline Benn was an unusual woman. Born into a conservative upper middle-class family in the American Midwest, the eldest daughter of a Cincinnati lawyer, a conventional and protected life awaited her should she have wished. However, from an early age, this determined young woman knew she was different. Even as a teenager, she questioned many of the social arrangements she saw around her; in a sea of Republicanism, she knew herself to be an instinctive Democrat. It was a process of radicalization that was to continue throughout her life. While always cherishing the family, friends and wider community from which she came, her politics and her work increasingly took her into a different terrain. Her marriage to a progressive young Englishman, who became, partly through her strong influence, a committed Socialist, took her far away from the mores and values of her highly traditional background.

Caroline's interests were many and varied. A natural academic, she also had a deep and abiding interest in the arts and literature; as a young wife and mother she wrote a very funny and highly regarded novel. But in terms of her life's main work, education became her abiding interest. She had found her own private schooling stifling and rigid. Sent away to board for some of her teens, she became convinced of the importance of, and pleasure to be had in, a local schooling. Raising four children in the centre of London, she began to look around at what was on offer and to weigh up the virtues of private schooling, the grammar school option and the newly developing comprehensive movement which was gathering pace in Britain in the late 1940s and 50s.

By the early 1960s, Caroline and Tony had made the decision to send their four children to the local comprehensive, Holland Park School, a decision which caused something of a storm: in that period, most Labour cabinet ministers and many MPs still educated their children in the private sector. But both Caroline and Tony stood firm. They believed that if the Labour Party was advocating comprehensives as good enough for *other* people's children, then Labour Party spokespeople and especially leaders should act with principle when it came to their own children.

Caroline's subsequent involvement with, and commitment to, Holland Park in particular and the comprehensive movement in general was to shape her life and work for subsequent decades. A governor of the school for 27 years, and Chair for 12, she cherished her connection to, and work with and for, the school. But she also engaged passionately with the wider cause. Never a sentimental polemicist, Caroline preferred to serve and further the purposes of the comprehensive movement through empirical research, effective campaigning and use of her considerable political acumen. Education ministers and civil servants recognized her expertise – often far beyond their own. She produced an annual report explaining in detail how secondary reorganization was being carried out throughout Britain. So great was her knowledge that, in the 1960s, education ministers would telephone *her* for information as to how the comprehensive reform was progressing in various parts of the country. *Half Way There*, written with Professor Brian Simon in the late 1960s, and *Thirty Years On*, written with Clyde Chitty in the mid-1990s, still stand as the two most thorough investigations of the early and developing achievements of the comprehensive movement.

Through campaign groups such as the Comprehensive Schools Committee, the Campaign for Comprehensive Education, the Socialist Education Association, the Hillcole Group and many others, Caroline worked tirelessly to pursue her aim of creating a more just and creative education system, in which all children, not just a privileged few, could develop their talents to the full. She loathed the principle and practice of selection, which she believed damaged children and society as a whole. Religious schooling, too, offended her belief in the importance of tolerance and, given the class-based nature of so much of the process of selection for these schools, her commitment to the goal of social equality. For her, a fair education system was a vital part of a flourishing democracy.

She would have been deeply disappointed at developments since her death, under the aegis of New Labour.

Since one of Caroline's chief concerns was to see an end to all forms of selection at 11, she was obviously keen to find a fair and workable method for allocating children to secondary schools, particularly in the large cities. She believed firmly that when any school was allowed to act as its own admissions authority, the result was a situation approaching anarchy. Her doubts and misgivings about a structure of secondary schools described by Tony Blair as an 'escalator' were obviously shared by others. In his Brian Simon Memorial Lecture, delivered at the Institute of Education in London in September 2002, Professor Tim Brighouse, formerly Director of Education for Birmingham and currently Commissioner for London Schools, argued that Conservative and New Labour education policy since the early 1980s had resulted in 'a giddyingly steep pecking order of secondary schools'. It was time to accept that 'in the large cities, the comprehensive school in practice had all but disappeared, if indeed it had ever existed' (see Brighouse, 2003).

Professor Brighouse's gloomy analysis was based both on his own experience of running the education service in Birmingham and on the message conveyed by Sir Peter Newsam, formerly Director of the London Institute of Education, in a lecture delivered to the Secondary Heads Association Conference in June 2002. At this event, Sir Peter argued that, in terms of intake, English secondary schools could be divided, with some degree of overlap between them, into eight main categories:

1. *Category 1*: super-selective (independent or state grammar) schools, taking children almost exclusively from within the top 10 per cent of the ability range at the age of entry.
2. *Category 2*: selective (independent or state grammar) schools, taking children almost entirely from within the top 25 per cent of the ability range, including some pupils from the top 10 per cent.
3. *Category 3*: comprehensive (plus) schools, taking children of all abilities, but with the intake heavily concentrated in the top 50 per cent of the ability range.

4. *Category 4*: comprehensive schools, taking a balanced intake of pupils of all abilities.
5. *Category 5*: comprehensive (minus), taking children of all abilities, but with few pupils in the top 25 per cent of the ability range.
6. *Category 6*: secondary modern schools, rarely recruiting any children in the top 25 per cent of the ability range.
7. *Category 7*: secondary modern (minus) schools, having no pupils in the top 25 per cent of the ability range and with only some 10 to 15 per cent of their intake in the next 25 per cent.
8. *Category 8*: 'other' secondary or sub-secondary modern schools, having no pupils in the top 25 per cent of the ability range, having 10 per cent or less in the next 25 per cent and, most significantly, having the remainder of their annual intake heavily weighted towards the lower end of the 'bottom' 50 per cent.

Sir Peter did not provide his audience with precise figures for each of these categories, but the mere existence of Categories 6, 7 and 8 gave those listening very real cause for concern (see Newsam, 2003, pp. 17–18).

In the face of all this gloom and despondency, Caroline would have been heartened by the debate triggered off by a feature in the *Observer* of 29 February 2004, timed to coincide with the broadcast of a Channel 4 documentary on 5 March, 'The Best for My Child', presented by parent, governor and former Downing Street aide Fiona Millar. It was Fiona Millar's contention that the present system favoured articulate, well-informed and invariably middle-class parents. These parents clung to the notion that had blighted British education for at least a century: that excellence was the right of an elite few. To make the system fairer, all selection at 11 should be ended, while publicly funded faith schools would lose their right to select children by faith. Parents would still be able to express a *preference* – but pupils would be chosen either according to the distance they lived from the school or taking into account the 'feeder' primary school they had attended. Sadly, Caroline would have been totally demoralized by the publication, in July 2004, of New Labour's *Five Year Strategy for Children and Learners* (DfES, 2004), which envisaged the creation of a 'post-comprehensive' world by means of an expanded programme of City Academies and Independent Specialist Schools.

Caroline's American background, her considerable personal glamour, her wit and wicked sense of fun, her modesty and preference for collective working over individual 'stardom' in some ways served to obscure her extraordinary seriousness of purpose during her lifetime. This book of essays is designed to celebrate her courage and commitment; every one has been written in honour of a lifetime of work in service of the aim of a fairer education system and a vital, humane democracy. During decades of work dedicated to the cause of a fairer education system, there was hardly any aspect of education that Caroline did not write or think about: further and higher education, women and education, ethnic diversity, special needs, lifelong learning, and many many more.

In editing this volume of essays, we have tried to reflect the full range of her interests over a lifetime. In the first and most personal of the essays, Tony Benn pays tribute to her remarkable energy, her capacity for hard work and her extraordinary ability to keep in close touch with an ever-growing network of family and friends. As Tony points out, her scholarly approach to education and politics was combined with a keen determination to campaign actively and collaboratively for all the causes in which she believed.

In the second chapter, Melissa Benn examines current perceptions of the urban comprehensive school. She argues that in a society where so much of life has been effectively privatized, the local comprehensive represents something of a threat because it is, by definition, one of the few modern public institutions which cannot grant or deny membership on the basis of religion, class or ethnicity. One of the very real problems facing us today is how to create community and social solidarity in the face of so many potential causes of division.

These first two contributions are then followed by insiders' accounts of life at two of London's early comprehensive schools: Holland Park, where Caroline was Chair of Governors for 12 years,

and Willesden High in Brent. Jane Shallice describes the
excitement of being a teacher at Holland Park in the 1970s after
the arrival of a new headteacher who was determined to make the
school 'truly comprehensive'. This was a time when many teachers
felt passionately that old assumptions had to be challenged, past
practices questioned and new alternatives developed. At Willesden
High, which opened in September 1967, Max Morris had the
difficult task of amalgamating a grammar school, a technical school
and a secondary modern. He points out that after just five years of
its existence, the school was able to show that, as far as examination
results were concerned, those who would have been selected for a
grammar school education under the divided system had done as
well as they would have done under that system, while the rest, the
great majority, had done substantially better.

In the next chapter, Roy Hattersley makes the case against
selection, arguing that a divided secondary system fails to provide
the best possible education for the largest possible percentage of the
population. He suggests that in those parts of the country where
genuine comprehensive schools have been established, there must be
a real bewilderment as to why the end of selection is still a subject
of controversy. In his view, the comprehensive system both unites
the nation and confirms that we all have a contribution to make to
the well-being of the community in which we live.

These ideas are elaborated upon in an essay by Sally Tomlinson
based on her Caroline Benn Memorial Lecture delivered at the
Institute of Education in London in November 2003. This piece
argues that defence of selective education is becoming increasingly
untenable as there is accumulating evidence that selection lowers
educational standards overall and that even the most 'able'
students would progress as well in comprehensive schools. Sally
Tomlinson believes that New Labour under Tony Blair has a naïve
belief in the self-evident virtues of a meritocracy – a term invented
by the late Michael Young for his 1958 satire *The Rise of the
Meritocracy* – where those who succeed believe that they deserve
their privileges and status on account of their superior talents and
intellect as demonstrated by a high IQ and other educational
qualifications.

Following on from this, Chapter 7 by Clyde Chitty looks at the history of intelligence testing, and seeks to show that the mental measurement movement has its origins in concerns about racial purity and mental degeneracy. It is the contention of this piece that false ideas about fixed innate ability have been used to justify the allocation of children to different types of secondary school at the age of 11 and that the comprehensive school movement needs urgently to take on board the essential concept of human educability.

Finally in this opening group of chapters on issues related to secondary selection and the comprehensive school, Geoff Whitty's contribution also asserts that New Labour is committed to a meritocratic model of society and to a system of education that corresponds to that model. In a chapter that also began life as a Caroline Benn Memorial Lecture, Geoff Whitty argues that we need to welcome specialist schools into the comprehensive fold while, at the same time, taking seriously the issue of admissions policies and seeking to curb the excesses of the 'quasi-markets' introduced by the Conservatives and, in too many respects, perpetuated by New Labour.

The nature of the secondary school curriculum has been touched upon in a number of these opening chapters, and this is now the main focus of the essay by Maurice Plaskow. This contribution argues that the current content-driven curriculum with its accompanying assessment and examination systems does nothing to encourage a creative approach to teaching and learning. We need to re-examine the chief purposes of education in the twenty-first century and then devise appropriate curricula with suitable, flexible strategies for implementing them.

The chapter by Rosalyn George, based on a major piece of research, explores the perspective of a group of pre-adolescent girls as they transfer from their primary to their secondary schools. It was found that for this particular group, issues of curriculum and school organization were less important than the continuity and development of peer group relations and friendships.

John Clay's chapter looks primarily at the implications of two and a half decades of unremitting change for the training of teachers. Two case studies are employed to exemplify how new 'regimes of truth' are being constructed in schools and teacher training institutions.

With its ambitious title 'Rethinking the Future', Mike Cole's chapter operates on a broad canvas, focusing particularly on the commodification of knowledge. It is argued that education should not exist for the glorification of capital, of consumption, of commodification. Teachers at all levels of the system need to foster critical reflection, alongside an ongoing debate about all the alternatives that exist for running our social and economic system.

At the heart of much of Caroline's work was a concern with the issues of social inclusion and exclusion; and it is in this context that Janet Holland's chapter examines the complexity of youth transitions to adulthood. Drawing on a longitudinal, qualitative investigation of young people in five contrasting locations around the UK, the chapter makes use of a number of illuminating case studies to give the reader some idea of the complex routes that young people now tread as they take on adulthood and adult roles and responsibilities.

Moving on to the FHE sector, Colin Waugh's chapter argues that the all-important issue is whether or not we seek to promote an education that furthers the *self-liberation* of working-class people. It is in this light that Colin Waugh argues that 'Improving Own Learning and Performance' should be a mandatory part of the Key Skills Programme.

In his chapter on HE, Pat Ainley draws on Caroline's own thinking on the subject to argue that all universities should be 'free' in every sense of the term. There should be no separation of teaching from research; and all universities should be transformed into centres of lively discussion and action, tolerating and even encouraging 'subversive' thought and activity.

Chris Searle's chapter focuses on the experiences of those young Yemenis who came to Britain from the 1950s onwards seeking work and a new life as part of the post-Windrush migrations. The chapter makes extensive use of accounts by Yemeni ex-steelworkers who attended English classes organized through Sheffield's Yemeni Community Assocation.

Finally, a long and detailed chapter by Andy Green and Susanne Wiburg attempts to set issues of comprehensive schooling and educational inequality in an international context. In terms of education system factors, what the more egalitarian societies appear to have in common are all the structures and processes typically associated with radical versions of comprehensive education: non-selective schools, mixed ability classes, late subject specialization and measures to equalize resources between schools.

1 Caroline Benn

Tony Benn

When Caroline died in November 2000 one of the many obituaries suggested that she had exerted greater influence on the politics of her time than had any other member of her family. It was a recognition that in her role as a writer, teacher and Socialist, she had devoted herself to the promotion of lifelong comprehensive education, having written and lectured about it throughout her adult life.

She was also by far the greatest influence on *my* life and her scholarly approach to politics was combined with a deep commitment and a determination to campaign actively and effectively for the causes in which she believed; she was the most powerful partner that anyone could hope to have – supportive and knowledgeable.

In 1948 a young American whom I had met the previous year in the United States wrote and told me that he thought I would like to meet a friend who was coming over to a summer school in Oxford. This I arranged to do by making an appointment to have tea with her at Worcester College, and there, on August 2nd, we met and talked, and over the next few days we met every day. Our last time together was to have been August 11th, when I had to return to London and she was going to France on her way back to Cincinnati where she was due to enrol at the university for her MA degree involving a thesis on Milton.

I realized that I would never see her again and that this was my last chance to propose marriage. So just after midnight, when we had had an evening together and I was walking her back to her lodgings, we passed the Church where the Woodstock and Banbury Roads converge, saw three benches in front of it and suggested we sit for a moment, carefully choosing the centre one so I could always remember where I had proposed.

Then I asked her to marry me and after a pause of five seconds – which seemed like a lifetime – she said yes, and we wandered joyfully through Oxford planning to have five children. I saw her only briefly again before she returned to her family to tell them the news.

That is how 51 years of our partnership began.

I planned to go to America early the following year and we decided we would use the intervening time to write long and detailed letters to each other describing our own families and our ideas across the whole spectrum of thought, which we called 'the great correspondence'. From her letters, which were written with immense clarity, I learned a lot about her father, a descendant of a family of Huguenots who went to America after the Revocation of the Edict of Nantes in 1685, settling first on the East Coast. Ezekiel and Mary Baker Decamp, who were married in 1799 and had 17 children, went by covered wagon, in the early part of the nineteenth century, to settle in Cincinnati. In less than a hundred years they had nearly 800 descendants. Caroline's mother came from an Irish Protestant family, and her father and her mother's father were lawyers in the Republican tradition, which was not surprising since Cincinnati was the home of the great Republican president William Howard Taft.

Caroline's own religious tradition was of non-conformist, hard-working men and women and she and I shared a commitment to human rights, internationalism and democracy which we had acquired in a similar way, although we were born three thousand miles apart and could hardly have come from more different backgrounds.

When she was at Vassar, Caroline organized a national inter-collegiate conference on the creative arts in contemporary society and brought a number of distinguished artists, including John Cage, to the college; it was a huge success and is still remembered by those who were there even though, at the outset, the college authorities thought it was too political.

From her earliest years she was an independent spirit and in 1948 she voted for Henry Wallace as president at a time when Wallace, having been dropped by Truman as his vice-president, stood as a progressive independent and attracted the support of the Left.

I went to America in early 1949, earning my living as a travelling salesman for my family's publishing firm, and we were married in Cincinnati on 17 June 1949. After our honeymoon in Michigan we went off to a conference organized by the Summer Institute for International Progress at Wellesley College, returning to London by ship. Here Caroline began a second MA on the co-operation between Ben Jonson and Inigo Jones on the Stuart masques.

We first lived in a flat in Hammersmith; I got a job at the BBC and a year later, when she had graduated and I had been elected to parliament, we began a family. She devoted herself to raising them while supporting me in every way as a candidate in my constituency.

Her view of parliament was steadily transformed from pride when I was first elected to the conclusion that it was a place of comfortable royal ritual to persuade those who believed they were really engaged in some serious process of social transformation that they had 'arrived'.

In 1952 we moved to the house where I now live, and our older children went to a little private primary school but later all four moved into the state system and went on to Holland Park Comprehensive School which had recently been formed as a result of a merger of three other schools.

She became a governor of the School, where she remained for 27 years and chaired it for 12, attending all the meetings faithfully including those which dealt with the appointment of staff, cases involving the expulsion of children and matters arising from the premises. Towards the end of her life she set up an association of former pupils and searched them out to include in the school record.

One of her great interests was adult education and she taught first for the Open University, and later at the Kensington College, and her interest in her students was such that they kept in touch with her and she encouraged them and read some of their theses, commenting in a way that was both radical and helpful.

In the 1960s she began her work for the advancement of comprehensive education and the Comprehensive Schools Committee used to meet at home in my office. Its publications had real influence on Labour's education policy at that time. It later became the Campaign for Comprehensive Education (CCE), and Caroline was invited to become president of the Socialist Education Association, which now honours her memory with an annual lecture.

She came to know as close friends Professor Brian Simon of Leicester University and Clyde Chitty, then a comprehensive school teacher, and many others, some of whom are contributors to this volume, and later worked with the Hillcole Group on issues related to education and democracy. With Clyde Chitty she co-ordinated work on the Hillcole Group book *Rethinking Education and Democracy*, which was published in 1997.

The arguments against selection gained ground in the Labour Party and on the Left, and in her view constituted an integral part of the move to more democracy in society, which she believed had to begin in schools. She was co-opted to the Inner London Education Authority, was an ILEA governor of Imperial College and Mary Datchlor Girls' School, and wrote some very powerful articles against selection, including some shrewd comments on the idea that some children were especially 'gifted' and therefore needed to be taken out of mainstream education and given special privileges to equip them, as cadets, for the ruling class.

She wrote about the need for teaching about all religions in all schools which, in the light of the present tensions between Christians, Muslims and Jews, has acquired a special political significance; and kept in touch with people in Northern Ireland who were concerned to bring the education of Protestants and Catholics together. Caroline always regarded religious schools as doubly divisive on both a theological and class basis, since they were so often selective in character as well.

With Clyde Chitty she wrote many articles and they worked together with Brian Simon on the book *Half Way There*, which chronicled the advance of comprehensive schools at the end of the 1960s, followed by *Thirty Years On* with Clyde Chitty, which looked back on the achievements so painfully secured. The work on these books required the most thorough inquiry of comprehensive education developments in every single local authority so that people could check on how far their LEAs had advanced. She also undertook studies on the Youth Training Scheme and the Manpower Services Commission in the Labour Movement Inquiry into it, which were detailed, factual and very critical.

Whenever we travelled abroad her main interest was educational development, whether in Cuba, where the educational programmes brought in people from all over the world, in China, where during the Cultural Revolution the mixture of theory and practice was held to be so central, or in America itself where public education has always played a leading role. She wrote about these visits on her return.

Her campaigning was not confined to education. When President Kennedy was assassinated she was invited to join a committee to investigate his death, because she was very suspicious of the explanation that it was done by Oswald and believed there was some conspiracy involved. As a result of this she was advised by someone from the US Embassy that she should detach herself from it, which somewhat strengthened her resolve. Indeed she was listed as a dangerous 'red', ahead of me, in the Economic League blacklist of subversives, which ran to 22,000 people and was circulated to companies to alert them to the risk they ran if any of these 'subversives' applied for a job.

She had a number of death threats, and one was reported to the Metropolitan Police who took it up with the FBI, because it came from America. They then interviewed her brother in the mistaken belief that he had actually made the threat, and it took a lot to persuade them that they had got the whole situation wrong.

She personally suffered as a result of political campaigns by the tabloids directed against me, and by lies that were printed about her which, among other things, had the effect of damaging her independent position. The BBC once even refused to refer to a book she had written on education on the grounds that it was published during an election and the requirements of political balance meant that it could not be reviewed.

Her working methods were very interesting because she was essentially collective in mind and spirit and many of the articles she wrote appeared in the names of others with whom she worked.

Caroline was always modest and self-effacing and never sought publicity for herself, unlike many who are engaged in political campaigns.

When our son Joshua got a BBC computer in the early 1980s she began to work day and night producing papers and documents and these are still on the discs; later models included her last laptop on which she worked in bed late at night during her long illness. She kept everything and her archives run into hundreds of boxes, the responsibility for sorting having fallen to our daughter Melissa as her literary executor; her papers will be of real interest to future historians of the Comprehensive School Movement.

She also did a great deal of public speaking and to watch her on a platform was a unique experience. She would stand absolutely immobile, her voice so low as to be almost inaudible but every word was listened to with rapt attention because of the quality of what she was saying, which she had prepared with meticulous care and which, as a result, read well.

Caroline also wrote a novel called *Lion in a Den of Daniels* about an American couple who came to live in England, the husband Hank being very boring, his wife sampling London life and commenting on it most entertainingly. That book was also published in America. But her greatest work was her *Keir Hardie*, a biography to which she devoted many years, travelling in Scotland, where Hardie was born, to Wales, which he represented as an MP, to Europe to read the archives of the Pankhurst family and to America where Sir Norman Angell's papers are held by a university. The book was published in 1992, and widely acclaimed with reviews by Tony Blair, Gordon Brown and others which reflected the depths of her understanding, not only of Hardie and his family, but also of the formation of the Labour Party. It is one of the best accounts of how Labour came into being and emerged as a major force.

She even followed the story of Keir Hardie's family after his death, and his granddaughter and great-granddaughter, who now live in Boston, came to London when her book was published and attended a celebration in the House of Commons at which Betty Boothroyd, then Speaker, was also present.

The book also allowed her to understand the nature of the Labour Party and the way in which it had developed since, and gave her a great insight into the contemporary arguments which have always existed and always will exist within our broad church, stretching from Marxists on the Left to right-wing Christian democrats who from time to time have surfaced within the party.

One Christmas she gave me the *Communist Manifesto*, which she knew I had not read, a gift which indicated the serious Socialist understanding which underpinned her own political perception. Although she was never tempted to be a Communist she had many Communist friends, including Professor Brian Simon, and when their book, *Half Way There*, was about to be published in 1970 a security officer at the Ministry of Technology came to see me with an ashen face and asked me if I knew my wife had written a book with a Communist!

Writing about her in this way gives a less than adequate account of the nature of her life, for she was a wonderful mother and grandmother and was the centre of the family at every stage, from the birth of our eldest son in 1951 to that of her youngest granddaughter who was only four when she died. She wrote stories for them and listened endlessly to their accounts of school and their friends. She was a keen photographer and her archives contain thousands of photos, mainly of the family, which she arranged to be distributed to them after her death.

Her love of her family also meant she kept in closest touch with her American relatives, including her brother and sister and their children. When she went to America she would hire a car and visit as many of them as possible, keeping us informed of their news and them informed of ours. Caroline remained an American citizen, was devoted to Cincinnati, and the *Cincinnati Enquirer* arrived by post every day for years and she pored over it. She greatly looked forward to her visits home to see her family and friends and later going for the music festival held every year in May.

Another great love was Stansgate, the house that my grandfather put up in the 1890s and which was in a pretty poor state of repair. She had it refurbished and her great pride and joy was an eight-acre field which she converted into a nature reserve.

She was very fond of music, especially opera, and with close friends would go regularly to the opera in London and to the Wexford Music Festival in Ireland, not to mention her trips to Cincinnati. She was also very interested in architecture and one of her very best friends, Peter Carter, together with an old college contemporary, Phyllis Lambert, always discussed their architectural projects with her. She was very proud to have been put on a panel one year to pick the best modern building.

She had a capacity for friendship which was quite phenomenal and she kept up a constant correspondence, so that a mass of letters would be received regularly and she would read all of them with care and write back fully. One man in Hungary who had read her *Keir Hardie* wrote with some information she did not have, and she kept up a correspondence with him. His Socialist magazine, with references to her in it, still comes to the house.

When she was in hospital in the last stages of her cancer one of the young cleaners turned out to have come from Columbia, and she was soon in deep conversation with him about the way the Left was treated there by the Government.

The greatest challenge in her life came with her cancer which was diagnosed late because it was then the practice not to offer a breast scan to anyone over 65. By the time it had been diagnosed, she learned that it had spread to the spine and knew in her heart that it was terminal, even though I liked to believe she might recover, and she never discouraged my hopes. She had the gift of eternal youth and even in the last months, when she was racked by pain, she looked young and often radiant. But she admonished those who said that to her, on the grounds that it was ageist – what was wrong with being in your mid 70s!

She tackled the question of her illness in a typically academic way, acquiring a huge library of books about cancer and searching the internet with the help of my son for reports of the latest treatments and taking them back to her consultant who became rather nervous of this lady who would question him about a research paper published the previous week by a doctor at an American university who claimed to be able to throw some light on her condition. When her friend Clyde was diagnosed as having prostate cancer, she spent hours looking for articles on the subject and passing them on to him.

She bore her disabilities with great courage and the house became full of equipment – wheelchair, hoists to get her in and out of the bath, and a chair which carried her up to the first floor. She took it all with great good humour, and on one occasion when the SEA (Socialist Educational Association) was meeting in the garden to which she had no access, she sat at the window in the first floor and joined in the discussion, planning a conference which was held just after her death.

It is only fair to say that she was bitterly disappointed by the education policy of the New Labour Government elected in 1997 which she felt had completely abandoned the comprehensive idea, and was committed to selection, the main influence for which she believed came from the educational adviser at Number 10, whom she had met and from whom so many of the present policies seem to have sprung. Her death did at least spare her from hearing about the growth of selection and religious schools which she regarded as divisive, reversing the generation of progressive thinking beginning when the National Association of Labour Teachers was set up in the 1930s. But her real joy remained the family and her books which still cram our shelves at home, her gardening and music and above all her friends who sustained her, as we all tried to do.

Her interest in education was transmitted to all our children, expressing itself in some of the work they did. Stephen was co-opted to the Inner London Education Authority, as she had been herself, and his work at the Royal Society of Chemistry where he is the parliamentary officer has concentrated on the need to encourage young scientists. Hilary, now in the Cabinet, was elected to the Ealing Council and became Chair of Education, subsequently working as an adviser to David Blunkett in his early years as Secretary of State for Education. Melissa has lectured at the City University on the history and practice of journalism and runs workshops for aspiring writers. Joshua was one of the first pioneers of computer use and trained many journalists in the use of computers in those early years. Indeed it was his training that brought Caroline from a very non-technical view of life to an understanding of the importance of this great new tool, which she used for her own writing.

When Caroline said that I should explain that I was leaving Parliament to devote more time to politics she launched me into a series of public lectures and to the discovery that the function of the old is to encourage people by acting as a teacher, even if only as an untrained classroom assistant.

She was a very remarkable woman, tough-minded and clear, independent in thought and action and with a capacity for caring which impressed itself on everyone she met. A memorial lecture every year has been established in her memory and I am regularly asked at public meetings what Caroline would have thought of this or that, and to autograph a copy of her *Keir Hardie*. It is an indication of the fondness and respect with which she will always be remembered by those in the Labour Movement whom she knew and loved.

Her advice to me checking my texts when I gave them to her was always based upon an enquiry into what I really wanted to say which she managed to disentangle from a mass of verbiage and make clear. She was very critical when she thought I was wrong and all the mistakes I made in my life were made when I rejected her advice.

Like every person who has a politically active partner she paid a heavy price in that, inevitably, her own work was often overshadowed and she was sucked into controversy that diverted attention away from her own formidable political contribution, and her account of Keir Hardie illustrated that in a very vivid way.

But it would be totally inadequate to end an account of her life without highlighting the fact that she was such fun to be with and her friendships were kept alive by her intense interest in every one she knew as well as in the work and lives of our children and grandchildren. Looking back on our years together that is the greatest loss of all for me, and for everyone who knew her.

Her ashes are buried in our garden at Stansgate and next to it is the bench where I had proposed to her.

I can never record or repay the debt I owe her and was sustained, when she died, by a huge flood of letters from people who recalled meeting her, reading her work or in some way being influenced by something she had said or done.

That and this book are some recognition of her life's work and I have been proud to have been asked to contribute this chapter and grateful to those who have agreed to write about her.

2 On Dreams and Dilemmas, Class and Cities: Some Thoughts on the Modern Politics of Comprehensives

Melissa Benn

INTRODUCTION

In many ways, I am the child of a dream. Born in the late 1950s, at the very time when the fledgling comprehensive ideal was taking root, my three brothers and I were mostly educated at local state schools. Nothing particularly unusual about that – except that all four of us had been taken out of the private sector in order to 'go comprehensive', a decision made on grounds of principle, not pragmatism, and one which, at the time, provoked considerable public and private comment and, often, enormous consternation. Family, friends and complete strangers warned of the risk this decision posed to our futures: of the human sacrifice our parents were making to a worthy but dangerous ideal. But our parents' commitment to local schools remained unswerving; my mother, Caroline Benn, became one of the most outspoken advocates of the comprehensive movement from the 1960s onwards, a cause into which she poured her considerable scholarly and strategic talents.

Thirty years or so on, I am now at mid-life, with two young children who are also at a local school. Revisiting the educational world as a parent has been an interesting experience. It has made me realize not only how deeply and unshakeably the comprehensive ideal has lodged itself in me but also how powerful and potentially disturbing this same ideal continues to be to so many others. Unlike the National Health Service or the principle of state education generally, both of which enjoy widespread popular support, the concept of the comprehensive can arouse intense fear and loathing, often to an inexplicable degree. In this chapter, I want to explore some of the hidden and not-so-hidden anxieties behind these modern antagonisms, and to say a little about why I still believe so strongly in the comprehensive ideal in these rather tetchy, highly pragmatic times.

CURRENT DILEMMAS

One of the difficulties that faces anyone with strong beliefs about the merits of the comprehensive system is that, to put it crudely, we don't really have one. It can feel peculiarly unjust to have to defend a principle which has not had the chance, in so many areas, to be put fully and creatively into practice, and, worse still, one which has been consistently undermined by successive governments, including New Labour, as well as by large sections of the press. Of course, as Roy Hattersley mentions in this volume, there are successful and well-supported 'all-in' schools in many small towns and rural areas. But in the big cities and large towns, where choice, in all its dubious allure, has become the mantra of the anxious and the ambitious, there is now such a plethora of educational provision, such a subtle and not so subtle ranking of schools – as outlined by Tim Brighouse, in his 2002 Brian Simon Memorial Lecture – that it is simply inaccurate to describe many local schools as truly comprehensive (Brighouse, 2003).

But let's not get too pessimistic. Many so-called inner city schools do still enjoy a wide enough range of parental support and are mixed enough in terms of class, ethnic background and gender to be considered functioning comprehensives; they also do very well. But as any comprehensive-supporting parent knows, it is an ongoing struggle to keep drawing in support from many middle-class parents, even (perhaps especially) when their children are at a state school. There can be something anxiously conditional, perpetually dissatisfied in much parental reaction to, and involvement in, such schools; unrealistic comparisons are constantly being made with the private, grammar or the faith school sector, which have far more selective intakes, usually far greater resources and altogether more controlled environments.

Very soon, a vicious circle is established: the more local parents fail to support neighbourhood schools, either by taking alternative options or by constantly emphasizing the achievements of these other educational institutions, with all their obvious advantages (and often doing so in ignorance of the wider political context), the more demoralized the atmosphere around the local school can become, often quite out of proportion to its considerable achievements. In some very troubled boroughs, the school then becomes a repository for all those children of families who cannot – or will not – find a so-called 'escape route' out. It is in such circumstances that 'comp' becomes synonymous with 'sink'.

All this is, inevitably, a reflection of the highly individualistic era in which we live. Comprehensives were first introduced, from the late 1950s onwards, in a period of profound if flawed idealism about the potential of human beings, political structures and collective action. Genuine social change was on the agenda: people were prepared to take risks, to engage across existing and often rigid social boundaries. We now inhabit a much more fearful period, in which the ingrained habit of consumer choice mixes oddly with deeper-rooted class and ethnic prejudices to reinforce a closed and highly pragmatic attitude to strangers and friends, family and work, past and future, all of which, in turn, affect school choice. Economic uncertainty, fear of urban crime, anxiety about asylum seekers, a sharp decline in belief in the potential of public politics – all of these and more mean that many parents have developed an obsessive focus on education as the prime solution to the problem of their children's future; highly selective schools are seen as a safe haven in a scary, unstable world.

Such anxiety has not been soothed by ambiguous and half-hearted government policy. As other contributors to this volume argue, New Labour has often eschewed strengthening existing schools in favour of jazzy new initiatives such as city academies, specialist schools, an increase in private sponsorship of education as well as outspoken support for the continued growth of faith schools. The Government has also consistently underplayed and undermined the achievement of the country's many comprehensives, as Sally Tomlinson argues in her contribution. We have seen, too, the intensification – not eradication, as promised – of selection at secondary level, even though recognition of the enormous damage this does to children, particularly working-class children, was one of the most important educational developments of the postwar period, and the key impetus to the original movement for comprehensive reform.

In place of the old 11-plus examination, we have selection in its tortuous, covert and occasionally comic 'mark-2004' version: young children started on one or more musical instruments from an early age partly in order to boost their chances of winning a place at one of the local specialist schools; parents who miraculously convert to Christianity or start attending Mass in order to secure a place for their child at a Church of England or Roman Catholic secondary; children coached from an early age in mathematics, creative writing or verbal reasoning in order to pass the intensely competitive exams for the private schools, grammar schools and so-called selective comprehensives that abound in the big cities.

But the effects of selection are anything but comic; they can be poisonous, as any primary school parent who has witnessed the bitterness, helplessness, and manoeuvring that goes on behind so much transfer to secondary level knows. Selective options within the state system tend also to benefit the middle-class families: those with the know-how and the spare cash to negotiate the shadowy world of tutors, Saturday schools and special scholarships, and of course the reassuring, winning manner when facing a headteacher's interview for a secondary school place. The 11-plus is dead; long live the 11-plus.

So what has gone wrong? And how can we put it right? Reflecting on this question over the years, both as a pupil and now as a parent, I have come to wonder if the comprehensive ideal is, in fact, much more daring and far-reaching than many of its original proponents recognized. Or perhaps it appears particularly daring or dangerously far-reaching in a period of 'small c conservatism', a conservatism which is itself fuelled by fear. Not surprisingly, it is about class and ethnic differences. But it is also about cities.

It is, perhaps, too easy or too lazy to caricature the attitudes of some of the middle and upper classes as snobbery, although it is certainly true that many people still hold to stereotyped views of the poor or those from different cultural backgrounds – yet often, oddly enough, also expressing desires for a rich cultural or social mix in their lives. But the attitude I am trying to divine and describe is something much more complex than mere snobbery.

For many parents, particularly in the big cities, the local school is the concrete and glass representation of their unexplored terrors of everything from the approaching chaos of adolescence, in their own and other children, to the effects of sharp social polarization which they see around them daily on the streets, on public transport and in the squares and streets of the large towns and cities in which they live.

Many modern families have successfully privatized large sections of their lives: they travel mainly by car rather than by public transport; they belong to the burgeoning numbers of member-only gyms; they have private health insurance, they build high walls round their middle-class estates. The local comprehensive – which is, by definition, one of the few modern public institutions which cannot select or reject membership on the basis of religious, ethnic or class backgrounds – becomes then the one place where these families must directly face those whom they perceive as profoundly, and often threateningly, different from themselves. Concerns about discipline and academic standards are the most common ways in which parents focus these more amorphous concerns.

Of course, learning and the atmosphere around learning are crucial. Yet both research and anecdotal evidence confirm that excellent academic achievement is possible in a socially and ethnically mixed school, and that overall achievement is increased by the participation of well-supported and academically able pupils. Personally, I would like to see a less rigid curriculum, smaller class sizes, fewer exams, more time to explore subject areas in depth. The 'reinvented traditionalism' of recent years means that some state schools have lost an important element in their approach to learning: creativity, openness to new ideas and more varied, interesting teaching methods.

But to concentrate only on academic standards is to take an unnecessarily limiting approach to education. Much of what is valuable in contemporary schools and schooling cannot be objectively measured by league tables, value-added tables, Ofsted inspections and the rest. It is often as difficult to describe and define what makes a good school as it is to pin down the qualities that make a good relationship or a happy family; one resorts to such terms as vitality, cohesion, calm, creativity, friendliness and openness.

I do not want to downplay parental fears about their children's safety at school. One of the biggest problems facing those secondary schools that are obliged to accept all children from the locality, regardless of so-called academic ability or parental wealth or religious faith, is that, almost inevitably, it is they and they alone who must deal with children from difficult backgrounds. Not surprisingly, children *with* a problem are then likely to *become* a problem. And, if they come from poor backgrounds, they are much more likely to be demonized than understood, far more likely to be exiled (or, in school terms, excluded) than endlessly supported through difficult times, like their middle-class peers. In the absence of wider social support for many families, and scant public understanding, teachers become the front line when it comes to dealing with many of these problems.

The deeper answer to these difficulties does not lie merely in behaviour management but in understanding the source of these young people's difficulties. Close up, most of these pupils look pretty much like anyone else. They may be troubled, yes; they may even be disruptive; but they are also young people with plenty of intelligence, humour, kindness and potential. The further you retreat from them, the more dehumanized they become, an attitude which accounts for what education writer Fiona Millar has rightly called 'the school gates' phenomenon: parents judging a school solely on their observation of pupil behaviour in the local streets.

It is largely personal experience that makes me question the extraordinary emphasis that parents who reject a local school put on the question of discipline or on academic standards, even at primary level. How much is this a substitute, a kind of code, for an unarticulated fear, or even distaste, of difference?

IN DEFENCE OF THE URBAN EXPERIENCE

In *The Uses of Disorder*, published over thirty years ago, the American sociologist and novelist Richard Sennett describes how respectable white families in America in the postwar period withdrew to the suburbs. They did so in order to preserve a mythic, false and ultimately fragile sense of identity based on sameness, and expulsion of the 'other'; such a move, not surprisingly, created a violent and stifling repression of its own. Yet, at the same time, the 1960s saw the revival of interest, particularly among the young, in the many creative, even anarchistic, possibilities of our cities, small and large. It is through city living, Sennett suggests, that we can learn how to negotiate difference, clashes of interests and identities, on a daily basis. This is certainly not the fashionable view of cities in the modern period, in which we almost obsessively muse on possibilities of threat and breakdown. Nonetheless, I would argue, it is a useful notion to revive and re-examine.

The young Sennett has a refreshingly unprecious view of neighbourhood schools as a 'focus for conflict and conciliation for the parents ... controlled by the community, but the community is so diverse that the schools cannot be pushed in any one direction' (Sennett, 1970, pp. 190–91).

Imagining an extremely bright little girl, who attends a neighbourhood school, Sennett writes:

> ... this little girl sees, every day, that the tensions and friendships in the community or school ... do not create chaos .... People are not sheltered from each other, but their contacts are more explorations of a constantly shifting environment than an acting out of unchanging routines. Therefore this little girl grows up in a neighbourhood that does not permit her family or her circle of friends to be intensive and inward turning. This fact has a liberating power for her as someone who is exceptionally bright. (*ibid*, p. 191)

Sennett here puts his finger on the vital connection between neighbourhood schools and the needs and demands of local democracy, something that it is easy to forget in this era of fatally weakened local authorities. He also makes an original and important connection between improving intelligence and not sheltering our young, which completely reverses modern received parental wisdom, which suggests that the more you shield a child from contemporary realities the more they are likely to learn.

Increasingly, the middle-class are withdrawing into tightly protected enclaves of housing, health, education and even leisure. In turn, this withdrawal increases fear, ignorance, misunderstanding and prejudice; it also leeches important energy from public services, and further weakens them, then allowing those who have so withdrawn to redouble their attack upon the so-called inadequacies of the services in which they no longer participate. Yet, as so many parents who continue to send their children to the local school will attest, something interesting and positive can emerge from the mix of so many children from such different backgrounds.

As a parent, I have seen some of this at close hand, if so far only at primary level. At our local primary school, over seventy languages are spoken. The school has one of the few purpose-built refugee centres in the country, established in order to welcome children newly arrived in our borough, and so to ease their passage into schooling. (Here, at least, we have learned the crucial lesson of recent European history: that the genuine welcoming of refugees is the litmus test of a humane democracy.) But children also come from every kind of family in the neighbourhood: poor, middle income and wealthy.

Perhaps the most important lesson to emerge from the mix of children from such different backgrounds is that there is a profound difference between learning *with* others and merely learning *of* them. To understand why a Muslim girl in the class cannot go swimming, to debate the story of Mussolini with an Italian Jewish classmate, to hear a traumatized silent child who has fled from a country at war suddenly recite a poem in his or her language of origin, is not only puzzling, challenging or deeply moving by turns; it also allows children to dig deep beneath the cheap and crude headlines of identity, day in, day out. How can Ofsted ever hope to capture the educational value inherent in these experiences?

There is clearly a social aspect to learning, with schooling the first important step in the acquisition of skills related to good citizenship, including active participation, tolerance, recognition of difference and so on. Surely we can only come to understand the true meaning of difference through proximity? It is not enough to take an intellectual interest in the lives, thoughts and practices of others. If one's education is spent largely with people like ourselves, whether in terms of class, faith, gender or all three, what richness and chance for understanding are lost?

We should not be blind to the very real difficulties that the experience of difference can create. In many ways, economic disparities pose the greatest challenge, particularly in big cities, where extremes of wealth and poverty live, cheek by jowl, in most neighbourhoods. As many parents will tell you, children, or, perhaps more importantly, their parents, often stick to same class or same faith friendship groups. But not always. Children from different social backgrounds may gripe at each other, but their friendship may also lead them to ask important questions about inequality.

One of the most pressing questions facing us today is how to deal with inequality and difference: how to create social solidarity in the face of so many potential causes of division. Will we create a more socially just society by hiding away from each other? No. My visceral objection to private schools and some selective schooling comes down to the implied monasticism of such choices: monasticism as defined in the *Shorter Oxford English Dictionary* is 'to forsweare the ful stream of ye world, and to live in a nooke'. Given the conflicts and upheavals of modern society, do we really want to reinforce the lessons of either religious difference or class privilege, particularly the latter, and to confirm children, far too young to know better, in an unjustified arrogance, which is often based solely on family wealth?

Little in the comprehensive option is easy, nor will it ever be. But in terms of the wider social good, it is surely far preferable to the route of educational apartheid.

I owe my mother a great deal in so many ways. From her, I developed a love of learning, for she was both a creative writer and a highly disciplined scholar. I also owe to her the deeply unfashionable belief that *every* child is of value, not just my own. Individual achievement and fulfilment are vital, but these need not be gained at the unnecessary expense of others. In other words, we must transcend narrow self interest or we are lost; we all have a contribution to make to the collective good. If public services, including education, are to have any real meaning or value in today's world, beyond acting as a form of safety net for the poor, then they require the active participation and support of all citizens. Without that full-hearted involvement, we risk undervaluing the skills and talents inherent in each and every member of society, and so harming the very fabric of our democracy.

3 In Praise of Sixties Idealism

Jane Shallice

The public nature of our services has been under attack for over twenty years, with enormous consequences for the collective good. Responsibility for key areas of life has slowly been devolved to individuals and their families, democratic accountability increasingly bypassed in favour of appointees, consultants and business 'experts'. In education, the direct reach of the private sector is evident in the growing numbers of private finance schemes for both school building and provision of services; it has even seeped into control of schools themselves. City academies are considered the answer to educational 'black spots', with business sponsors required to find initial capital and government providing the additional building and running costs. Many of these schools are run by religious bodies, and 'user pays' is the current iniquitous terminology governing ideas about the modern school. Even the rather notional 'democratic' control of the education committees has been abandoned as council cabinets decide local policy and scrutiny committees cast a vague eye over proceedings.

At a conference organized by the Hillcole Group in October 1999, having listened to the litany of defeats and reverses that progressive educational policies had suffered, Caroline Benn argued forcefully against any diminution of our demands (see Benn, 2001). She urged us not to fall into the trap of mythologizing some kind of golden past but to make even greater efforts to develop and offer meaningful alternatives for the future. Part of this task is surely to recall the ways in which many schools changed in the 1960s and 70s. In doing so, we do not seek to replicate the past, but to use our knowledge of it as a reminder both of the huge political and social gains achieved during that period and to deepen our understanding of the simple truth that, acting together, people *can* make a difference.

Although comprehensive education was part of Labour Party policy postwar, the comprehensive model was always expected to operate within a system that retained private schools and some selective and grammar schools, just as it does today. In London in the 1960s with a large number of grammar schools, around 17 to 20 per cent of pupils were selected through the 11-plus, which had an inevitable impact on any comprehensive. However, the London County Council was in favour of comprehensive education and had set up eight experimental comprehensive schools in the late 1940s which had been formed by amalgamating existing secondary schools. The successes achieved by these institutions encouraged the extension of the policy, and with the release of more resources, more comprehensives were opened, some 'custom-built' and some created by the expansion of existing grammar schools.

One such purpose-built comprehensive was Holland Park School in the wealthy Royal London Borough of Kensington and Chelsea. Established on a large, beautiful site, it was bounded by luxury private flats and houses and, along one side, by Holland Park itself. (One of the nearby buildings was the residence of the High Commissioner for South Africa who insisted that the students did not use the road alongside his house in case they disrupted his garden parties. During the first years of the school, students were forbidden to use the entrances that led them on to that road.) The land had been bought by the London County Council on behalf of the people of London and, in the teeth of bitter opposition from the wealthy residents and ratepayers of the borough, the school opened in 1958.

The large purpose-built building stood in extensive grounds, which included Thorpe Lodge (a fine building and the former residence of the Governor of the Bank of England) which was used for sixth form teaching, a very well kept large garden and a magnificent stand of trees. Holland Park appeared to have every facility necessary for a genuine comprehensive school. It opened with over 2000 pupils, after two local schools had been closed and other schools in the area had been instructed to send an allocation of their pupils.

In its early days, however, Holland Park was a 'comprehensive' in name only – being run more along grammar school lines. The school had Houses, named in traditional fashion after bygone political figures (Fox, Addison, Maine, Macaulay, Hunter, Wilberforce), a school uniform and a prefect system. All years were streamed into 12 classes, identified by the letters A1, 2, 3, B1, 2, 3, etc., down to the two remedial E classes. Later the groupings were altered under pressure to six 'fast learning' classes and six 'slow learning' classes, with the academic and non-academic classes being named after the initial letters of the school: six Hs and six Ps, and the two remedial classes being called S1 and S2. Students placed into the School Leavers Group in the 4th year could not change their mind and stay on at the school. When one teacher expressed a wish to enter some of these pupils for an examination, a senior member of staff could only remark, 'Well, they should be truanting by now'. The other feature of the school, which indicated its early grammar school aspirations, was the High Table at lunchtime. Senior staff, all gowned, sat on a stage perched above the children and were served by Domestic Science students.

Real change in the school came with the arrival of Dr Derek Rushworth. The Head of Modern Languages when the school opened in 1958, he left to take a headship elsewhere and returned as the head teacher in 1971. A highly intelligent and political man, Derek Rushworth was determined to make the school 'truly comprehensive' in place of what he considered to be merely an artificial mix of different types of schools. Although (it being Kensington and Chelsea) a large number of children were hived off to the private sector, the school still had a significant number of middle-class children whose parents were supportive of comprehensive education, and consequently the school had a broad social mix. Derek Rushworth, an active member of the National Association of Head Teachers, was also adept at ensuring that all grants and sources of funding from the ILEA were tapped. He certainly gained a reputation both at school and at County Hall for being a head who could – and would – not have the wool pulled over his eyes. As all who taught and worked in the authority would testify, the ILEA had a huge range of services, including a large inspectorate and advisory service which provided a wealth of expertise and support and myriad centres, facilities and funds. It also benefited from the intellectual legacy of the LCC's Education Library (see Maclure, 1970, p. 84).

Holland Park also had a group of highly committed and dynamic teachers. A young teacher who arrived in the early 1970s said, 'You had brilliant people, scholarly intellectuals who were never patronizing to the kids'. There was an extremely active parents' group and a governing body which had decided the year of Derek Rushworth's arrival, against the advice of the previous head teacher, to initiate mixed ability groupings throughout the first year.

Dr Rushworth recalls how when he was still head of languages, the heads of department and heads of year had been asked to meet a group of parents wanting to set up a parent/teacher association. (It was at this meeting that he first met Caroline Benn.) In the early period of Holland Park's existence, many of its teachers were opposed to anything that might impinge on their authority and they were prepared only to countenance such a body if it restricted itself to providing funds. In fact, it later became the Holland Park School Association whose members included parents, teachers, non-teaching staff and students, and which became an effective body mobilizing support for positive developments in the school.

Initially involved with the parents, Caroline Benn became a governor and played an important role at the school for the rest of her life. No one can overestimate her contribution; with her profound commitment to comprehensive education, her tremendous political acumen and her clarity of vision, she was a strong support for staff, both teaching and non-teaching, and for the rights of students.

One of the teachers who had been working at the school for three years described the impact of Derek Rushworth's appointment: 'He was the engine of change. Shortly after he arrived we started to discuss the changes that were required. And I suppose there was a part of us that was thinking it was never going to happen ... because we were frightened of it. We had been used to teaching these streamed groups and you knew how to gauge your level. The idea of teaching mixed ability groups shocked a number of people, but, all of a sudden, it was there and you slipped into it. Most people had worried about it, but it worked.'

This teacher went on: 'There was such a drive, such a belief that it ought to happen, that the school ended the academic year in July as a streamed school and returned in September with all the lower school organized along mixed ability lines. We all had this determination and had, I suppose, subconsciously been teaching in this way all along. We had learned an approach and a skill that we probably hadn't realized.'

In many secondary schools at that time there was a fever of discussion and debate as many of the teachers, having themselves, as school students, experienced the iniquities of the selection system, believed that schools ought to change. It was felt, too, that change was possible. This was a period of tremendous social and political upheaval and with the lessons from the Civil Rights Movement in the USA, anti-imperialist struggles, opposition to the Vietnam War and the demands of student radicals throughout higher education, it was possible to 'be realistic *and* demand the impossible'.

Many teachers felt passionately that old assumptions had to be challenged, past practices questioned and new alternatives developed. This was also reflected in the growth of organizations and lobby groups, as well as groups within the NUT; conferences were organized, pamphlets, journals and books produced in abundance. Obviously for many teachers in schools where entrenched conservatism ruled and there was little or no support for new ideas or methods, they could initiate new practices only within their own classrooms. But it was far more difficult to feel any success or to sustain such attempts at change. However, in schools where there were like-minded groups of staff or where there were liberal head teachers, there seemed to be a continuous debate about teaching methods, about the content of courses, about the rights of students, about the organization of the school and its relationship to the community outside. Those of us who were young teachers at the time thought that schools should and could be far better and were quickly drawn into these discussions. Obviously in almost all schools there was a very clear hierarchy of undisputed power, but in some schools the ideas and energies of young (and old) teachers were welcomed. Such was the case at Holland Park.

Derek Rushworth wanted to develop a comprehensive school in the widest sense of the term, and in this he was lucky to have a governing body (with members like Caroline Benn) who were both willing supporters and participants. He championed the development of a liberal, creative, open curriculum and a structure within which students could delay specialism choices for as long as possible. He opposed vocational education on the grounds that such courses would restrict choice, and this policy was constantly under debate and review. The debate about 'typing or no typing' ran for years! In his view, staff were professionally able to develop their own courses and he encouraged all forms of collaborative and integrated work. He was eager to support the development of a wide range of out-of-school activities, and clubs and societies thrived. Sporting activities were encouraged, the Debating Society was particularly strong, there was lots of music, an orchestra, and a dynamic drama group which from the 1970s took their performances annually to the Edinburgh Festival.

At his first staff meeting, Dr Rushworth suggested that the school should try operating without corporal punishment for one term. Apart from his own personal opposition, there were many staff opposed to it, including many of the heads of houses who found it objectionable that they were being asked to wield the cane on behalf of other teachers. At the start of the next term, nobody even suggested a vote to reinstitute it. The uniform question was also quickly settled. The school agreed that uniform would not be compulsory and there was no real lobby to retain it.

But crucially Derek wanted to develop democratic structures within the school. Staff meetings were *de rigueur* in most schools but here they were a site for debate and challenging discussion, with papers written and presented and many passionate arguments aired. A school council was established with a vast election process which was run by the Social Education Department. Its various committees had the right to examine departmental curriculae, access to information from the head, and funds (which, according to Derek, they only ever spent on litter bins). Dr Rushworth worked on the principle that – in his own words – 'everyone should know everything'.

Derek Rushworth has said that, in retrospect, perhaps he was not the most traditional of heads. He wanted discussion and believed that the challenging of received ideas was the way to change the views and practices of teachers rather than through the issue of prescriptive edicts. He reflected, 'I don't think that I showed much leadership!' But staff disagreed. One said that he was seen as a considerable figurehead. 'He was someone who had ideas and who, even if you disagreed with him, you respected. He was exceptionally approachable and had an open door policy for both staff and pupils.' It was clear that staff, even if they disagreed with him, respected him and his views, and felt that he did accept arguments and criticism if well-founded.

Another teacher recalled him with great fondness. 'Everyone respected him. He was very human. He had a bad temper and at times was like Rumplestiltskin. He would stamp his foot or blow up. But he was utterly respectful of us and of all the students as people. He really valued what we did. I always remember him doing the assembly after having been to Sartre's funeral. When he returned he gave a whole school assembly on it and every child listened to every single word.'

Throughout the school there was a high level of commitment from the teachers and tutors, who were expected to make home visits, a practice virtually unheard of today. There were annual visits to France, plays and concerts, an activity week at the end of the summer term when large numbers of children went on school journeys and the others enjoyed a huge range of activities; there was always the HPSA to fund children who needed financial support. In short, there was a genuine sense of a school community.

In many comprehensive schools at this time, the curriculum developed in many creative ways. There was a genuine attempt to provide a truly liberal education, which opened up the world to the children in the classrooms. We worked with a belief that knowledge is 'seamless' and however much we had been squeezed or corralled into disciplines, boundaries between subjects were hazy if not truly permeable. Affective knowledge rather than a cognitive approach was the basis of our work.

Much of the new thinking and theorizing in the 1960s was built upon the more progressive experiments begun in schools like A. S. Neill's Summerhill in the independent sector or during Michael Duane's depressingly short period as head of Risinghill, schools where affirmations of the children and their experiences were the basis of practice. There was also more of an understanding that the culture into which a child is born and raised is paramount in their own thinking, and therefore in their intellectual and emotional development and their relations with the world around them. For many this was a revolutionary understanding – particularly so for those working in a system which imposed *tout court* a middle-class culture, one, of course, deemed to be better.

The ranked and tiered classroom in which children were rigidly placed and controlled was gradually dismantled. In the old days, movement had been prohibited in the classroom. There was no flexibility of classroom organization; all were supervised under the teacher's gaze, as the guard or warder in Panopticon. Slowly group work flowered and, with it, recognition of the value of embracing new ideas.

Comprehensives were not without their critics, and from the late 1960s the writers of the Black Papers were demanding streaming, regular testing, the assertion of 'excellence', 'value free' education and the removal of 'ideology' from the classroom. As a large and high-profile school, Holland Park was subject to much vilification, with papers claiming that it was all sex and drugs and rock and roll, and little education! Despite this pretty constant barrage of criticism and distortion, by the start of the 1980s the school had developed and matured. The curriculum was structured into faculties: CDTMS (Craft, Design, Technology, Maths and Science); HUMS (Humanities, English and Languages); CAPE (Creative Arts and PE) and PALSS (Pastoral and Learning Support Services) which ensured that all students had access to all areas of knowledge. Integrated courses had developed in Humanities, Science and the areas of Design Technology, and there was a series of initiatives such as all-girl groups in Physics and DT. There was a Women's Group and a Black Teachers' Group.

Unquestionably, for large numbers of children, comprehensive education, which taught them without resort to selection and labelling, had hugely liberating effects. However, just as comprehensive schools were beginning to make a difference, Margaret Thatcher won the 1979 Election and at government level all the anti-progressive arguments held sway.

The 1988 Educational Reform Act had a dramatic and immediate impact on all schools, an effect compounded by the disbanding of the ILEA a couple of years later. The Act introduced a form of marketization into the schools system. Through open enrolment, *per capita* funding and school managers taking on the responsibilities previously the work of the LEAs, school was pitted against school. There was a dramatic movement away from the precepts of the 1960s and 70s and New Labour has only built on the foundations laid by the Tories. A functionalism now pervades classrooms with the underlying, if not stated, assumption that there are right and wrong ways of writing, looking, talking, interpreting texts – indeed, of understanding the world.

This is not a plea on my part for a 'postmodernist' approach, but instead for a realization that the institution of 'levels' is one of the most alienating of concepts. All areas of knowledge benefit from crossing set boundaries and stages. For many of us who were radical teachers in the 1960s, 70s and early 80s there was a large overlap in techniques, skills, vocabulary and content. Today, attaining knowledge is conceived of as a linear or sequential activity.

New Labour has created a Byzantine structure of secondary education. Technology colleges, specialist schools, non-specialist comprehensive schools and the increasingly important city academies compete against each other for customers. There is, of course, no debate at all about the private sector.

With this return to the old pre-welfare state educational and social divides, it is essential that we turn again to consider the tasks that face us. In her speech in 1999 Caroline warned us against pessimism which could only paralyse and prevent us effectively contesting the policies of those in power. In all her tireless efforts, she demanded both rigour and commitment, wanting to preserve education as a public right and to extend its democratic accountability. 'The greatest act is to ... teach those we teach to question, to continue to question ourselves, to interrogate every part of the system and all we are told and read and view – and never accept what we have been given at face value until we are satisfied' (Benn, 2001, p. 4).

4 The Route to My Comprehensive

Max Morris

From the moment I entered educational politics in the 1930s I became convinced that the ending of the divided post-primary system and the abolition of privilege within it was the crucial step needed to give working-class children their birthright in education. The questions were, how? And what would be the structure we would put in its place?

I was not alone in my commitment. That the system had to be replaced was the objective of the group of left-wing teachers in the NUT with whom I associated as soon as I began teaching. They were an informal grouping belonging to the Labour Party and the Communist Party, who were concerned not only with radicalizing the NUT but with Socialist educational reform. The bible of educational reformers at that time was Tawney's *Secondary Education for All*, written in 1922, but this did not advance major structural reforms, only demands for more and better opportunities, for equality in separate schools. The Hadow reform, allowing advanced classes in senior elementary schools, was heralded by many as the way forward, but it could in practice impose iron chains on secondary education by creating separate and different types of secondary school.

Our group discussions developed from this the idea of the 'multilateral' school, either a single institution with 'modern', technical and grammar streams, across whose boundaries transfer would be easy and, most importantly, with parity of conditions, or three different streams in separate buildings on a single campus site. However, the obnoxious division of children into fixed types requiring different kinds of schooling in the Spens Report (1938) and the Norwood Report (1943) clarified our group's discussions and we moved from multilateralism towards the idea of a common or single school. This became our objective when the War ended and we were faced with the operation of the 1944 Education Act, which embodied the theoretical position taken in the Norwood Report.

The Act provided secondary education according to 'Age, Aptitude and Ability'. Such innocent and common-sense sounding words! But they became the foundation of a postwar secondary system every bit as divided and class-biased as in the bad pre-war days. It was put over by the con trick of renaming the old 'senior schools' as 'Modern Schools'. Whoever thought up that title deserves the accolade due to genius. Modern? It was modern apparently to leave school earlier than in the grammar schools, to have larger classes, and to lack specialist teachers, for example in maths, science and modern languages. It was modern to spend less on those that needed education most.

'Comprehensive' as a title to describe our objective dated later on from Circular 144 of 1947 in which the Ministry defined the different possible types of secondary school. It was a title redolent of civil service jargon – we would have preferred common or single.

In the educational press, in the NUT and above all in the local Labour Parties opposition grew for a multitude of reasons to the 11-plus, and we vigorously pressed the idea of the comprehensive school. It had received a major fillip from an event which at the time had an enormous impact, especially on the Labour Movement. With incredible stupidity the New Labour Ministry under Ellen Wilkinson took over from the Tories what became the notorious Pamphlet No. 1, 'The Nation's Schools', which contained the golden sentence that the education of the overwhelming majority of children was to be determined by the fact that 'their future employment will not demand any measure of technical skill or knowledge'. They were to be the hewers of wood and drawers of water in our capitalist society!

No formulation could have been more deliberately calculated by the civil service mandarins, public schoolmen almost to a man, to raise every hackle in the Labour Movement. There were stormy scenes at the first Labour Party Conference after Labour took office when, to everyone's astonishment, 'Red' Ellen in tears defended the abominable monster produced by her Tory predecessors. Conference defeated both the platform and the minister and ordered that the offending passages in this classic statement of class-ridden education be revised. But later it was all too plain that the ghost of 'The Nation's Schools' still walked. It was to become the spectre which haunted the development of post-1944 secondary education.

The limited objective accepted by many in the Labour Party was the widening of access to grammar schools, which catered for about 20 per cent of the secondary school population, but although more resources, better buildings, smaller classes, nursery schools, more university places, better welfare services and so on were all essential reforms, the educational structure itself remained fatally flawed because of the divided secondary system.

Intelligence testing was the intellectual fig-leaf used to cover up the nakedness of the class-biased educational structure, expressed especially through the boosting of the secondary modern school, the lower tier of the secondary system. At the time I summed up the 'theory' of the modern school as 'It doesn't matter what you teach them, it's how you teach it. Content doesn't matter as long as you keep the children happy. High attainment and sound knowledge, the avenue to the seats of power, are not for the masses. Keep them happy with "practical" work – you don't need brains for working a lathe or the tools of the "modern" equivalents of the hewers of wood and drawers of water.'

Looking back on those days, one can feel pride in having belonged to a group of left-wingers that took on in theoretical combat the pillars of the educational establishment; that dared to examine critically the mighty Professors Spearman, Burt and Vernon. I remember how small I was intended to feel when, bold enough to utter a few words of doubt on Spearman's views on intelligence at a conference at the London Institute, I was lambasted from the platform for daring to question the master. But Spearman was wrong, terribly wrong, in his theories that placed the working-class in permanent intellectual servitude.

We fought the good fight for high standards, for raising the educational level and demanded that all artificial barriers be removed from secondary modern children staying on and entering for the examinations hitherto exclusively oriented towards the grammar school minority; we had many allies in the profession and among educational administrators and academics.

A growing movement towards a broad consensus against selection so early in the child's life was considerably pushed forward by the undermining of confidence in intelligence testing, not just its procedures but its whole theoretical foundation in the false concept of immutable innate intelligence. Intelligence tests, we said, tried to pour the holy water of 'science' on the essentially reactionary political and social process of selection. The lie was also given to the prevailing theory by the creation in several areas, e.g. London, Anglesey, Coventry, the West Riding, etc., of successful comprehensives as islands of progress despite all the difficulties imposed by a non-comprehensive environment.

During the Tory period 1951–64 the Labour Party, influenced by these developments, by the effective propaganda of NALT (National Association of Labour Teachers, the forerunner of the Socialist Educational Association), and by a number of brilliant educational publicists including Caroline Benn, began to adopt a much clearer commitment to the Comprehensive Idea, although in 1955, Gaitskell could still say he 'saw no need to be "violently dogmatic" about the comprehensive school'. The vital decision was made in 1958, when the Party committed itself to a comprehensive system.

It is interesting to note that the cause of education crossed Right/ Left lines in the Labour Movement. The keenest advocates of democratic educational thinking I came across in the Labour party before the Kinnock era were not my friends among the Bevanites, apart from Jennie Lee and Stephen Swingler, but right-wingers like Ted Short, Fred Peart, Michael Stewart and, later, Roy Hattersley. It is ironical to remember that the 1959 Labour Party Conference was won for an anti-public school policy because of the conversion of the extreme right-wing leader, Arthur Deakin, General Secretary of the T&GWU.

What appeared to be final success was achieved by the Wilson Government, which after debating the organizational and political issues decided that rather than setting up a compulsory system throughout the country, which was urged by the Secretary of State, Michael Stewart, it would replace the existing divided system by a comprehensive system under the aegis and effective control of the LEAs. The process of reorganization was to be carried out according to the principles laid down by Circular 10/65 produced by Anthony Crosland, who had replaced Stewart. Crosland, himself a passionate believer in equality, was like Stewart personally in favour of a compulsory national system, but the Government was too timid.

Under the momentum created by the circular most LEAs responded quickly and from 1967 on comprehensives began to cover the country. Many of these, however, could not be truly comprehensive because of the continued existence of grammar schools and because of the difficulty of developing the new type of schools within existing unsuitable buildings which could not be replaced for financial reasons. So the new system was flawed: the money was not made available, hybrid systems continued for years in some LEAs and many comprehensives were so only in name.

Another and vital weakness was that no lead on the curricular issues created by the new system was given from the Government. The magnitude of the problems created by a changeover from a selective to an unselective system was simply not appreciated. Yet Britain was about to undertake an unprecedented transformation of its educational structure, an immense challenge. The challenges of developing comprehensive schools were in practice left to be solved by each LEA in its own way in the face of its own difficulties.

Among the LEAs that responded speedily to Circular 10/65 was my own, Brent, where I was head of a secondary modern school. Brent wanted ultimately to create a system of 11 to 18 comprehensives and I was appointed to one of the first of them, Willesden High School, in November 1966, with the school planned to open in September 1967.

Until then it had all been theory; but now it was to be practice. I had the task in Willesden High School, formed by amalgamating a grammar, a secondary technical and a secondary modern school, of planning a comprehensive. Instead of political campaigning for the comprehensive, I had the job of organizing one and the responsibility for running it. A positive factor was that the technical school (in which I had once taught) had already begun the process of integration within the grammar school.

There were serious problems to solve arising from the nature of the entry and the curricular base from which I had to begin. In the Brent scheme, the authority had regrettably – from expediency not principles – decided to pay for children who opted out of the system into grammar, denominational, direct grant or independent schools elsewhere. So a fair number of academically able children were lost to the school. Although my catchment area, as I used to say, stretched from Rolls Royce land to slumdom, it was clear we would not have a totally unselective entry. On the contrary, we would become an almost exclusively working-class and increasingly black neighbourhood school. I was not alarmed, as some were, about this. If the job of the comprehensive was, as I firmly believed, to raise the educational standards of the majority, how better to begin than with a school population previously denied full educational opportunity?

Could we really be called comprehensive with such an obviously flawed composition whose flaws were intensified by the departure of very many middle-class children, removed by their parents who obviously did not like the massive majority of working-class including ethnic minority children? My answer was, yes, a comprehensive in course of development. If we were to wait for ideal conditions to exist – 100 per cent entry from the local child population, an absolutely new or suitably modified set of buildings properly equipped, a thoroughly trained comprehensive-dedicated staff, and so on, that is for ideal conditions before we started – we would have had to wait for the Greek Kalends. We had to start with an educational landscape disfigured by the private sector and grammar schools in neighbouring boroughs. We had to get on with the job with the conditions we had inherited.

We were to be a ten-form entry school, occupying two sites twelve hundred yards apart, one site being the grammar/technical school in reasonably modern and well-equipped buildings; the other a very old-fashioned secondary modern. Whereas the grammar tech under its previous head had a good reputation locally, the secondary modern, though it had a good staff, had had no head for a year and was very depressed.

My instructions from the Education Committee were to carry out its pledge to continue existing courses for all children in the school at the time of the merger. So, while we could organize a comprehensive curriculum for the new entry, for some considerable time we would be running this side by side with grammar, technical and modern courses for the majority of the children.

Problems enough, one could say. But I was determined to interpret my remit very broadly. While carrying out the Committee's pledge, I would not only create something new for the comprehensive entry but also would weld the different elements of the existing schools together in every way possible, especially in curriculum. I was going to maintain the grammar-technical children's standards and offer them new opportunities while substantially improving the education available to the modern school pupils.

I began a long process of consultation. I interviewed every member of staff both to learn what I could about them and to explain what we would be trying to do. I attended school assemblies and social functions, met the PTA of the tech – no PTA existed in the grammar school and the one in the modern school was defunct. I had frequent and useful meetings with the Chairman and Vice-chairman of the Education Committee and the Chief Education Officer, all of whom gave every possible help.

May I at this point make something clear? I have written here in the first person and this must seem rather strange these days when the approach to school organization and in particular the head's role is rather different. The fact is that, having been appointed, I was simply told to get on with the job in the time given to me. No one suggested that I should prepare plans for the approval, far less the decision, of a governing body or in consultation with any organization of parents. Brent still at that time operated a system of joint governing bodies for groups of secondary schools but my experience up till then had been that such governing bodies played very little part in the life and work of schools. I was expected to be able to plan all aspects of the school's work and any consultations with staff and parents were entirely up to me. The Authority made it clear that it had appointed me because they thought I could do the job and I was expected to get on with it and produce a viable school organization by the following September.

Such a modus operandi would of course be impossible today. Thus I was left to produce my own scheme of appointments and allowances; to interview and make recommendations for all of them that could be filled internally. Other appointments would be made in the normal way by advertisement and the Committee's routine procedures. I recall having difficulty with only a couple of the numerous recommendations I made which, for some reason or other, the chairman did not approve. A fair number of the grammar school staff sadly left due to unwillingness to work in a comprehensive; others left for promotion elsewhere.

My consultations with members of staff were genuine and would continue after the school opened. I was not enamoured of mass meetings of what would be a very large staff for the conduct of business, though these would be necessary from time to time (in fact I called them once a term and had no complaint as far as I recall). I worked through heads of department and heads of pastoral work (which I had to build up), who would be expected to have regular and frequent departmental meetings and inform me of their problems for discussion and possible resolution. I had ultimate managerial responsibility and was answerable to the authority for the conduct of the school. Of course when the Authority created new governing bodies, I reported regularly to them. I was very fortunate in having as my chair of governors the Chairman of the Education Committee of the Authority.

I had no hesitations about staff deployment. We were one school and would be one staff. Thus my timetabling instructions to heads of department (to whom I gave a great deal of autonomy) were to use all their staff throughout the school, especially for the new entry, consistent with the maintenance of existing grammar-tech courses. I also wanted heads of departments to teach if possible in both lower and upper forms. There was no reason why modern school staff should not take grammar-tech classes where able, and it would be good for the others to get used to teaching the slower learners. The children had to get the best we had to offer.

Though organization occupied much attention, its only point was to subserve curriculum. Curriculum is all in a school – so much else flows from the right decisions here. The new entry would have a genuinely comprehensive education with everything that anyone could reasonably include in a 'common core' – science, technical and practical studies, art, music, French, as well as the staple subjects. This we wanted to continue for the first three years. We were also thinking of a course system in the fourth and fifth forms which would allow the continuation of a broad education consistent with examination demands.

For nearly all the children coming in this was a substantial extension of opportunity over what would have occurred under the old system and, for many in both the grammar-tech and modern schools, we were able to offer new technical facilities. The new entry would also have mixed ability teaching though provision was made for setting French and Maths if the departments wanted. We could not go beyond this at that stage because of the committee's pledge.

Having studied the records of the children in the modern school and, later, seeing the composition of the new entry, I made what I believe was the most crucial decision of all if we were to succeed as a comprehensive, which was to deploy a substantial part of our generous staffing allocation in creating what was to become through growth the largest remedial department in the country (later re-named, after the fashion, special education).

All my experience as a classroom teacher and head had been with working-class children. It is a cliché these days that low expectation seriously affects very many such children's educational development. But I always believed that responsibility for this lay with the two- or three-tier system of secondary education built upon a foundation of under-resourced primary schools. I saw my job as trying to redress the wrongs of the old divided educational world through the liberal conditions of the new comprehensive dispensation informed with the spirit of what my old mentor, G.C.T. Giles, called 'mass educability'.

When we began the comprehensive with the prospect of large numbers of children requiring such attention, the big problem was getting staff properly trained for the job. These were not very thick on the ground, nor, indeed, were people suitable to run a large remedial department, a job which required considerable expertise, devotion, optimism, imagination and, most of all, patience. Lack of professional expertise had to be compensated for in our circumstances by enthusiasm. The fact that most remedial teachers were volunteers for a very trying job was a big plus in their favour. On the whole we were lucky with our recruitment, though to some applicants, glowing with educational and social idealism, we had to explain that their job was not to apply Paolo Freire's theories in downtown Willesden.

We had no infallible way of deciding admission to a remedial class for the simple reason that no such criteria existed then or now. Children are 'backward' for all sorts of reasons and we decided to adopt a pragmatic approach including primary school reports and reading tests which were usually very valuable and reasonably accurate. Most important it was essential to recognize that any initial placement was provisional and what mattered was how after a while their teachers in the new school estimated each child's ability to cope. The objective was to move children out of a remedial class into the mainstream.

We estimated a need for seven remedial classes, two (after a term's experience three) in the first year, two in the second, one in the third (soon two) and two in the fourth, plus specialist groups for reading and English as a second language (ESL). The work was to be done in small classes mainly under a single teacher and, in addition, we would withdraw children from ordinary classes for extra reading and maths. Without these arrangements subject teachers, untrained for and unused to coping with what would have been massive and extraordinarily difficult teaching problems, would have sunk into despair and become resentful under the burden.

The overall aim of the remedial work and the best criterion of its success would be when we judged children had advanced enough to be absorbed painlessly into the mainstream classes. To abolish the remedial department altogether would have been the biggest success of all! Alas remedial work did not always produce the hoped for results – permanent improvement of attainment. Children can fall back. We still know too little how children learn and how to deal with their learning difficulties. Even with our generous staffing (almost as good as in the public schools thanks to Brent's generosity and understanding) we still did not have enough to do what we would have liked.

Other problems seemed insignificant beside the immensity of this one. I outlawed corporal punishment, though not everyone agreed. We began building what was to become a highly successful pastoral system based on forms. This seems commonplace today but I am writing of the 1960s when it was far from commonplace. There had been no experience in any of our constituent schools of an organized pastoral system. Indeed, pastoral systems had to be built up in all the new comprehensives – those who criticized deployment of staff on pastoral work can have had no idea of how absolutely essential they were if we were to succeed.

A PTA was organized. I visited all the feeder primary schools to meet the children coming in and their staffs and heads. We held meetings for the new parents. We opened in September 1967 with what I hoped and expected to be a smoothly running organization.

Six months after our opening we held our first Speech Day, christening our brand new assembly hall, with Christopher Hill, the Master of Balliol, an old friend and keen comprehensive advocate, as guest speaker. He entertained us with superb wit and unconventional wisdom. As I listened to his warm words for what he had seen, I felt relaxed for the first time in 15 months. Thanks to the magnificent response of my colleagues to the difficult problems they had faced we seemed set fair for the future.

Five years later, when the first entry had completed the statutory secondary school course, I listened to another Speech Day guest, Vic Feather, General Secretary of the TUC, kiss the blarney stone ('the best Comprehensive school I have seen yet') after I had made my fifth annual report. That had shown conclusively (we had researched thoroughly) that in exam results all those who would have been selected for grammar school education under the old system had done about as well as they would have done under that system, while the rest, the great majority, had done substantially better. Whether a school is a success or not depends on many factors. But, I reflected, we had beaten the Cassandras on the one factual criterion they had forecast we could not fulfil. In that particular aspect of educational attainment we had beyond any shadow of doubt proved that, while we were advancing the education of the slower, those ahead in the race did not suffer.

I worked in the school as head for 11 years until I had to retire. With the support of my deputies, senior and junior staff, I feel we accomplished something very positive for the children of the neighbourhood which would have been impossible under the old divided system and which proved the value of comprehensive education as the right way to handle the community's schools.

5 The Case Against Selection

Roy Hattersley

The case for comprehensive secondary education is beyond rational dispute. Were I to fear for a fleeting second that the argument *for* selection had the slightest merit, I would remind myself of the way in which 'the grammar school lobby' advances its outdated cause. Opponents of comprehensive schools – especially in those local authorities whose parents have battled to end the 11-plus – always choose to campaign on a single fraudulent argument. The comprehensive ideal, they claim, destroys 'good schools' and depresses the general quality of education. They know – or at least they ought to know – that the end of selection has had quite the opposite effect. Comprehensive education is one of the success stories of the twentieth century.

It is the comprehensive schools which have produced the boom in higher education. The explosion in student numbers – so great that it can no longer be financed by government grants – is the direct result of ending selection. The old municipal and county grammar schools which comprehensive reorganization replaced were – even on the limited criteria of examination results – a disgrace. A hundred and twenty 11-year-olds – designated by examination to be the brightest and best of their age group – enrolled in the first form. Most of them came from highly supportive homes. They were taught in small classes by highly qualified teachers and enjoyed both 'superior' facilities and the encouragement that came from being told that they were 'special'. Yet only about twenty members of the original intake found their way into higher education. A comprehensive school with results like that would face the humiliation of 'special measures'.

Sadly the failure of the old grammar schools is not just part of our education history. Where they still exist, the problem of under-achievement persists. Results in Kent – where the Conservative-controlled Local Education Authority defends its grammar schools as 'centres of excellence' – are worse than those in many of the London boroughs which are derided as examples of the comprehensive system's failure. In 17 of the county's schools less than 30 per cent of the students were awarded five or more GCSE passes at grades A to C in 2003. Worse still, in terms of those schools' performance, many of them showed no 'value added'. They were, of course, the 'community schools' – secondary moderns by another name.

Of course there are some unsuccessful comprehensive schools. Since comprehensive institutions are responsible for the education of around 95 per cent of all English school students, that is hardly surprising. But most of the 'failures', about which the supporters of selection make so much noise, are 'comprehensive' only in name. By definition, comprehensive and selective schools cannot exist side by side. Once a percentage of pupils is 'creamed off' to grammar schools, the essential all-entry intake is impossible. The name may be changed on the school gate notice board. But the school remains a secondary modern. Many of them do their best for the pupils in their care. But to compare their results with those in the grammar school down the road – and then to declare the whole comprehensive system a failure – is fraudulent nonsense.

Naturally enough, the highly selective Kent grammar schools produce very good results. And so they should. The case for comprehensive education has never been built on the pretence that modern grammar schools do badly – though many of them do not perform as well as they should. The problem in those areas where grammar schools remain is the effect that selection has on the whole secondary system. It meets the needs of a minority at the expense of the majority of pupils who are deemed 'unsuitable' for an 'academic education'. And it is important to understand the inadequacy of the process by which the minority is chosen. In theory, the test – examination, continuous assessment or interview – identifies the ability and aptitude. We know that the margin of error is more than 10 per cent. But the mistake – the allocation of 'academic' pupils to secondary modern schools – is not its worst fault. Testing – and especially testing at 11-plus – is inevitably socially biased. The middle classes enjoy a built-in advantage. If you doubt it, look at the incidence of free school meals in the areas where selection remains. Very few of the very poor find their way to grammar schools. Free school meals are a feature of the secondary modern.

That is one reason why the idea of selection providing 'escape routes' from the inner-city ghettoes is sentimental nonsense. In the selective system, thousands of 'bright' children are written off because of their social backgrounds. But the real argument against 'escape routes' is more fundamental. And it goes to the heart of the argument for comprehensive education. The creation of 'escape routes' accepts – by definition – that there are parts of the education system from which 'escape' is necessary. And any process which allows one or two 'talented' boys and girls to find refuge in a grammar school allows the rest to suffer the deprivations and disadvantages from which the fortunate few have 'escaped'. A civilized country – indeed any country which wants to maximize the potential of its people – seeks a general system of education from which no 'escape' is necessary. The 'ladder of opportunity' argument is just a sop to the conscience of that selfish minority which wants to enjoy an education which is 'superior' to that available to most of the country's students.

The case for comprehensive schools is, therefore, the need – the obvious, self-evident, undeniable need – to provide the best possible education for the largest possible percentage of the population. Selection fails that test in primary as well as secondary schools. For it unavoidably diverts the curriculum from genuine education to 'passing the test'. Kent again provides the example of what should *not* happen. In that highly selective county, primary school pupils sit 'familiarization tests'. Some heads expect all of Year 6 to complete the practice papers – whether they are taking the examination or not. Others separate potential grammar school 'sheep' from community school 'goats'. The result was summed up by Charles Clarke, the Secretary of State for Education and Skills:

According to Ofsted, Kent's KS2 results are below those of its statistical neighbours. Clearly, as the research concluded, emphasis on tests at the expense of a balanced curriculum is not in the best interests of all the pupils.

Here we have the view of a 'New Labour' minister who is committed to the principle that education policy should be based on 'what works' rather than on any ideological or social precept. And those of us who argue in favour of a comprehensive system must never forget that by the Government's own – admittedly intellectually inadequate – criteria it 'works' better, far better than the segregation which follows selection. It works – in terms even of examination results – because it does not discourage and depress those pupils who are 'written off' in the selective system. It works because it is based on the knowledge that the school population possesses more intellectual ability than the grammar school enthusiasts allow and because it believes that encouragement is essential to the development of a student's full potential. It works because it boosts the morale of staff as well as of students and makes a whole school realize how much *all* its members can achieve.

The success of the comprehensive system is now accepted in most of the country. In those counties where genuine comprehensive schools have been created – meeting the needs of every pupil from the intellectually 'gifted' to those in special needs – there is only bewilderment about why the end of selection is still a subject of controversy. Part of the answer is London – where the 'comprehensive schools' are rarely genuine and all the problems of an overcrowded capital are reflected in the education system. Go to Derbyshire or the West Riding of Yorkshire, Oxfordshire or the county of Nottingham, and parents of every sort will express their unequivocal support for the comprehensive system.

Yet little pockets of resistance to progress remain. Regrettably they often coincide with those provincial suburbs in which general elections are won and lost. In consequence, a government obsessed with extending its mandate panders to the prejudices of 'swing voters'. In Solihull, a town ballot in the 1980s which offered a return to selection, confirmed that the prosperous burghers of that West Midlands borough wanted to keep their comprehensive schools. I have no doubt that an honest poll would produce the same result in the areas where selection remains. Unfortunately the 'parents' ballot', introduced in 1999, was a confidence trick – intentionally geared to ensure that the result maintained the status quo. The campaign in Richmond, North Yorkshire, confirmed that the Government had organized a classic 'gerrymander'. Parents likely to vote against selection were excluded from the list of voters. Parents likely to vote in favour – including a number from outside the city who sent their children to private schools – were allowed to take part. That was an admission by the Government that comprehensive schools are popular with a majority of voters. So they should be, since they offer a good education to a majority of our school students. But it is important to recognize the reason why an influential minority remains in passionate support of selection.

The case for selection is *social* rather than *educational*. For we know that many students whose parents have chosen grammar schools would do just as well in the comprehensive system. A grammar school place is what economists call 'a positional good' – a possession which is valued as much for the status which it confers as for the inherent benefits which it provides. The selective system is a relic of the characteristic which has held this country back for five hundred years. The English like hierarchies. We feel most comfortable in societies in which class is clearly delineated and accept that some people rise while others fall. It is a peculiarly English disease. The Scots and the Welsh have always taken a more rational view about social division. In neither country is the creation of a complete and genuine comprehensive system an issue. Selection is regarded as a relic of the discredited past. Only in England does a vocal and influential minority cling on to the symbols of a divided society. Never forget that the grammar school enthusiasts are 'social engineers' who want the secondary school system to perpetuate the sort of society in which they believe.

I make no apology for being motivated by a parallel determination to want to live in a society which *unites* rather than *separates*, a society in which all individuals are treated with equal respect because they are acknowledged to be of equal value. The comprehensive system has a social purpose. It unites the nation and confirms that we each make a contribution to the progress of the community in which we live. It is one of the elements of government and public administration in which ideals and pragmatism both point to the same conclusion. A society which rejects secondary selection both increases the general level of educational attainment and encourages the spirit of community which is the highest mark of civilization.

6 Comprehensive Success: Bog-standard Government*

Sally Tomlinson

Governments over the past forty years have demonstrated a bog-standard[1] commitment to the principle of equal value of every individual's learning capabilities, free from prior judgements about who has more 'ability' or 'aptitude' than others. There has also been a very limited commitment to the equal resourcing and funding of all schools and colleges. A major project of the political Right throughout the second half of the twentieth century and into the twenty-first has been to deny any recognition of the successes of democratic education reform, and to keep or reintroduce the sort of selection which works for the creation of an hierarchical society. No government so far has come near to resolving the contradictions involved in securing greater investment and training for all, in a society that still regards educating the working-class and the disadvantaged with ambivalence. Initiatives to expand vocational programmes, especially from age 14, and engage the truants, the disaffected and the socially excluded are not aimed at the middle-class. The retention of overtly selective schools and the introduction of education markets in England which are intended to provide choice and competition between a diversity of schools are proving extraordinarily effective in reintroducing a complex system of selection and inequitable resourcing in which the working-class and disadvantaged are the obvious losers. There has been an astonishing lack of support for teachers, local authorities, parents and

* This chapter was originally given as the Third Caroline Benn Memorial Lecture at the Institute of Education, London, on 15 November 2003.

communities who have worked to carry out what, despite the immensity of the task, has actually been a *successful* transformation of secondary education. Attacks on comprehensive schools by those in or near government have persisted, and attempts to destabilize the principles, infrastructure and purpose of comprehensive education continue.

In 1996 Caroline Benn and Clyde Chitty, in a study of some 1560 schools and colleges – all LEAs in England, Scotland and Wales being represented – asked whether comprehensive education was 'alive and well' or 'struggling to survive'. As almost 90 per cent of young people attended comprehensive schools by the 1990s, they had clearly survived. But Benn and Chitty found:

> a severe and debilitating contradiction at the heart of the majority's education over the past thirty years in Britain. On the one hand, governments were ostensibly supporting the comprehensive principle to which most schools and colleges were becoming committed; while, at the same time, they were either failing to support it adequately or working hard to undermine its principles and practices, and, in some cases, making it clear that they had no confidence in an education that did not prejudge an individual's worth or facilitate an escalation of enclaves for the favoured few. (Benn and Chitty, 1996, p. 468)

The contradictions in New Labour's education policies, and lack of support for comprehensive principles, became apparent early on. While the 1998 Education Act was permitting continued selection for grammar schools by 'ability' and allowing all schools to select a percentage of pupils on 'aptitude', Prime Minister Blair was writing in *The Times Educational Supplement* about his vision of an inclusive society (Blair, 1998). By the following year he was committing the Government to the achievement of a meritocracy – 'ladders of opportunity for all ... no more ceilings to prevent people achieving the success they merit' (Blair, 1999), with no mention of those on the lower rungs of the ladder. By 2001 he was enlisting 'post-comprehensive education' to support meritocracy by 'diversity' and his advisers and ministers were openly attacking comprehensive schools. Alastair Campbell, his communications director, referred, in February 2001, to 'bog-standard comprehensives' in cities, and Estelle Morris, Secretary of State for Education for a year until October 2002, asserted during her tenure that there were 'some schools she would not touch with a barge-pole'. Conservative Shadow Home Secretary Oliver Letwin joined in, claiming in October 2003 that he would 'rather go out on the streets and beg' than send his children to the local comprehensive in London (see Aaronovitch, 2003).

This chapter briefly documents some of the successes of comprehensive education, refuting the assertion, repeated in ministerial pronouncements and press releases, that there has ever been a 'one-size-fits-all' system. It points out the bog-standard policy of retaining and expanding selection of pupils when evidence is mounting that selection does not contribute to raising educational standards. It examines the dubious strategy of promoting 'modernizing diversity' via the creation of specialist schools and more faith schools. It revisits the late Lord Michael Young's book *The Rise of the Meritocracy* (1958) in which he satirized the rise of a class who believed their 'merit' entitled them to endless privileges above those who had not demonstrated sufficient merit. This situation, he believed, had come about by 2001, and 'as a result, general inequality has become more grievous ... and without a bleat from those who once spoke up so trenchantly for greater equality' (Young, 2001).

VERY OLD LABOUR

The New Labour Party has made much of repudiating policies that were considered to belong to 'Old Labour'. Yet support for selection for separate schools is very Old Labour. The 1944 legislation was based on educationally spurious notions of three types of mind – academic, technical and practical. Children were separated at 11 on the basis of supposedly 'scientific' testing and the result was that from 1946 some 80 per cent were placed in secondary modern schools with inferior resources. A 1945 Labour pamphlet argued that these schools were for children whose future employment 'would not demand any measure of technical skill or knowledge' and the Labour Party argued against comprehensive education until 1952. Even when comprehensive education was party policy, the leadership was satisfied that grammar schools should continue to educate small selected groups. Tony Benn recorded in his diary in 1953 that Hugh Gaitskell – soon to be leader – 'still wants an educated elite learning Latin verse' (Benn, 1994, p. 172). The ideology of meritocracy has always had a strong appeal for privately schooled Oxbridge educated Labour leaders. However, both the Conservative Government and Labour in opposition in the early 1960s recognized that educating more young people to higher levels was an economic necessity, and this coincided with – mainly – Labour politicians' view that educating all children together, rather than selecting a few for a higher status, better-resourced education, was a desirable egalitarian aim.[2] Deterministic theories of intelligence began to be rejected, and before Labour was elected in 1964, 90 out of 163 Local Education Authorities had plans to end selection. Mrs Thatcher, in her period as Education Minister in the 1970s, while lamenting that she was unable to slow down the comprehensive movement, approved more plans for school reorganization than had any other Education Minister, and by the early 1990s some 88 per cent of young people in England were in comprehensive schools. Wales and Scotland developed fully comprehensive non-selective systems, and were not tempted by the subsequent return to selection and unequal funding of some comprehensive schools as grant-maintained or specialist.[3]

By 2003 the New Labour Government was presiding over an hierarchical secondary education system which included some 1528 private schools, three city academies – private schools financed by the state – with 30 more planned, 15 private city technology colleges which were about to become academies, 164 grammar schools, 992 specialist secondary schools (with more planned) and some 2300 notional comprehensive schools. After the 1998 Act schools had designated themselves as either foundation schools (and most schools which had had preferential funding as grant-maintained schools under the Conservatives chose this label), voluntary aided or controlled religious schools or community schools. The word 'comprehensive' did not appear in New Labour's first big Education Act. Foundation or community special schools catered for some 1 per cent of pupils considered to have special educational needs. There was an expansion of Pupil Referral Units which selected out disaffected and disruptive pupils, and there were designated programmes to select 'gifted' and 'talented' pupils and those needing Learning Support Units. Sixth form, tertiary and Further Education colleges variously educated pupils to A Level, with an increasing number of predominantly working-class pupils attending vocational or work experience courses in colleges and on employers' premises from age 14.

COMPREHENSIVE SUCCESS

The success of comprehensive education, as both an education project that raised standards and, to a lesser extent, an egalitarian project has been remarkable. It was not to be expected, in a class-conscious country like England, that educating all social classes together would be popular, and despite the professional and managerial classes doing best out of comprehensive education, middle-class strategies for avoiding their children being educated with the poor have become more and more ingenious and expensive (see Reay, 1998; Ball, 2003). Nevertheless standards, as measured by those entering and passing public examinations, have been steadily rising since the 1960s. In 1962, when some 20 per cent were selected for grammar schools, 16 per cent of pupils obtained five O Level passes. In 2001 51 per cent achieved the equivalent of five GCSE passes. The A Level exam, originally designed for less than 10 per cent of the population, was achieved in two or more subjects by 37 per cent of young people in 2001. In 1970, 47 per cent left school without any qualifications; by 2000 this had fallen to 10 per cent. In the early 1960s less than 10 per cent went on to higher education. The Robbins Committee, which published its findings in 1963, recommended an increase to 17 per cent (Ministry

of Education, 1963). By 2002 some 40 per cent are in higher
education, with a government aim of increasing this to 50 per cent.

Those who assert that more working-class students made it into
higher education when grammar schools were the norm are
contradicted by the Robbins Committee. Their survey showed
that in 1961/2 some 64 per cent of students in higher education had
fathers in professional or management jobs, only 4 per cent had
fathers in semi-skilled jobs and 2 per cent came from unskilled
homes. Eventually thousands who had 'failed' their 11-plus
obtained degrees through Harold Wilson's great success – the
Open University – and millions more obtained further education in
comprehensive institutions. By 2000 some 450 FE colleges,
although underfunded, were providing a comprehensive education
and skills training for nearly five million students and a million
more were enrolled on adult education courses.

A major success of comprehensive education has been the
education of groups not previously considered 'able' enough for a
subject-centred secondary education, calling into question notions
of 'ability'. Grammar schools always educated predominantly
middle- and lower-middle-class children, with enough 'bright'
working-class children selected to maintain an illusion of 'equality
of opportunity'. Although arguments continue to be made that
grammar schools facilitated social mobility – and this was certainly
true for many originally lower-middle-class public service professionals who reached more secure middle-class positions – it was
comprehensive schooling that enabled widespread occupational
mobility. In 1960 three-quarters of the male working population
were in manual jobs. Owing to comprehensive education and a
changed occupational structure, their children are predominantly in
a wide variety of non-manual jobs. Offering all girls the chance of
more equal study in comprehensives led to a closing of the gap in
male and female achievements, although accompanied by moral
panics about low-achieving boys. Ethnic minority groups have
never done well in systems of selection in England, but have
improved their achievements overall through comprehensive
education, and the partial inclusion of disabled young people
must also be regarded as a success. Primary education has remained

largely comprehensive, despite recent calls for returns to selection by streaming children, and a very 'un-bog-standard' policy of the New Labour Government has been to offer free pre-school comprehensive education to all children from age 3 years.

Part of the attack on comprehensive secondary education, and a defence of the diversity strategy, has been to continually assert that comprehensives were based on a 'one-size-fits-all' model. The supposed sameness of comprehensives has been constantly disproved. Smith and Tomlinson (1989), Benn and Chitty (1996), Pring and Walford (1997) and others have all demonstrated the efforts the schools have always made to respond to their locality, teach all children effectively and develop a distinctive ethos. The jibe of similarity became somewhat ridiculous after the introduction of the National Curriculum. Research studies have also found no demand for 'specialism' at secondary level, beyond the 'broad and balanced education' the National Curriculum was intended to provide. The parents Benn and Chitty researched in 1994 wanted:

> broad-based comprehensive schools specialising in a full range of learning, with high standards throughout in *each* field in *each* school. (p. 323)

In 2003, the Chief Eduation Officer in Hertfordshire told the House of Commons Select Committee on Education and Skills that:

> What Hertfordshire parents say to me is that they want a high quality local school. Education is a public service and people have a right to a good local school and not to have to shop around to get it.

OVERT SELECTION

In 1996 David Blunkett, then Shadow Education Secretary, pledged 'no more selection under a Labour Government', but while in office presided over an increasingly selective school system. Stephen Pollard, a politically well-connected commentator, wrote in 2001 that the provision of a diversity of schools and programmes for 'the gifted and talented' meant that 'selection is back as a centrepiece of educational policy' (Pollard, 2001). Private education continues to be the major source of selective education, the better schools selecting by both money and testing. The private sector is highly significant as although only around 7 per cent of children overall are in private education – rising to over 30 per cent in Richmond on Thames – some 26 per cent of those who take A Levels come from private schools and over 40 per cent are found in the 'best' universities. Private education continues to translate into privilege in the labour market, a 1990s study concluding that a superclass of top professionals are now an almost entirely privately schooled elite (Adonis and Pollard, 1997). Privately schooled pupils are also increasingly part of a new global elite, moving on to world-class universities and top multinational jobs (Ong, 2003).

The remaining 164 grammar schools constitute the major source of state school selection, affecting the intake of some 500 'comprehensive' schools, 15 LEAs remaining wholly selective and 21 partially selective. Admissions to grammar schools increased by 20 per cent in the 1990s, with a corresponding increase into secondary modern schools. The grammar schools remain largely middle-class enclaves, around 2 per cent of pupils on free school meals (the poverty measure in schooling) compared to 18 per cent nationally, and are heavily oversubscribed by intensively tutored children. Despite promises of 'no selection' while in opposition, the Government introduced six pages of legislation into the 1998 Education Act concerning balloting of parents for the retention of grammar schools. This was probably the ultimate 'bog-standard' policy, as it allowed parents with children at private schools to vote, and denied many local parents a vote. In addition, the Government has encouraged philanthropic schemes based on 'escape' from supposedly less attractive comprehensive schools.[4] Unequal resourcing between grammars and secondary modern schools is a major, but undebated, issue of social justice. In Buckingham, Bucks Grammar accumulated a surplus of £900,000 over three years, while the local secondary moderns accumulated a similar deficit. Ministers continue to play down the issue of overt selection, Schools Minister David Miliband asserting that 'the ending of the 11-plus in most parts of the country was a victory over structural inequality of opportunity' (Miliband, 2003); and the current Secretary of State for Education, while criticizing the 11-plus, being reluctant to take measures to forbid practices which affect selection (see Hattersley, 2004).

Defence of selective education is becoming more untenable as there is accumulating evidence that selection lowers educational standards overall and that even the most 'able' pupils would progress as well in comprehensive schools. A 'value-added' analysis of public examination results in comparable LEAs concluded that the differences in progress in comprehensive and selective systems are not striking, although they do appear to operate in favour of the former, especially at higher levels of attainment (see Schagen and Schagen, 2003). The first publication of government value-added league tables of schools in January 2004 also showed comprehensive schools adding most value to pupils' learning. Kent, the county famously sticking with selection, has been the subject of several studies demonstrating the malign effect of selection on overall standards and the distortion of the primary curriculum to accommodate preparation for the 11-plus (Jesson, 2001; Hattersley, 2004), and a study in Northern Ireland documented that selection was socially divisive, damaged self-esteem, disrupted teaching and reinforced inequality of opportunity (Gallagher and Smith, 2002). The widely quoted programme for international student assessment (the PISA study) demonstrated that countries with non-selective systems achieved the highest overall standards of education (OECD, 2002).

COVERT SELECTION

Overt selection of up to 10 per cent of pupils by 'aptitude' is legally permitted in all secondary schools, the lawyers drafting the 1998 Act producing miracles of legal jargon to differentiate between tests of 'ability' and tests of 'aptitude'. The House of Commons Education and Skills Committee were later to report that they could find no meaningful distinction between 'ability' and 'aptitude', but schools designated as specialist are able to take advantage of the notion of selection by 'aptitude', especially those Foundation, Voluntary and Grammar specialist schools which are their own admissions authorities. Despite attempts to introduce fairer admissions policies – the DfES producing the latest Code of Practice on school admissions in late 2003 – the evidence so far is that some schools employ a variety of covert methods for selecting some pupils and rejecting others (see West and Hinds, 2003). This is not entirely unexpected. Education reforms designed to create 'quasi-markets' signalled a deliberate move away from secondary schools as local or community institutions to schools as competing providers and parents have been encouraged by league tables and inspection reports to shop around for 'best buys'. As competition for entry to 'good schools' intensified, so schools increased their methods of covert selection, by interview and other means. Entry to faith schools – Anglican and Catholic schools doing well in league tables – has encouraged large numbers of parents to discover their faith roots. Selection by mortgage, a growing practice from the 1980s as those able to afford it moved house to be near desirable schools, has recently been quantified by estate agents as a £42,000 premium to be near a 'good' primary school, and £23,000 to be near a good secondary school (Garrett, 2002).

The Government has also encouraged *within* school selection. The *Excellence in Cities* action plan launched in 1999 (DfEE, 1999) was largely an attempt to retain the middle classes in inner-city schools, and to reassure influential and vocal ethnic minorities about the quality of education offered to their children. The programme included more setting by ability, more learning support and mentoring of low-ability pupils, and selection of 'gifted and talented' pupils – the most able 5–10 per cent to attend summer schools, do more extra-curricular activities and take 'world-class' tests. Warwick University won a bid to establish an Academy for Gifted and Talented Youth, at which the fortunate 'gifted' would pay for courses. Early evaluation of these programmes found white middle-class children more likely to be selected as 'gifted' and the programme did not appear to raise educational standards overall.

FAILING SCHOOLS

While policies which encourage overt and covert selection do not appear to raise standards overall, the bog-standard policy of labelling schools as 'failing' and in need of special measures appears to be one of the most pointless policies instigated by a Conservative government and continued by New Labour. Failing schools are demonized institutions whose heads, teachers and governors are deemed personally responsible for the under-performance of students. Research has subsequently demonstrated that despite 'parachuting' in heads to 'turn around' failing schools, such schools lose their headteachers twice as fast as the national average. At the time of the 1997 General Election, press coverage of failing schools became almost hysterical in its negative portrayal of 'the worst school in Britain'. Politicians competed in macho style to 'name and shame' failing schools, almost all comprehensive or secondary modern schools attended by the children of the poor, by minority pupils and those with special educational needs. These were pupils not wanted in schools attempting to boost their league table positions (see Tomlinson, 1997). Although market forces were helping to create failing schools, it was not until the end of 1998 that the public humiliation of schools and teachers was abandoned, although the pressure placed on schools to drive up their GCSE results, usually by concentrating on pupils on the borderline of obtaining a C grade, continued to have negative effects (see Gillborn and Youdell, 2000). The contradiction involved in attempting to raise standards in disadvantaged areas while retaining parental preference has become more obvious as schools have become more polarized by social class. Schools with high levels of disadvantage have become more so, and very few schools with poor children attending achieve good examination results (Bradley and Taylor, 2002). After studying the wide variation in achievements between social classes shown up in the PISA study, German researchers pointed out that the comprehensive system in England was being undermined by a competitive market system.

MODERNIZING DIVERSITY

In January 2001 the Government published a remarkably self-congratulatory Green Paper announcing that 'we have got the basics right in primary schools' and that standards of literacy and numeracy had been transformed. The mission was now to bring about a transformation in secondary schools, moving away from a comprehensive system that had apparently not differentiated between individual abilities and aptitudes, or provided for those of high academic ability or vocational and work-related routes. After presenting this travesty of comprehensive education, the Paper went on to assert that comprehensives, apart from church schools, had had little scope to develop a 'distinctive character or mission', had been built on a 'one-size-fits-all' model and did not cater for 'individual needs and aspirations'. The promised transformation was not to be achieved by funding and resourcing all schools fairly, but by promoting an unfair diversity through the specialist school programme, establishing more faith schools, and private City Academies, and separating out pupils of high ability and those on vocational or work-based routes. Extra money and resources were also given or promised to Beacon schools, 'Leading Edge' specialist schools, Teacher Training Schools and Extended Schools incorporating social services. By 2003, the diversity agenda of specialist schools had become a basic plank of New Labour education policy that was, as several ministers noted, 'not negotiable'.

The specialist schools programme had its origins in the Conservative introduction, in 1988, of City Technology Colleges, schools to be funded by business. In the event the 15 colleges ended up largely funded by taxpayers and eventually incorporated into the City Academies programme of more privately run, state-supported schools. From 1993 the Conservative Government added to the specialist programme, attempting to increase education market-ization via choice and competition and business influence. To qualify each school had to raise £50,000 from private sponsors, to be matched by £150,000 plus £123 for each pupil, from the government. Among the first schools to bid for specialist status in

1994 were grant-maintained (later foundation) schools which had already had extra government money. Specialist schools coming on-stream during the 1990s have thus accumulated extra finances running in some cases into millions. Of the schools in operation early in 2003 some 173 specialized in arts, 18 in business and enterprise, 4 in engineering, 157 in languages, 12 in maths and computing, 24 in science, 162 in sports and 443 in technology. Cyril Taylor, adviser to Mrs Thatcher and knighted by her for services to the City Technology Trust, became chairperson of what then turned into the Specialist Schools Trust and received a special extra knighthood from New Labour in 2004. Numbers of schools actually operating as specialist were unclear into 2004. The DfES Paper in 2003 announced that from September 217 more would become specialist, bringing the total to 'at least 1209', with new specialisms in music and the humanities to come on stream in September 2004. However, the Paper also noted that the Government's key reform was 'to create a new specialist system where each school has its own specialist ethos'. It certainly appeared that the Government could not decide whether to persist with the unequal funding of some secondary schools or recognize the gross inequalities they had put in place.

Just as proponents of grammar schools had from the 1960s published research purporting to show that grammar and secondary modern schools produced better examination results than comprehensive schools, so the Specialist Schools Programme had barely begun operating than research ostensibly showing that it produced better results began to appear. The Specialist Schools Trust, with an obvious vested interest, reported at the end of 2003 that of pupils in 938 specialist schools they surveyed, 56 per cent achieved five or more A–C grades at GCSE, as against 47 per cent of pupils in 1193 non-specialist comprehensive and secondary modern schools (see Jesson, Taylor and Ware, 2003). With no sense of irony, the Trust reported that the longer a school had been 'specialist' the more it improved, perhaps a relief to the Government to know that millions had been well spent. An Ofsted evaluation of 327 specialist schools also noted their improved academic performance, except for sports colleges, predominantly to be found in inner cities. Even Cyril

Taylor conceded that this could be due to the lower-ability intake of these schools. It is also the case, as reported by the manager of the Trudex Textile Company, which supplied most of the school uniforms in the country, that specialist language and arts schools chose traditional uniforms of blazers, shirts and ties, while sports colleges clothed their pupils in sweatshirts and jumpers. The assumption that specialist and non-specialist schools can be compared without taking into account extra resources and funding over ten years, overt and covert selection, and the history and location of every school, is non-sense (in the literal meaning). However, this will not deter those seeking evidence to prove their policy of creating a hierarchy of schools is right.

THE RISE OF THE MERITOCRACY

New Labour's rationale for its policies is primarily that all members of a society have a duty to invest in their own human capital which will, in turn, improve national economic productivity in a global market. But since all cannot acquire the desirable jobs in a high skills economy, there must be meritocratic competition between individuals who have different abilities and aptitudes – or, according to most of the recent government publications, have different needs and aspirations. The government, in this scenario, will provide the ladders of opportunity, there will be equality of opportunity for all to climb, unhindered by social class, gender, ethnicity, or disability. In these meritocratic terms it presumably makes sense that any belief in educating all children together in comprehensive schools, without prior selection for unequal and different provision, has to be jettisoned. The notion of a diverse school system creating a stratified workforce which corresponds to economic and business needs is very attractive to governments. A report produced for the European Commission in 1996 unambiguously asserted that 'education systems are required to function as a hierarchical talent filter' (see Reiffers Report, 1996). Selection, diversity and inequality of provision make sense if education is seen primarily as the means by which young people are prepared for work at different levels in a flexible labour force, with a curriculum increasingly influenced by economic interests.

But there are considerable problems associated with the notion of a meritocracy. Goldthorpe, reviewing the history of the concept in 1997, concluded that throughout the twentieth century the working-classes have always had to demonstrate considerably more merit than have others to achieve desirable positions, and that attempts to provide the structures of inequality within modern societies with a meritocratic legitimation do not succeed (Goldthorpe, 1997). The history of sponsoring 'meritorious' poor children into private or selective schools has been one persistent attempt to legitimate a system geared to social inequality.

The late Lord Michael Young, who invented the term in his satire *The Rise of the Meritocracy* (1958) showed that a meritocracy involved the creation of a new social class who believed their privileges and superior status were deserved because of their pure merit, as demonstrated by high IQ and educational qualifications. While the good intentions of the government in Young's satire were to separate individual merit from birth, wealth, nepotism, bribery, patronage or purchase, the rise of the new class led to considerable problems. The book took the form of a journal written by a hero of the people killed in a violent encounter between the Meritocracy and the Populist Party at Peterloo in 2034 and it described how the government had attempted, by 'scientific' testing, to create the meritocracy. The threat of the comprehensive school was 'seen off' as clever children were progressively separated from the stupid who remained or were demoted to the lower classes. The meritorious climbed the ladder into the higher class. They acquired new accents and joned BUGSA (the British Union of Grammar School Attenders), and intelligence tests became so refined that all members of the public were required to carry a National Intelligence Card, issued by HQ Eugenics House. Alas, the children of lords were not always happy to be demoted because of their dullness, living in council houses and doing menial work. Women were not keen on producing their IQ card before marriage. A hard core of envious egalitarians became a danger to the state, and a member of the elite was forced to write a pamphlet urging a *Fair*

Deal for the Upper Classes. Eventually a populist movement challenged the meritocracy and the mass confrontation took place at Peterloo!

This cautionary tale has presumably not been read by Prime Minister Blair or his ministers, and the sad situation of dull demoted lords was never a possibility. The point Young made, in an article written in 2001, was that while it is good to appoint people to jobs on their merit, there are dangers that the meritocracy will harden into a self-regarding group without room in it for others (Young, 2001). In our modern social environment the rich and powerful are doing very well and are encouraged to think their advancement comes from their own merit. The obverse of this is that those judged to be without merit can feel demoralized and resentful. Young was right that general inequality becomes more grievous with every year that passes. New Labour no longer speaks up for equality, but for 'fairness' to get up the ladder. Within this rationale, there is a need to prejudge children's worth and eschew the comprehensive principle. Hence the bog-standard policies supporting selection and diversity.

The current policies are creating educational structures which encourage genuine fears of parents from all social and ethnic groups about the future of their children in the global economy and in the English social class hierarchy. Despite persistent reforms, the structures of the education system and the chances it gives to all young people are not designed to bring about a fair, democratic egalitarian society. Unless bog-standard policies are recognized for what they are, we are all losers.

NOTES

1   The term bog-standard is used here in the *Chambers Dictionary* definition of 'spongy'.
2   Edward Boyle, Conservative Minister for Education in the early 1960s, was a supporter of experiments in comprehensive education.

3   The Conservative 1988 Education Reform Act introduced
     Grant-maintained Schools, to be funded directly by central
     government, bypassing Local Education Authorities. Mrs
     Thatcher appeared on television to say she hoped all schools
     would opt out of LEA control, and a Grant-maintained Schools
     Trust, financed by business, was set up. The schools were given
     considerable capital and extra running costs. Labour abolished
     grant-maintained status, but continued to fund some schools
     over others via the specialist schools programme.
4   One such scheme is operated by the Sutton Trust, financed by
     businessman Peter Lampl, who was knighted in 2004.

7 *Eugenic Theories and Concepts of Ability*

Clyde Chitty

INTRODUCTION

The principal message that I want to put across in this chapter is that the comprehensive reform has no meaning unless it challenges the fallacy of fixed potential in education. It should dismantle the structures rooted in this fallacy that act as barriers to learning while, at the same time, facilitating practices that enable everyone to enjoy a full education. It is not concerned merely to offer *opportunities* to learn. It recognizes and proclaims the *right* to the full range of learning that is available for each age group in the compulsory period of schooling – with a full choice of learning at the other stages of life.

These ideas were already half-formed in my mind when I began my teaching career in London in 1966. I had just spent a really exciting PGCE year in the School of Education at Leicester University, where one of my teachers had been the late Professor Brian Simon. Brian was one of the country's leading campaigners for comprehensive education and had already produced two important little books, *Intelligence Testing and the Comprehensive School*, published in 1953, and *The Common Secondary School*, published in 1955, arguing that the divided secondary system was based on a whole set of false assumptions, notably the idea that it was possible to say, from the results of mental tests applied at the age of ten or eleven, what a child's future accomplishments might be.

It was actually through Brian Simon that I first came to meet Caroline Benn. Before leaving Leicester, I asked Brian how I could play a part in the burgeoning campaign for comprehensive education, and he told me about the Comprehensive Schools Committee. This had been launched in London in the autumn of 1965, two months after Tony Crosland's Department of Education and Science issued the famous Circular 10/65 requesting local education authorities to prepare plans for comprehensive reorganization. This new Committee was composed of parents, teachers and researchers, with Brian Simon as one of the original sponsors. There was to be a new magazine called *Comprehensive Education*, which would carry details of local campaigns and publish accounts of research carried out by classroom teachers in individual comprehensives. The editorial board was looking for willing volunteers to help with its production; and from my very modest involvement in 1967, I went on to co-edit the magazine with Caroline (and others) for the best part of thirty years.

The mid-1960s was indeed a blissful time to be alive (and young!), and my early work with Caroline coincided with a very happy period in my life teaching English and history at Malory School in south-east London.

Back in 1966, Malory was a large, very successful mixed comprehensive school with around 1450 students, the vast majority of whom lived on a forty-year-old working-class housing estate on the outskirts of Bromley in Kent. At the age of 11, students were allocated to one or other of ten streams arranged in a strict hierarchical order and labelled: X, Y, A, B, C, D, G, H, R and S. They remained in those streams for the next four years; and only a very small minority of students did either sufficiently well, or badly, to move up or down. At that time, 19 per cent of London children still went to selective schools; and despite its 'comprehensive' label, Malory contained very few students who would have 'passed' the old 11-plus, with this small group concentrated each year in the X stream.

Before the autumn term of 1966 had even got under way, I found that I had earned the sympathy of many of my new colleagues by being given 3D for history for three 40-minute periods a week. 3D was hardly the most popular class in the school; and teaching these students any subject was regarded by most members of staff as something of an ordeal. To make matters even worse, I was scheduled to teach them for the last period of the day on Tuesdays, Thursdays and Fridays. Yet for reasons that even now I find very difficult to articulate, they rapidly became my favourite group of students. They were bright, funny and, above all, surprisingly easy to motivate. In those early days in the classroom, I was very nervous, and although I was well-organized and spent several hours each evening on detailed lesson preparation, my teaching was relatively cautious and unadventurous. Yet, despite all my obvious shortcomings, the students in that class somehow picked up on the fact that I liked them and expected great things of them. At no point did I ever have cause to reprimand the class as a whole or individual students within it. Somewhat arrogantly, I later identified with Mr Wilkins, a young teacher in *This Right Soft Lot*, the late Edward Blishen's brilliant second novel published in 1969 and based, like the first, on his own experience of teaching in a tough secondary modern school in a deprived part of north London. This is how the author describes a rather nervous teacher who, though very formal in his approach, nevertheless earned the respect and affection of the children he taught: 'Young Mr Wilkins ... after a year of teaching, was still very stiff and four-square in the classroom, but the children yielded to him ... Everything was against Mr Wilkins: his slightness, his gentle middle-class voice, the anxious formality of his teaching. And yet he was rarely in trouble. I had overheard some of the boys talking about him, once. "He's all right, Wilkie. I mean, he helps you, don't he. I mean, he tries to help you get on. He don't just roar at you all the time. He don't just bore you stiff." It was Mr Wilkins's real, quiet concern for them that they detected; and that had value for them' (p. 29).

Well, I hope that 3D did, in fact, realize that I looked forward to the lessons I had with them. In any event, when they became 4D, I opted to take them for English as well as for history, which meant that I now saw them for 10 periods a week, accounting for a third of my teaching timetable. This was the period *before* the raising of the school leaving age to sixteen (which eventually took place in 1972/73), and in the fifth year at Malory (now Year 11), the ten streams were reduced to six. 4D became 5B1, and all the students were entered for CSE English and history. They all did extremely well, and a large number of them secured a CSE Grade One in both subjects (then considered to be the equivalent of an O-level pass). Considering this class had once been the *sixth* stream in a school with very few grammar school students, this was a remarkable achievement; and it served to reinforce all the ideas with which I had come into teaching. It led me to question the whole validity of banding, streaming and setting and to take a special interest in the issue of human intellectual capacity – and especially in the degree to which it is capable of change and development. It also led me to spend many years studying the development of eugenic views on ability to which we will now turn.

THE ORIGINS OF SOCIAL DARWINISM

Within the space of just over 10 years in the middle of the nineteenth century, two tracts were published which were to have an enormous impact worldwide and change forever existing perceptions of human development and social progress: *The Communist Manifesto*, drafted by Karl Marx and Friedrich Engels and published anonymously in London in February 1848, and *The Origin of Species*, written by Charles Darwin and published in November 1859. We know that Marx and Darwin communicated with each other and took an interest in each other's work. Darwin's evolutionary theories challenged the forces of tradition, conservatism and especially religion; and Marx immediately hailed *The Origin* as 'the basis in natural science for our views' (quoted in Hobsbawn, 1975, p. 305). Yet being a man of moderate liberal views, Darwin was in no sense an advocate of social upheaval; and he politely rejected Marx's suggestion that he should be the dedicatee of the second volume of *Capital*.

In the years that followed the publication of *The Origin of Species*, many of Darwin's views were used, or rather *misused*, to support arguments that *nature* was more important than *nurture* and that *heredity* was more important than *environment*, itself a term capable of many different meanings and embracing a number of qualitatively varied influences, both natural and social. Darwin's theory that the process of 'natural selection' had been responsible for the 'superiority' of human beings was now extended to support the view that natural selection had also determined the fact that some human beings were obviously 'superior' to others. Ideas that had initially appealed chiefly to socialists and social democrats were now taken up by a number of right-wing philosophers and political thinkers who contemplated the possibility that natural selection could produce a new race of 'supermen', destined to dominate 'human inferiors' in much the same way that human beings dominated and exploited members of the animal kingdom.

It was, above all, Darwin's second cousin, explorer and scientist Francis Galton (1822–1911), who sought to apply Darwinian principles to human society and to provide 'scientific' justification for a process of selective breeding designed to maintain and, where possible, improve the genetic condition of the human race. Galton was particularly concerned to ensure that 'racial purity' should not be undermined in increasingly democratic and egalitarian societies where the average level of ability and creativity might be in danger of declining as a result of those at the bottom end of the social scale 'over breeding'. Whereas, for Marx and Darwin, current social developments represented progress and achievement, for Galton, the idea of increasing working-class numbers and influence had appalling implications. In seeking to clarify the principles of 'Social Darwinism', Galton was also concerned to establish psychology as a *biological* science. In his first book, *Hereditary Genius*, which appeared in 1869, he published the results of a genealogical study of scientific families, claiming thereby to demonstrate that 'genius' was inborn and confined almost exclusively to certain types of privileged families with innate qualities and abilities.

On the very first page of *Hereditary Genius*, Galton extolled the virtues of 'judicious marriage', lamenting 'the degradation of human nature' by 'the propagation of the unfit' and invoking the 'duty' of the authorities to exercise power by the enforcement of strict breeding policies. Fourteen years later, he coined the term 'eugenics' – now commonly defined as the study of methods of improving the innate quality of the human race, especially by selective breeding – in the first edition of *Inquiries into Human Faculty*, published in 1883. In this work, he explained that the term came from the Greek word *eugenes* which was used to describe someone who was 'hereditarily endowed with noble qualities'. In 1909, Galton himself defined eugenics as 'the science which deals with all the influences that preserve the inborn qualities of a race and also those that develop them to the utmost advantage' (quoted in Brown, 1988, p. 295).

In the light of the above, it is not difficult to understand why Francis Galton is often seen as one of the evil spirits of the nineteenth century, condemning succeeding generations of psychologists to pursue a sterile debate between the absurd extremes of environmental and genetic determinism and inspiring ideas and policies which would cause misery and cruelty to millions of people in the century to come. Yet within his lifetime, Galton's eugenic theories soon acquired a remarkable number of adherents, and, if anything, their popularity grew in the twenty or so years following his death in 1911. At the same time, it is important to stress that their appeal was *not* restricted to those on the Right of the political spectrum. Eugenic themes could be found in the ideological writings of liberals, social reformers, Fabian socialists and pioneers of the birth control movement.

While Galton's eugenic creed was steadily gaining in popularity and respectability in England, educational psychology in a number of countries was increasingly preoccupied with the development of the pseudo-science of 'psychometry' – the measurement and testing of mental ability states and processes. In France in 1904, the Ministry of Public Instruction entrusted Alfred Binet (1857–1911) with the task of devising tests for Parisian school-children designed initially to distinguish between those pupils who were 'mentally retarded' and those who were 'performing badly' for a variety of other reasons. Binet's first tests were published in 1905, and before Galton died, these had been improved in 1908 and again in 1911. And as these tests were refined, so their scope and usefulness apparently broadened: they could identify not only the 'mentally retarded' but also the 'above average' and 'very bright'. Other psychologists on both sides of the Atlantic joined in this kind of research, and in 1916, the Stanford-Binet test was devised, purporting to be able to predict future ability on the basis of current scores. It was at this time that the concept of Intelligence Quotient came to the fore, this being an expression of the relationship between 'ability' and chronological age translated into a convenient number by means of the beguilingly simple formula: IQ equals Mental Age divided by Chronological Age multiplied by 100. According to this formula, an IQ of 100 was, by definition, the norm or average score, and marks above or below 100 indicated the possession of 'above' or 'below average' intelligence. These tests were used during World War I for selecting key personnel and allocating individual recruits to suitable jobs. In England, it was Galton's disciple Cyril Burt (1883–1971) who did more than anyone to advocate the widespread use of IQ tests for the purpose of pinning permanent labels on schoolchildren at the age of 11.

THE POPULARITY OF EUGENIC THEORIES

The period from 1907 to the early 1930s has been described by Cyril Burt's biographer Leslie Hearnshaw as 'the heyday of Eugenics' (Hearnshaw, 1979, p. 48). November 1907 actually saw the founding of the Eugenics Education Society (known simply as the Eugenics Society after 1926), with the aim of 'furthering eugenic teaching and understanding at home, in the schools and elsewhere'. The Society quickly became a very influential pressure group, and recruited a considerable proportion of its membership from scientists, university teachers and doctors concerned with preserving the 'virility' of the Anglo-Saxon 'race'. Although some writers have given the impression that the Society was at its strongest in the years *before* World War I, in simple numerical terms this is not the case. It was in the 1920s that the Society enjoyed an appreciable increase in numbers, culminating with the highest recorded annual membership figure of 768 in 1932 (see Brown, 1988, p. 300). It was of considerable benefit to the Society's prestige and respectability that in his will Francis Galton bequeathed

£45,000 to University College, London to establish a chair of eugenics. Galton's friend and disciple Karl Pearson, who had been Professor of Applied Mathematics in the college since 1884, transferred to the new chair in 1912 and held it until his retirement in 1933. As one of the explanations for the popularity of eugenic theories in England in the first three decades of the last century, it is important to note that between the latter years of the Victorian period and the early 1930s, the average size of families fell by around two-thirds. Since many members of the professional classes were now practising methods of birth control, there was a pronounced fear that the ranks of the affluent and the educated would soon be heavily and irretrievably outnumbered by those of the urban masses and assorted groups of undesirable immigrants.

Professor John Carey has advanced the thesis in his 1992 book *The Intellectuals and the Masses* that many of the prominent novelists and poets of the first half of the last century were also profoundly influenced by the new 'science' of eugenics, and by the writings of the German philosopher Friedrich Nietzsche (1844–1900), in deploring the advent of mass culture and the changes brought about in England by the educational legislation dating back to 1870.

W. B. Yeats joined the Eugenics Society and T. S. Eliot was hugely sympathetic, with anti-semitic themes running through much of his work. Among a number of respected and widely read writers, Aldous and Julian Huxley, George Bernard Shaw and H. G. Wells were all heavily influenced by eugenic thinking. In this respect, it is interesting to note that far from being the clever and liberal satire it is often assumed to be, Aldous Huxley's *Brave New World*, which appeared in 1932, actually presented a vision of the future that Huxley found very palatable, with democracy overthrown by force, people educated to know their place and society governed according to strict eugenic principles.

We know that Yeats's own keen interest in the beneficial potential of eugenics was reinforced by his reading of Raymond B. Cattell's *The Fight for our National Intelligence*, which was published in 1937. Both Cattell and Yeats were excited by the passing of a Eugenic Sterilization Law in Nazi Germany in 1933 and they congratulated Hitler's Government on being the first administration in Europe to have the courage to enforce sterilization of the unfit and mentally retarded as a means to secure racial improvement. It was *On the Boiler*, which was written in 1938 and then published in 1939, the year of Yeats's death, that contained the poet's most forthright and unequivocal exposition of eugenic theories. As far as educational issues were concerned, Yeats accepted Cattell's view that innate intelligence – or what Yeats termed 'mother-wit – could now be measured, especially in children, with great accuracy. If, for example, you took a pair of twins and educated one in wealth, the other in poverty, tests administered at various stages in their adult lives would show that 'their mother-wit remained the same'. Then again, if you picked a group of 'slum children' and moved them to 'a better neighbourhood' with all the benefits of 'better food, light and air', the move would have no effect on their intelligence. It followed that all social welfare schemes and educational reforms were useless as 'improvers of the breed'. Yeats quoted with approval a saying popular with George Bernard Shaw to the effect that 'you couldn't make a silk purse out of a sow's ear'. Sooner or later, in Yeats's view, ways would have to be found of limiting the average family size of the urban masses and unintelligent classes (Yeats, 1939, republished in Larrissy, 1997, p. 391).

Another prominent writer of the period who viewed any attempt to educate the masses with a mixture of alarm and derision was D. H. Lawrence, and here the key influence was the controversial work of Friedrich Nietzsche and, in particular, *Also Sprach Zarathustra* which Nietzsche worked on between 1883 and 1885. The young Lawrence actually 'discovered' Nietzsche in Croydon Public Library in 1908, and seemed very happy to accept the idea that the breeding of a future 'master race' would necessarily entail the annihilation of millions of 'failures'. He also shared the view put forward in *Also Sprach Zarathustra* that the very concept of universal education was one to be deplored and discarded. It was Nietzsche's firm belief that education should remain a 'privilege' so that higher beings could dominate written culture: 'Another century of mass readership and spirit itself will stink ... That everyone can learn to read will ruin in the long run not only writing, but thinking too. ... Once spirit was God, then it became man, and now it is even becoming the mob'

(Nietzsche, 1883–5, translated by Hollingdale, 1961, p. 67). For Lawrence, it was essential that all schools for the masses should be closed immediately. Without the demands imposed by formal education, the working-class would be free to lead a purely physical life. If there had to be some forms of instruction, boys would be expected to attend craft workshops, girls would study domestic science and it would also be compulsory for boys to learn 'primitive modes of fighting and gymnastics'.

CYRIL BURT AND THE ISSUE OF INTELLIGENCE

It is now important to concentrate on the process by which the eugenic theories put forward by Francis Galton and his disciples exerted a powerful influence on concepts of 'ability' and 'intelligence' with profound implications for social planning. It is indeed the chief purpose of this chapter to trace the development of a view of ability, education and social class which found its most complete expression in Britain in the works of Cyril Burt. According to this view, all individuals can be seen as hereditarily endowed with a certain level of 'general intelligence' which then acts as a major determinant of one's social position within the hierarchy of occupational classes.

As a family doctor working in the village of Snitterfield, some five miles from Stratford-upon-Avon, in the 1890s, Cyril Burt's father numbered Francis Galton among his neighbours, friends and patients (see Hearnshaw, 1979, p. 23). The young Cyril, who often accompanied his father on his rounds, was impressed by Galton from the very beginning, describing him later as 'one of the most distinguished-looking people I have ever known – tall, slim, neatly-dressed, with a prominent forehead like the dome of St Pauls' (quoted in Norton, 1981, p. 305).

Having spent seven years as a pupil at Christ's Hospital in the City of London (1895 to 1902), Burt gained a scholarship to study classics at Jesus College, Oxford, and this was how he spent his undergraduate years, despite a strong wish to switch to science in preparation for a medical career. On leaving university, Burt decided to specialize in psychology; and it was in 1909, during a five-year period as Lecturer in Experimental Psychology at the University of Liverpool, that he wrote his career-establishing paper for the *British Journal of Psychology* entitled 'Experimental Tests of General Intelligence' (Burt, 1909). The conclusion he reached was that intelligence was inherited 'to a degree which few psychologists have hitherto legitimately ventured to maintain' (p. 177).

It was largely on the strength of this 1909 paper, which had a very good reception, that Burt was appointed three years later to the position of official educational psychologist to the London County Council (LCC), a post which he held from 1913 until his transfer to University College in 1932. This LCC post gave Burt unprecedented power and influence, for, by the terms of the 1902 Education Act, local education authorities had responsibility for a wide range of educational and social activities covering a broad spectrum of the community.

During much of his time with the LCC, Burt was engaged in routine clinical work, particularly with the 'subnormal' and the 'delinquent'. As was the case with others working in the field of child psychology at the start of the last century, it was a eugenic concern with the problem of mental deficiency – often referred to as 'feeblemindedness' – that caused Burt to take a keen interest in the whole issue of intelligence testing. In an article for Volume 4 of *The Eugenics Review*, published in 1913, he emphasized that his growing interest in the data to be obtained from intelligence testing did indeed derive from his concern with the twin problems of mental degeneracy and national deterioration, arguing that refined statistical techniques were necessary in order to identify those children who were simply not capable, by reason of mental defect, of benefiting from the instruction given in an ordinary elementary school. Insisting that there was no such thing as 'acquired' or 'manufactured' feeblemindedness, Burt's conclusion was simple and dogmatic: 'The fact of mental inheritance can no longer be contested, its importance scarcely over-estimated. ... There assuredly could be no problem upon which experimentalist, statistician and psychologist could so fruitfully concentrate their wisdom as the problem of heredity and its influence upon the mind' (quoted in Lowe, 1980, p. 4).

Burt's own classic definition of 'human intelligence' was clearly stated some twenty years later in *How the Mind Works*, a book for popular consumption based on broadcast talks by a number of experts on the new 'science' of mental testing delivered in 1933. Here Burt argued that:

> By the term intelligence, the psychologist understands *inborn, all-round intellectual ability*. It is inherited, or at least innate, not due to teaching or training; it is intellectual, not emotional or moral, and remains uninfluenced by industry or zeal; it is general, not specific, that is to say it is not limited to any particular kind of work, but enters into all we do or say or think. Of all our mental qualities, it is the most far-reaching; fortunately, it can be measured with accuracy and ease. (Burt, 1933, pp. 28–9)

As Professor Brian Simon, one of Burt's foremost critics, observed in 1974: 'Here was a simple, clear, straightforward statement about the precise functioning of the human mind, admitting no doubts, inviting no argument' (Simon, 1974, p. 241).

The implications of such a theory for the structuring of the British education system were indeed profound, as Burt himself acknowledged in a Third Programme talk broadcast in November 1950: 'Obviously, in an ideal community, our aim should be to discover what ration of intelligence nature has given to each individual child at birth, then to provide him [sic] with the appropriate education, and finally to guide him into the career for which he seems to have been marked out' (reprinted in *The Listener*, 16 November 1950).

Such views, expressed with real conviction and absolute certainty, undoubtedly encouraged a fatalistic attitude among large numbers of classroom teachers who were being led to believe that the level of 'intelligence' any child could reach was already determined by biological mechanisms. In other words, a child was born with *all that he or she could become*. As the American philosopher James Lawler has pointed out, theories of the innate intellectual inferiority of certain classes of children meant that schools should not be thought of as providing an enriching and creative environment, but should simply be charged with the function of sorting out and selecting the 'bright' from the 'dull', as determined by nature, and as basically reflected in the existing social hierarchy. ... Where educational institutions *should* aim at the *development* of intellectual and cultural abilities, the main thrust of the theories of Cyril Burt and others was that the level of intelligence that children could reach or fail to reach was basically decided once and for all in the genes. (Lawler, 1978, p.3)

CHALLENGES TO THE PRACTICE OF INTELLIGENCE TESTING

It was in the first half of the 1950s that two books appeared which powerfully attacked the whole idea of intelligence testing as a means of determining a child's future at the age of 11. Brian Simon's *Intelligence Testing and the Comprehensive School*, published in 1953, argued that intelligence tests not only 'exclude, or attempt to exclude, any emotional response', but also 'isolate the individual from all social relations and any "real life" situation' (Simon, 1953, p. 60). Alice Heim's *The Appraisal of Intelligence*, which appeared the following year, maintained that 'intelligence ... cannot be separated from other aspects of mental activity' and insisted on the necessity of 'studying intelligence as part of the total personality' (Heim, 1954, p. 1). Leslie Hearnshaw has suggested (1979, pp. 59, 227–8) that these two books, and especially the one by Brian Simon, played a major role in causing Burt to search for and indeed *fabricate* data in order to substantiate his theories. Thanks largely to the meticulous research carried out by Professor Leon Kamin of Princeton University (see Kamin, 1974) we now have evidence that most of Burt's later work, and particularly his papers on identical twins reared apart, had little or no basis in reality; but it is not clear exactly when the psychologist resorted to unorthodox and fraudulent methods to defeat the arguments of his critics. (It is also fair to point out that there are those who argue (see, for example, Wooldridge, 1994) that the attacks against Burt were motivated by a mixture of professional and ideological antagonism and that Burt was entirely innocent of the charges of fictitious research and data falsification.)

At a time when Burt's theories about innate ability and his fanatical commitment to mass intelligence testing were just beginning to cause disquiet and alarm among sections of the academic community (and this was twenty years before charges of deliberate deception were made), it was, paradoxically, the development of the divided secondary system itself which played a large role in challenging and undermining the hard-line 'classic' views of the leading psychometrists. In particular, the unexpected passes secured by many secondary modern candidates in the new GCE Ordinary Level examination introduced in 1951 had the obvious and immediate effect of exposing the fallibility of the 11-plus selection procedure. By the end of the 1950s, it had become much more difficult to argue that every child was born with a given quota of 'intelligence' which remained constant throughout his or her life – and that this key quality was a direct product of genetic endowment and not therefore in any way susceptible to the influence of schooling.

One secondary modern school for girls serving a working-class district in a large industrial city, which took in only those children who had *failed* to gain entrance to either a grammar or a selective central school, entered a number of its 16-year-old girls for the GCSE Ordinary Level examination in 1954. Of those who gained five or more passes, one had had an IQ of 97 on entry to the school in 1949; another an IQ of 85. (This was at a time when an IQ of 115 or over was generally considered to be necessary to succeed in examination courses.) And other secondary modern schools were soon in a position to boast of similar achievements, so that there were real problems involved in defending the psychometrists' standpoint (see Simon, 1955, pp. 64–6).

It was in these unfavourable circumstances that some psycho-metrists did, in fact, feel obliged to tone down some of their more doctrinaire statements and put forward a modified and more sophisticated view of human intellectual capacity. This subtle change of emphasis came in a report of a special working party set up by the British Psychological Society with the intention of responding to some of the well-informed criticisms of the practice of universal testing and of the very concept of the IQ examination as an accurate measure of *innate* ability. This Report, published in 1957, conceded that since it was now clear that many children could actually *enhance* their IQ scores, it must be true that 'environmental' factors had *some* effect on 'intelligence' – and particularly in the early and teenage years. But although this report expressed reservations about all the claims made for the 11-plus and was critical of the practice of streaming within the junior school, it had nothing to say about *education* as the key to human development. A refusal to challenge the narrow assumptions of the past meant that only 'heredity' and the vague and generalized category of 'environment' (comprising a wide range of 'active' and 'passive' influences) were recognized as determining factors in a child's intellectual development. As Brian Simon observed at the beginning of the 1970s: 'From a theoretical point of view ... the psychometrists, by abandoning heredity for environment, were merely switching from the roundabout to the swing, without giving any evidence of an intention to leave the fairground' (Simon, 1971, pp. 22–3).

In *The Comprehensive School*, first published in 1963, Robin Pedley argued that none of the tests conceived and tried over the course of sixty years could satisfactorily distinguish 'natural talent' from 'what had been learned'. It was his view that heredity and environment were too closely entangled to be clearly identified. This meant that children from 'literate homes', with 'interested and helpful parents', had an enormous advantage over 'children from culturally poor homes' where books were unknown and conversation was 'either limited or unprintable' (Pedley, 1963, pp. 16–17).

Of even greater significance, the first chapter of the 1963 Newsom Report, *Half Our Future*, a report concerned with the education of 13- to 16-year-old students of 'average or less than average ability', contained the now famous unequivocal statement:

> intellectual talent is not a fixed quantity with which we have to work, but a variable that can be modified by social policy and

educational approaches. ... The results of recent investigations increasingly indicate that the kind of intelligence which is measured by the tests so far applied is largely an *acquired* characteristic. (Ministry of Education, 1963, p. 6)

In his Foreword to the Report, Conservative Education Minister Edward Boyle implicitly rejected the psychometrists' theories when he stated that the essential point we have to grasp is that 'all children should have an equal opportunity of acquiring intelligence, and of developing their talents and abilities to the full' (*ibid.*, p. iv).

Yet, despite such confident pronouncements, a number of leading psychometrists and eugenicists, both in Britain and America, were simply not prepared to listen to opposing arguments and admit to past mistakes. In an article in *Black Paper Two: The Crisis in Education*, published in 1969, Cyril Burt not only reiterated Galton's view that mental differences were wholly or largely inherited, but also argued that, owing to recent 'progressive' education reforms carried out by the Wilson administration, standards in basic education were lower than they had been 55 years earlier, in the period just before World War I (Burt, 1969, p. 23).

It was also in 1969 that Arthur Jensen published an extraordinary article in *The Harvard Educational Review* entitled 'How Much can we Boost IQ and Scholastic Achievement?' (Jensen, 1969). Jensen had been a pupil of Hans Eysenck, author of a popular work, *Sense and Nonsense in Psychology*, published in 1957, and Eysenck had himself been one of Burt's postgraduate students. This very long 1969 paper, running to over 120 pages, soon acquired considerable notoriety because it set out to reiterate Burt's theory of fixed innate intelligence in terms not only of 'class' but also of 'race'. It began with the assertion that compensatory education had been tried and had failed. In particular, it had failed to improve the scores on IQ tests of 'under-privileged children' – and especially of black children. As measured by standard IQ tests, black children apparently scored an average of 15 points below white children. According to Jensen, 'environmentalists' who had argued in favour of massive compensatory education programmes designed to equalize opportunities had been guilty of seriously misleading the American Government. As a consequence, resources had been wasted and a great deal of effort expended on a pointless exercise. In Jensen's view, just as working-class white children were inferior (in terms of measured intelligence) to middle- and upper-class white children, so black children were innately inferior to white children. Any attempt, however well-intentioned, to compensate for this 'natural' state of affairs was obviously a waste of time and money.

RECENT TRENDS AND FUTURE POSSIBILITIES

For reasons we have had space only to touch upon in this chapter, eugenic proposals in a number of related fields had an extraordinary allure for policy-makers and intellectuals in Britain in the first half of the twentieth century. As Professor Desmond King has emphasized: 'Eugenics attracted support from an eclectic group of scientists, Fabians, upper-class Conservatives and civil servants, and enjoyed support from across the ideological range of views held by politicians' (King, 1999, p. 68). For a period of at least thirty years, the Eugenics Society certainly enjoyed a degree of influence out of all proportion to the actual size of its membership, which was never particularly large. Cyril Burt's work on ability and intelligence, growing fears about the physical and moral deterioration of the English 'race' and well-publicized campaigns for strategies, including sterilization, to deal with the problems of 'feeblemind-edness' and mental deficiency, all combined to keep eugenic ideas and solutions in the forefront of the intellectual debate.

It is, of course, true that the savage policies carried out by the Nazi Government in Germany after 1933 did much to discredit eugenic theories, particularly in matters relating to such dubious medical practices as compulsory sterilization and euthanasia. Yet ideas about innate ability and intelligence inspired by eugenic theories persisted throughout the century.

As late as October 1974, the late Sir Keith Joseph was including the distinctly eugenic sentence 'the balance of our population, of our human stock is threatened' in a now notorious speech delivered to the Edgbaston Conservative Association in Birmingham's Grand Hotel. The speech had been advertised in the local press as 'offering a night out which will linger in your memory for ever'; though it is likely that its long-term effects were far greater than Sir Keith himself intended and it certainly ended his chance of standing for the leadership of the Conservative Party in 1975. The speech achieved its notoriety because it appeared to be arguing that the nation was moving towards degeneration on account of the high and rising proportion of children being born to mothers 'least fitted to bring children into the world'. In the words of the speech:

> These are the mothers who were first pregnant in adolescence in social classes four and five (the unskilled and lower skilled). Many of these girls are unmarried; many are deserted or divorced, or soon will be ... Some are of low intelligence; most of low educational attainment. They are unlikely to be able to give their children the stable emotional background, the consistent combination of love and firmness which is more important than riches. They are producing problem children, the future unmarried mothers, delinquents, denizens of our borstals, subnormal educational establishments, prisons, hostels for drifters. Yet these mothers, the under-twenties in many cases, single parents from classes four and five, are now producing a third of all births. A high proportion of these births are a tragedy for the mother, the child and for us ... If we do nothing, the nation moves towards degeneration, however many resources we pour into preventive work and into the over-burdened educational system. (Reported in *The Sunday Times*, 20 October 1974; see also Denham and Garnett, 2001, pp. 265–76)

Sir Keith went on to propose that birth control facilities should be extended to the destitute, poor and inadequate, though some of his right-wing supporters argued that forcible sterilization was the only logical solution to the problems he was highlighting. One Labour MP summarized the message of the speech as 'castrate or conform'.

Then again, one of the most controversial and headline-grabbing contributions to the debate about 'race', class and intelligence was *The*

Bell Curve: Intelligence and Class Structure in American Life, co-authored by the late Richard J. Herrnstein and Charles Murray, and this was published in America as recently as 1994. Here the authors reiterated many of Arthur Jensen's earlier claims, maintaining that there was an enormous amount of very credible evidence showing that the mean IQ of Asian Americans was a little higher than that of European Americans which was, in turn, considerably higher than that of African Americans. Much of the explanation for this phenomenon apparently lay in genetic rather than environmental factors.

When extracts from the book appeared in the American magazine *The New Republic,* edited by Andrew Sullivan, a number of irate contributors denounced the work as blatantly 'racist', using terms like 'racist chic' and 'newspeak about racial inferiority'. Many found it reminiscent of the work of Hans Eysenck, who always maintained that negroes and the Irish were intellectually inferior to the English, and of William Shockley, the Nobel prize-winning physicist who advocated sterilization for people with low IQs and sperm banks for 'geniuses'.

In defending the work of Cyril Burt and Arthur Jensen, Herrnstein and Murray were very critical of rival views of intelligence and, in particular, of the theory of 'multiple intelligences' advanced by Harvard psychologist Howard Gardner in his 1983 book *Frames of Mind.* Rejecting the notion of a general intelligence factor, often known simply as 'g', Gardner argued the case for *seven* distinct 'intelligences' combinable in different ways to form the intellectual repertoire of all human beings. Two of these, logical-mathematical intelligence and linguistic intelligence, were what IQ tests already focused on. The remaining 'intelligences' in Gardner's list comprised: the musical, the spatial, the bodily-kinaesthetic and two forms of 'personal intelligence', the intrapersonal and the interpersonal.

Gardner accepted that his approach was distinctly radical and unusual in that he made no attempt to defend his theory with quantitative data. In a field that had been intensely quantitative since its inception, his particular contribution was uniquely devoid of psychometric or other quantitative evidence. At the same time, he rejected the criticism that he had merely redefined the term *intelligence* by broadening it to include what should more properly be called *talents*: 'I place no particular premium on the word *intelligence*', he wrote in 1983, 'but I do place great importance on the equivalence of various human faculties. If critics of my theory are willing to label language and logical thinking as talents as well, and to remove these from the pedestal they currently occupy, then I will be happy to speak in terms of *multiple talents*' (Gardner, 1983, p. xi). Without abandoning his basic approach, he later added to the original seven intelligences both the classificatory intelligence of the naturalist and – although he had reservations about this – spiritual intelligence. He was fond of claiming, half-seriously, that while Socrates viewed human beings as rational animals, he himself saw them as animals possessing eight-and-a-half intelligences.

It is, of course, possible to criticize Gardner for the particular way in which he has constructed his 'charmed circle of intelligences' (see, for example, White, 1998), but there is no doubt that the idea that intelligence or ability is not necessarily tied to IQ-tested skills has had a liberating effect on those children, often from deprived backgrounds, who have been encouraged to think of themselves as 'dim' or 'thick'. Thousands of so-called 'MI schools' have sprung up in recent years in America, Canada, Australia and elsewhere, all based on Gardner's theory. Some of Gardner's disciples, particularly in parts of Australia, actually believe that the school curriculum should be based on the development of all his 'intelligences'. MI theory has also become a powerful liberating force in school improvement projects across Britain, from Birmingham and Sandwell in the West Midlands to Govan in Scotland.

It was, above all, the practical day-to-day implications of adopting particular views of intelligence and ability that so concerned Caroline Benn. She well understood that even though words like 'intelligent', 'backward', 'more able', 'average' and 'less able' may not be spoken in their hearing, young people soon appreciate the nature of the category to which they have been allocated and where they and their friends fit into the pernicious hierarchy of ability. In her view, even the term 'mixed-ability teaching' was flawed in that it did not necessarily imply a radical break with ill-conceived notions of fixed ability.

For Caroline, comprehensive schooling was all about developing the abilities and talents that *all* children possess; and this was a point she emphasized in two articles written for *Forum* in 1982 (Benn, 1982a and b) in which she set out to challenge what she called 'the myth of giftedness'. It is surely appropriate for me to end this piece with a marvellous quote from Caroline on an issue about which she cared so deeply.

We give up our commitment to looking for gifts, talents and abilities in the vast majority of children once we have accepted the argument that the search for 'giftedness' is limited to the hunt for a few ... The way we can support 'giftedness' (whatever it may mean) is by encouraging a flexible, alert, high-standard, stimulating and supportive comprehensive education service for everyone at every stage of their lives ... A comprehensive system is the only way we can openly ensure attention to all equally and, at the same time, protect and reveal the full range of human gifts. Encouraging human ability in all its various forms is just one more reason why we must continue to work to get a genuine comprehensive education system safely started in Britain – and to promote it relentlessly when we have. (Benn, 1982b, p. 84)

8 Developing Comprehensive Education in a New Climate*

Geoff Whitty

INTRODUCTION

Prior to the 1997 General Election, Benn and Chitty's book *Thirty Years On* (Benn and Chitty, 1996) suggested that, despite the setbacks of the Tory years, achieving their vision of comprehensive secondary education remained in sight, if only an incoming Labour government would seize the opportunity and keep its nerve. As we now know, that didn't quite happen and New Labour has, at best, been half-hearted in its support of comprehensive schools. A recent press report claimed that 'the state comprehensive is now in a clear minority' (BBC News Online, 2004). Should we conclude that comprehensive education is effectively dead and that we would do best to accept that it was an experiment that failed?

As Caroline Benn herself recognized, the struggle to develop genuinely comprehensive education goes well beyond the issue of selection at 11-plus. I shall nevertheless concentrate in this chapter on the conventional terrain of comprehensive, non-selective, secondary schooling. Of course, even the term 'comprehensive school' has never had an entirely unambiguous meaning. Sometimes it has meant having carefully balanced intakes, at other times taking all-comers from the local neighbourhood. Balance has sometimes meant academic balance and sometimes social balance.

* This chapter has been developed from my lecture 'A Comprehensive Vision of Education', the first Caroline Benn Memorial Lecture, sponsored by the Socialist Educational Association and delivered at the Institute of Education, University of London on 17 November 2001.

Furthermore, there has never been agreement as to whether a single-sex comprehensive school, or a denominational comprehensive school, is a contradiction in terms. During the 1970s, there was also considerable debate about whether we were aiming for meritocratic or egalitarian comprehensives (Daunt, 1975; Jackson, 1976). And, although Hargreaves (1982) saw the nature of the comprehensive curriculum as one of the challenges for the comprehensive school, there was little consensus about what it should be like.

Whatever some supporters of comprehensive schools might want in the long-term, certain definitions of a comprehensive school are unlikely to be on the official policy agenda under New Labour. New Labour is committed to a meritocratic model of society and hence is looking to the education system to serve that. With the toleration (at least) of the remaining state grammar schools, gone is the firm conviction, as expressed by Ted Short back in the 1960s, that 'if it is wrong to select and segregate children ... it must be wrong everywhere' (quoted by Kerckhoff et al., 1996, p. 34). At times, there have even been some people close to New Labour arguing that it should formally rethink its opposition to academic selection, certainly at 14 if not 11. Meanwhile, there are still many schools that are secondary moderns in all but name and creation of quasi-markets in education has made it increasingly difficult to ensure balanced intakes (Newsam, 2002; Riddell, 2003). The encouragement of a diversity agenda through the expansion of specialist and faith schools has made it less likely that all schools will be put on the same legal footing and created fears of a two (or more) tiered system.

So, in the current climate, we are certainly not where, back in the 1960s, the early advocates of comprehensive education might have expected us to be by now. I know I then expected that well before the turn of the century we would have had a fully comprehensive system, little demand for private schools even if they still existed and, indeed, probably no single-sex or denominational schools. But we are not there and indeed society has probably changed sufficiently for some of those issues not to be quite as straightforward as I (for one) thought they were then. Many of the unresolved definitional issues remain and have themselves been complicated by the changing nature of British society. But none of this necessarily means that the comprehensive dream need be at an end.

ACADEMIC PERFORMANCE

Even in terms of conventional academic achievements, the record to date of schools labelled 'comprehensive' is hardly a dishonourable one – especially when we consider Newsam's claim that only a minority of so-called comprehensive schools in our major cities can be considered comprehensive in terms of academic and social balance. With colleagues, I recently produced a book called *Education and the Middle Class* (Power *et al.*, 2003). The original research on which it is based was carried out in the 1980s in the context of an evaluation of the Thatcher Government's Assisted Places Scheme, ostensibly designed to enable bright children from poor backgrounds to attend academically excellent private schools (Edwards *et al.*, 1989). The subsequent work that we did from that study, and which forms the core of the recent book, compared the careers of 350 academically able pupils attending different types of secondary school from age 11. The mean A-level subject score for those who studied in elite independent schools was 7.7 (just below grade B), while it was 7.2 for pupils in state grammar schools and 6.5 (just over grade C) for those who attended state comprehensives.

At first sight, these findings may not seem a great advertisement for comprehensive education. They suggest that comprehensive school pupils of high academic ability do rather less well at A-level than their peers in state grammar schools and both do less well than those in academically selective private schools. Our study also showed that those from the private schools were more likely to attend high status universities, read high status subjects and then enter the labour market in higher paid and more prestigious jobs. Today's brightest young people often have relatively successful careers whether they have attended public or private, selective or non-selective schools, when measured by crude indices such as entry to higher education or entry to professional and managerial jobs.

But it apparently remains the case that certain choices at 11 are still likely to bring a significantly greater chance of success than others, particularly when competing for the 'glittering prizes' associated with elite universities and elite occupations. So it is perhaps hardly surprising that our findings were featured on the front page of *The Times* as suggesting that it was well worth ambitious parents spending up to £100,000 on their children's education (O'Leary, 1997).

However, if we look at the figures another way, what is remarkable is how *small* the difference at A-level was – just over half a grade per subject. It is difficult to justify the translation of this difference into such large subsequent advantages when the elite private schools in our study had a narrower mission than the comprehensive schools, more selective intakes, better qualified teachers and better facilities. Those universities looking for 'the brightest and the best' would therefore do well to recognize that those who have gained slightly lower grades at some comprehensive schools may have at least as much potential as those with straight As from private schools. The other thing that is remarkable, given their differences in mission, is that within the overall sector differences in our study is hidden the fact some of the comprehensive schools actually performed better than some of the private and grammar schools. The aim, of course, must be to ensure that more comprehensive schools are able to do this, drawing on our developing knowledge of good practice.

The academic success of comprehensive schools to date is also evident when one looks at other evidence about the relative performance of academically able children in comprehensive and grammar schools. In a review of a range of studies of this issue a few years ago (Crook *et al.*, 1999), the differences in academic outcomes between selective and non-selective systems were found to be marginal overall. The evidence suggested that comprehensive schools benefited most children academically but possibly not the most academically able group. Subsequent studies have found similarly small differences, but slightly differing costs and benefits for different groups (Jesson, 2000; Schagen and Schagen, 2003). Indeed, some of this more recent evidence even throws doubt on the suggestion that non-selective systems operate to the detriment of the academically able. This is actually a remarkable testament to the academic success of comprehensive schools. If the most able children in comprehensive schools can perform neck and neck with – and in at least some studies outperform – those in schools which have a mission that is geared directly to their needs and not much else, then comprehensive schools can hardly be regarded as unequivocal failures.

It may appear odd that, in a chapter about comprehensive education, which should surely involve giving equal value to all learners and to all forms of learning, I chose to start by focusing on a study of academically able children most of whom were from middle-class backgrounds. I did so to make a point, not because I think that their education is more important than anyone else's. The point is that, even in terms of the academic criteria that inform so much of the debate about success or failure of comprehensive schools, they have not done badly. When we add to the equation the important fact that comprehensive schools are part of the inclusion agenda as well as the standards agenda, it is particularly puzzling that the present government should often appear so suspicious of comprehensive schools. Rather, one would expect it to be celebrating their achievements. Instead, in the name of modernization, it has too often suggested that we should now go post-comprehensive, a term that could seem to imply that the new order is somehow other than comprehensive.

THE DIVERSITY AGENDA

For some supporters of comprehensive education, that implication reflects a reality in which the raft of specific policies introduced by New Labour constitutes a retreat from comprehensive secondary education in all but name. Like many of them, I have had some real worries about the diversity agenda of specialist schools, faith schools and so on recreating the tripartite system, both academically and socially. That a government ostensibly committed to evidence-based policy should suggest that there are absolutely no grounds for such fears is especially worrying. There is one paragraph in the White Paper *Schools: Achieving Success* (DfES, 2001, p. 40) that is particularly disturbing in this respect. It said: 'There are those who have said that specialist schools will create a two-tier system. They won't.' End of story. This reminds me of when, in October 1987, BBC weatherman Michael Fish said, 'Some people have suggested that there is a hurricane heading this way. There isn't'; and we all know what happened that night!

As long as the basis of their success is open to question, there are some entirely legitimate concerns about the potentially divisive effects of specialist schools. Nevertheless, in the context of the national curriculum, having a curriculum specialism may not in itself differentiate schools significantly. The far more serious threat to the concept of the comprehensive school comes from the effect that the extra resources and the cachet of the specialist school label may have on recruitment. The early evidence on free school meal eligibility in specialist schools suggested that the intakes of such schools might well be socially unrepresentative, though this may be more associated with prior school type than with specialism *per se* (Gorard and Taylor, 2001). Others have claimed that, as the proportion of such schools increases – potentially now to 100 per cent – this phenomenon is decreasing (Taylor, 2001). The extent to which specialist schools are academically selective is also unclear, although critics almost certainly exaggerate the amount of formal selection that takes place even by using the dubious concept of aptitude (West *et al.*, 2000).

Official data based on Key Stage 4 results not only show specialist schools as performing relatively better than supposedly comparable non-specialist schools, they also show them performing relatively better in value-added terms (Jesson and Taylor, 2001; Smith, 2004). This evidence too is highly contentious and has rarely been subjected to adequate peer review in advance (Schagen and Goldstein, 2002), so we really do now need some much more rigorous research studies to determine the validity of the claims on either side and to assess the impact of specialism, selection and resources on the relative performance of specialist and other schools (Edwards and Tomlinson, 2002).

However, in the absence of conclusive evidence on these matters, it would seem inappropriate to dismiss the claims of many specialist schools to be comprehensive. Indeed, despite concerns about the possible threat to comprehensive education from some specialist schools, the statement on BBC News Online (2004), quoted at the beginning of this chapter, needs to be challenged. Well before the increase in the number of specialist schools under New Labour, Benn and Chitty (1996) argued that 'if schools merely make a particular activity their speciality ... but keep their entry itself non-selective, they are a comprehensive school with a special facility or activity' (p. 322). We can therefore legitimately claim that those specialist schools that achieve their results without unbalanced intakes should be seen as part of the success story of comprehensive education. After all, advocates of comprehensive education have never actually denied the importance of a degree of diversity – it was not we who coined the term 'bog standard'! Those of us who have worked in comprehensive schools know that each such school has its own ethos and we celebrate that. Indeed, the Government's new-found agenda of what it calls 'personalized' education, now apparently associated in ministers' minds with specialist schools (DfES, 2004), was pioneered in some of our flagship comprehensives in the 1970s and 1980s.

Furthermore, there are those who see specialist schools as a cunning ruse to make state schools more socially inclusive and thereby help to realize the comprehensive vision. For example, Penlington (2001) has argued, without any apparent sense of irony, that 'it is unusual [for a government] to base an entire policy on spin'. But in the case of specialist schools, she goes on, 'spin may be the most effective way to achieve two antagonistic goals: encouraging the middle classes to use the state sector while simultaneously raising levels of provision in Britain's worst-off communities'.

Clearly, in the absence of rigorous research studies and adequate monitoring of intakes, it is difficult to judge whether this outcome has actually been happening. And it is certainly too early to judge whether or not the expanded specialist schools programme will have this desirable effect. Significantly, though, John Dunford from the

Secondary Heads Association has recognized that we may now be moving away from the two-tier approach that he had earlier criticized and he is 'greatly encouraged by the speed with which the Government appears to be moving towards this more inclusive belief in specialist schools' (BBC News Online, 2004). Even in an earlier phase of the specialist schools initiative, it was the case that some dedicated comprehensive heads had, sometimes reluctantly, sought specialist school status in order to gain extra resources to pursue comprehensive ideals (see, for example, Imison, 1999). It would be unfortunate if their schools were to be regarded as outside the comprehensive fold. It would help, though, if more ministers would say openly, as Estelle Morris once did, that specialist schools are 'only modern comprehensive schools' (Morris, 2001). Unfortunately, one suspects that this is not a message high on the agenda at 10 Downing Street.

There can anyway be little doubt that, one way or another, diversity in secondary education will remain the name of the game for the foreseeable future. What we must do in this situation is to find ways of preventing legitimate differences becoming unjustifiable inequalities and to stop particular social groups monopolizing particular sorts of schools. As Benn and Chitty (1996) put it, 'the sooner selection masquerading as specialisation ends, the sooner genuine diversity and alternative approaches can flourish' (p. 324).

Thus, in my view, while accepting a degree of diversity between and within comprehensive schools, it is the issue of academic and social balance that must remain at the centre of the struggle for comprehensive education and the one that should be at the heart of policy. All sorts of schools that are nominally comprehensive lack balanced intakes, both socially and academically, and specialist schools are by no means the only offenders. School choice policies have made it possible for many schools to select covertly as well as overtly, thereby producing some schools with grossly unbalanced intakes – in both directions (Gewirtz *et al.*, 1995; Newsam, 2003).

PURSUING INCLUSION

Inclusion, as part of the comprehensive vision, should not be seen as just a matter of engaging disadvantaged groups. Inclusive comprehensive schools surely need to embrace both middle- and working-class pupils wherever this is geographically feasible. As Giddens (1998) has pointed out, 'social exclusion' is a dual process. It operates at the 'top' as well as the 'bottom' of society, with the wealthy often excluding themselves voluntarily from state-provided services. The ruling and upper middle classes in England traditionally 'self-excluded' themselves from mainstream educational provision by their use of elite private education. The rapid growth of the middle classes since World War II did not, however, lead to a similar growth in the size of that sector of education. So, although some of the newer fractions of the middle classes have made increasing use of private sector provision, others have successfully colonized parts of the mainstream public education system in ways that make it feel 'safe' for their own children. This is perhaps one of the reasons for the re-emergence of differentiated forms of public provision and for the 're-invented traditionalism' that we find in some comprehensive schools. But the effect – and sometimes the intention – has too often been to exclude 'other people's children' from the best public provision.

That is why social inclusion in the comprehensive vision must, in my view, involve social and academic balance in a way that is too often ignored by New Labour. I believe that, for comprehensive education to move forward from here, it is vital to ensure that the middle classes see mainstream public education as the right place for their children rather than opt out into their own schools, whether public or private. School choice policies have often facilitated a strategic withdrawal of the middle classes, making it even more difficult for schools in some areas to succeed because, as Maden (2001) has indicated, it is important for such schools to have 'a "critical mass" of more engaged, broadly "pro-school" children to start with' (p. 336). We therefore need to have schools that meet the aspirations of all children and thereby provide that social and academic mix that has been shown to be essential for maximizing the achievement of all. We know, as I said earlier, that there are comprehensive schools that perform with the best as far as academic achievement is concerned, while also doing many other things that private and grammar schools do not do. The aim must surely be to learn from those schools and help other comprehensive schools to do the same, rather than finding ways for pupils to escape from them.

As Young (1999) has pointed out, exclusion 'at the top' and 'at the bottom' are interdependent in quite specific ways. Families with high enough incomes to afford alternatives avoid the state secondary schools in some inner London boroughs precisely because many of the students in such schools are from families who would on any criteria be classified as being among the excluded 'at the bottom'. The falling quality of public services in some areas is thus partly an outcome of the withdrawal of support for them by relatively better-off people. But in boroughs where better-off families continue to use public secondary schools, they often use another mechanism of 'exclusion at the top', such as moving house into the catchment area of what they perceive to be the best state schools. This helps create, in the areas they forsake, the 'secondary modern' comprehensive schools identified by Newsam.

Meanwhile, the sponsorship of a few 'meritorious' working-class children into the suburban schools of the middle classes, whether public or private, helps to legitimate the system without threatening the so-called critical mass of middle-class children in such schools. The broader problem of working-class failure is barely addressed by the existence of privileged routes out for the few – and their very existence can serve to reduce the pressure for a more fundamental reform of provision. Individual success stories of the sort that politicians like to cite as evidence of the success of their policies – such as their annual photoshoots during the 1980s with some of the few unambiguously working-class pupils in the Assisted Places Scheme – do not address the issue of structural inequalities and indeed can have the effect of legitimating them.

Particularly in the context of specialist schools, and the continuing difficulties of achieving parity of esteem between different schools, it is important that all schools see themselves, and are seen, as part of a comprehensive system of secondary education.

This must involve curbing the excesses of the quasi-markets introduced by the Conservatives and, in too many respects, perpetuated by New Labour. To avoid diversity producing a hierarchy, all schools in an area need to work together in the interests of optimum provision for all pupils. My own view is that genuine collegiality among schools would be much easier if they were all put on a similar legal and budgetary footing, whatever private and voluntary sector partners are involved in their governance. Yet, even without that now unlikely occurrence, it might be possible to achieve something like it through federations or 'collegiates', collections of schools working collaboratively (Brighouse, 2002).

Whether we are talking about individual schools or collegiates, the key issue for a comprehensive future – certainly in London and other big cities – is admissions policies. It is clear that the degree of social polarization between schools increases with the proportion of schools controlling their own admission policies (Gorard and Taylor, 2001). While the Government still appears unwilling to address this issue head on, it has at least made some changes such as admissions forums and harmonization of admissions timetables. But I fear it will need far more than that to encourage some schools to be genuinely comprehensive in their intakes. For all its faults, the former Inner London Education Authority's banding arrangements prevented extreme polarization, while prior to the Greenwich judgement some degree of planning could take place at LEA level. But even with the present system, one would have thought that a government so imbued with the audit culture, would, at the very least, institute a far more rigorous and regular audit of actual admissions practices.

BEYOND INTAKES

Even if we achieved fair admissions policies, a comprehensive system needs to go much further than an aggregate of comprehensive schools and involves the creation of a comprehensive and inclusive approach to education within those schools. So, although I have hitherto focused heavily on issues of academic and social balance, I now want to touch briefly on other elements that would characterize a genuinely comprehensive approach to secondary education.

Successful comprehensive education requires a closer relationship between education and other areas of social policy if disadvantaged pupils are to gain more equal opportunities. Education Action Zones have provided some examples of multi-agency working between education, health and welfare services to tackle multiple disadvantage. However, I suspect the New Community Schools initiative in Scotland may well provide a better model for comprehensive school-based services and greater community involvement in schools. These schools are intended to be genuinely inclusive schools, both socially and educationally, and it is worth noting that greater inclusion rather than greater specialization is seen as the future for comprehensive education in Scotland (Sammons *et al.*, 2003).

Then there is the question of the comprehensive curriculum, one of the key challenges for the comprehensive school identified by Hargreaves (1982) in the 1980s. The relationship between individual need and social entitlement requires careful consideration if the point of having comprehensive intakes is not to be lost. In this respect, and in others, both 'specialization' and 'personalization' have their dangers as well as their strengths. The original National Curriculum may have been far too rigid, but the importance of a 'broad and balanced curriculum' remains and is especially important in specialist schools. In my view, Labour should look to enrich rather than narrow the curriculum, while certainly making it more challenging and engaging for different groups of pupils.

Thirdly, we need to foster a teaching force committed to comprehensive education. It is clear that many comprehensive school teachers do a quite remarkable job, especially when you consider the multiple demands made upon them. But too many people today are put off teaching because it is seen as a bureaucratic rather than a creative profession. Incentives and rewards for creativity and innovation need to be put back into the system and give teaching some of the excitement as well as the challenge that those of my generation felt when we started teaching in comprehensive schools in the 1960s. However, the greater flexibility now being offered to successful schools must not be allowed to lead to the most creative teachers avoiding the very schools that arguably need them the most.

These then are just some of the further issues we need to pursue if comprehensive schooling is to develop and flourish, particularly in our big cities. However, my main argument here is that, particularly in those cities, we need to ensure that comprehensive schools are both academically and socially comprehensive even when they have other diverse characteristics. New Labour needs to recognize, as did Caroline Benn throughout her campaign for comprehensive education, that a school cannot be considered truly comprehensive if particular social groups are effectively excluded from its benefits, either by choice or by default.

PROSPECTS FOR THE FUTURE

As I conclude the writing of this chapter, there is some cause for optimism that the climate for comprehensive education is actually improving in some respects. The 2003 statistics for Key Stage 4 published by the government were heralded by *The Times Educational Supplement* as 'A Comprehensive Win', with just three of the top hundred secondary schools in the value added league tables being incontrovertibly academically selective schools (Mansell and Wright, 2004). Such a claim does, of course, involve using an approach that remains methodologically questionable (Goldstein, 2004), but the main point I am making here relates to the way in which the figures were received. It also involves accepting specialist schools into the comprehensive fold and does not fully compensate for earlier claims about grammar school value added performance 11–14. However, it certainly does nothing to bolster the case for the overall academic superiority of selective schools.

Perhaps even more significant is the continuing conversion of some key opinion leaders to the cause of comprehensive education.

Former *Observer* editor Will Hutton, for example, once regarded the lack of academic selection as damaging to Britain's global competitiveness and argued for the revival of grammar schools 'in order to attract members of the middle-class back into the state system' (Hutton, 1996, p. 311). By 2001 he had already revised his position somewhat and was warning New Labour of the dangers of undermining comprehensive schooling (Hutton, 2001). Now, in an *Observer* column in January 2004, he writes that 'these friendless institutions are beginning to mount a comeback, and in some improbable places'. He cites the case of a massively improved specialist comprehensive school in Hackney as showing 'the way forward for all our schools' (Hutton, 2004). He sees the added resources from specialist status and Excellence in Cities rather than the specialism itself as the key and comments that even a small increase in resources can lead to significant improvement and help mount a challenge to the hegemony of the private sector. He concludes with an appeal to readers to send their own children to comprehensive schools and to demand that elite universities recruit more undergraduates from them.

When people as close to New Labour and its supporters as this argue that 'the (comprehensive) dream lives', we can be sure that it has been well worth sustaining – and developing – Caroline Benn's vision through these difficult times. While I can agree with many of the specific proposals for the future put forward recently by Brighouse (2003), there really is no need to 'draw a line in the sand and create a new ideal'.

9 The Process Curriculum

Maurice Plaskow

In a lecture on *The Lost Tools of Learning* given at Oxford in 1947 and published in 1948, the novelist Dorothy L. Sayers suggested that 'although we often succeed in teaching our pupils subjects, we fail lamentably on the whole in teaching them how to think'. She went on: 'modern education concentrates on teaching subjects ... mediaeval education concentrated on forging and learning to handle the tools of learning, using whatever subject came to hand, as a piece of material' (Sayers, 1948, pp. 7, 10).

Kenneth (now Lord) Baker's 1988 Education Act set out the framework for a national curriculum. To many, what emerged was more a *syllabus* than a *curriculum*. The curriculum was set out largely in terms of *subjects*: *what* children should be taught (whether they learn it or not is another matter) rather than *how* they should be taught. This content-driven curriculum is still largely in place.

Her Majesty's Inspectorate in *The Curriculum 11–16* (The 1977 Red Book) attempted to structure a curriculum based on 'areas of knowledge and experience'. It was a challenging concept. What is interesting about statements of intent, desired outcomes, skills and aptitudes is that they are almost all expressed as processes, capabilities, attitudes and values.

In 1981, the Schools Council (remember that body?), in the introduction to its *Practical Curriculum*, suggested that: 'a useful starting point is to consider each pupil's right of access of different areas of human knowledge and experience. The heart of the matter is what each child takes away from school. For each of them, what she or he takes away is the effective curriculum' (Schools Council, 1981, p. 3).

In its opening statement on the *Core Curriculum for Primary and Secondary Schools*, issued by the Norwegian Ministry of Church, Education and Research in 1994, the principal aim was stated as:

Schools shall provide intellectual freedom and tolerance, human equality and rights and emphasize the establishment of a cooperative climate between teachers and pupils and between school and home.

There is very little detail about subjects in the booklet, but a great deal about human development, the learning process and a civilized environment. To illustrate this, there are reproductions of paintings, drawings and sculptures throughout the publication.

The 1981 *Practical Curriculum* quoted with approval on page 14 the general educational aims expressed in the 1978 Warnock Report on *Special Needs*:

first to enlarge a child's knowledge, experience and imaginative understanding, and thus his [sic] awareness of moral values and capacity for enjoyment; and secondly to enable him to enter the world after formal education is over as an active participant in society and a responsible contributor to it, capable of achieving as much independence as possible.

This philosophy can be found in various government papers in the 1970s. See, for example, the 1977 DES document *Education in Schools*, where it appears under six general aims:

- to acquire knowledge, skills and practical abilities and the will to use them;
- to develop qualities of mind, body, spirit, feeling and imagination;
- to appreciate human achievements in art, music, science, technology and literature;
- to acquire understanding of the social, economic and political order, and a reasoned set of attitudes, values and beliefs;
- to prepare pupils for their adult lives at home, at work, at leisure, and at large, as consumers and citizens;
- to develop a sense of self-respect, the capacity to live as independent self-motivated adults and the ability to function as contributing members of co-operative groups.

This is a long way from a narrowly prescribed, instrumental curriculum, or a conformist programme of citizenship studies. It is far closer to the 1994 Norwegian document which acknowledges on page 10 that:

> intellectual freedom implies not only allowance for other points of view, but also the courage to take a stand, confidence to stand alone, and the strength of character to think and act according to one's own convictions. Tolerance is not the same as detachment and indifference.

The authors go on to point out that even within a common culture there are wide variations between individuals due to social background, gender and local origin.

The cultural baggage that leavers carry with them often determines which explanations and examples have meaning. In a society such as ours which is multicultural, multi-faith, pluralist and diverse these caveats hold especially true.

In any class teachers must expect there to be children from different faiths or none; one-parent families; children whose parents are separated or divorced, and whose parents have different partners. Where is a value-consensus to be derived that will have universal meaning? Is it possible to encourage students – of whatever age – to explore divergence, if not through Dorothy Sayers' Trivium of Grammar, Dialectic and Rhetoric, then by giving as much attention to the *process* of education as to its *content*?

Many schools are still not harnessing the experience which pupils gain outside the classroom, particularly from their home. The pressures of the National Curriculum and the associated tests put rigid constraints on how teachers spend their time. Charles Desforges points out in the summary to his report on *The Impact of Parental Involvement*:

> In the primary age range the impact caused by different levels of parental involvement is much bigger than the differences associated with variations in the quality of schools.

We need to re-examine the purposes of education in the twenty-first century and devise appropriate curricula with suitable, flexible strategies for implementing them. We are still tinkering with a curriculum tradition derived from nineteenth-century public schools.

Young people grow up in a complex, often confusing world, facing challenges which are rarely simple and never susceptible to single answers. The expectation of 'a job for life' or a *single* career path has long disappeared. The vocabulary now resounds with *adaptability*, *flexibility*, *continuous professional/skill development*. Employers increasingly seek evidence of a portfolio of skills, of an ability to work with other people and a capacity to think through problems.

This is the effective content of a process curriculum; not unrelated nuggets of information. Literacy and numeracy are necessary skills within the process which are needed to analyse issues, seek relevant information, interrogate sources and then construct possible outcomes. It is the working method of both scholar and designer. Lawrence Stenhouse once described the aim as 'turning pupils into students'.

And there is now a marvellous array of technologies to help in this task. Teachers can assume that from an early age children will have access to television, and increasingly to computers at home, and mobile telephones which already have the capacity to produce a range of visual and audio information as well as text.

Yet relatively few classrooms are equipped with interactive whiteboards which allow teachers to use audio-visual material to design lessons to which pupils can respond using similar technology. In many classrooms the model is still that of the transmission of information which pupils may or may not transform into knowledge, still less understanding. It is unsurprising that a significant number of young people are alienated, not so much from school – which is often an enjoyable and collegial institution – but from the curriculum, over which they feel no sense of ownership and which they find difficult to relate to the lives they lead, and hope to lead in the future.

The assessment and examination systems reinforce the content-driven curriculum and do not encourage a creative approach to teaching and learning which might actually realize the aspirations quoted above.

It is interesting that ex-Chief Inspector Mike Tomlinson in his report on the way forward for the 14–19 phase points the way to an English Baccalaureate, believing that all 14–19 year olds should follow programmes of learning which contain a balance of the general skills and knowledge which everybody needs for adult life and to undertake further learning and employment. The aspiration is to make connections (not differences) within knowledge, and to acknowledge that it is a skills-content bundle, not the acquisition of inert information.

We are only now exploring the notion of a 14–19 phase which will lead to the possibility of continuing education for everyone, not just for those who achieve the requisite 'academic' qualifications to enter 'higher' education. If this does become the aspiration then the assessment system will also need radical change, as will the content and approach to HE courses. More does not necessarily mean worse: it certainly means different. We can no longer sustain GCSE as a 'school leaving certificate' giving the impression to young people that their education is over at that age. There needs to be an articulated, developmental structure in which there can be transition points where students can understand the nature of choices open to them, and the routes to their achievement.

The *Record of Achievement* initiative (more recently called the *Progress File*) was an attempt to formalize this. Students did have ownership of the RoA, which gave them more insight into their own progress and learning tasks, and uses a much broader picture of the potential candidate. As the Assessment Reform Group has pointed out there needs to be a shift from assessment *of* learning to assessment *for* learning.

To achieve this shift is little short of a *transformation*; changing schools from *learning organizations* to *learning communities*. As Mitchell and Sackney express it in *Profound Improvement: Building Capacity for a Learning Community*, it means:

moving from a technological model that is concerned with targets, efficiency and hierarchical modes of accountability to one that is characterized by metaphors of wholeness and connections, diversity and complexity, relationships and meanings, reflection and enquiry, collaboration and collegiality. (Quoted in Rudduck and Flutter, 2004, p. 139)

In the Schools Council Report of its Working Party on the *Whole Curriculum 13–16* (1975), the Group highlighted what it called its key concepts. Central to these was the notion of the school as a centre of curriculum development:

All worthwhile proposals for curriculum change are put to the test in classrooms and only come to fruition if teachers have the resources, support, training and self-confidence to implement them. (Schools Council, 1975, p. 17)

Some of the studies in the large ESRC *Teaching and Learning Research Programme* are currently attempting to explore these territories. Students are, for example, being consulted about their learning, instead of being presented with small pieces of a map which they then somehow have to fit together. In another study, parents are being actively and purposefully involved in their children's learning, with pupils encouraged to bring their home activities into school, and parents helped to understand and contribute to the curriculum.

Another key concept of the 1975 *Whole Curriculum* report was that of the *educational covenant*. This was a long way from the current *Home-School Agreement*. The controversial and negotiable nature of the curriculum required the commitment and co-operation of pupils, parents, teachers and others:

We believe reconciliation between these groups will not be possible unless each is prepared to make concessions as well as to lay down claims. (Schools Council, 1975, p. 25)

The report expanded its notion of the educational covenant in terms of the 'reasonable expectations' of pupils, parents and teachers, and the claims of society which was providing the resources for the educational enterprise. It was based on the premise that education was a co-operative enterprise in which parents had an important contribution to make:

> Society may reasonably expect that schools will help their pupils gain a general knowledge of the democratic process and a respect for the law, as well as an understanding of how to participate in political processes, to change the law and defend oneself from injustice. It is difficult to encourage young people to behave responsibly if they have no experience of responsibility. Hence the importance of pupils' involvement in the educational endeavour and the concept of entitlement, along with reciprocal responsibility. (*Ibid.*, p. 27)

The report replaced Dorothy Sayers' *Trivium* with Phenix's six *Realms of Meaning* and set out a range of studies and their presentation which would contribute to understanding and meaning. It quoted with approval Jerome Bruner's criterion for the worthwhileness of a subject as whether when fully developed it is worth an adult's knowing, and whether having known it as a child makes a person a better adult. If the answer to both questions is negative or ambiguous, then the material is cluttering the curriculum.

In *Primary Practice*, its follow-up booklet to the *Practical Curriculum*, the Schools Council bravely entitled its Introduction *The Year 2000* and pointed out that:

> The silicon chip is already transforming our factories, offices, and household appliances. We can hardly imagine what changes it may now bring to the content and practice of (primary) education. (Schools Council, 1983, p. 11)

It went on:

> What we can be sure of is this: our own age is one of extreme turbulence. The structure of established industries ... the pattern of family life, are in ferment. Television by satellite and information by cable are only two of the obvious changes our children will need to take in their stride. (*Ibid.*)

The booklet went on to expand on planning, structuring and organizing a curriculum which took account of imagination, feeling and sensory expression and the contribution which pupil assessment and record-keeping (*not* SATS) could make to progression and continuity. It also considered the contribution which parents and others outside the school could make. It quoted from the 1978 DES report *Primary Education in England*:

> The general educational progress of children and their competence in the basic skills appear to have benefited where they were involved in a programme of work that included art and craft, history and geography, music and physical education, and science as well as language, mathematics and religious and moral education, although not necessarily as separate items on a timetable. (DES, 1978, p. 28)

Not everything in the past was good; nor was it all bad. Some ideas are worth revisiting. Child-centred education has become a term of abuse. But there is no doubt that the best teaching aid remains a highly motivated student.

10 The Importance of Friendship during Primary to Secondary School Transfer

Rosalyn George

It has only been in relatively recent times that the perspective of the child's experience of transfer from one phase of schooling to the next has begun to be explored (Measor and Woods, 1984; Reay and Lucey, 2000; O'Brien, 2003). Until this time, research into primary school transfer tended to concern itself with the organizational arrangements, for example, assessment procedures and selection, with the importance of friendship within this process of transfer being marginal to concerns of academic attainment and curricular demands. In this chapter I explore the perspective of a group of pre-adolescent girl friends as they transfer from their primary to their secondary schools and argue that children lay far greater emphasis on the importance of having not only a best friend, but also in the significance that they attach to peer group membership at this point in their schooling. As schools are seen as one of the major sites where peer relationships are formed, as well as the arena where future social identities are shaped (George and Pratt, 2004), I would suggest that children need such friendships in order to make sense of their new situation and in the development of their own identity.

Using the girls' own voices, I will document the extent to which their existing social relationships are disrupted as they adapt to and engage with a new school setting. The semi-structured interviews, conducted during the final year of primary school and at the end of the first term and third term of secondary school, identify the girls' concerns regarding their experiences of friendship. I examine the priorities of the girls and suggest that schools do not take sufficient account of them and, instead, privilege organizational structures, a prescribed curriculum against a background of school improvement.

STUDIES OF TRANSFER

Measor and Woods's (1984) highly celebrated ethnographic study of transition was one of the first studies to acknowledge the importance of friendship within the process. Their study focused on the pupil's attitudes to transfer rather than the teacher's, and explored the whole experience of transition from the pupil's perspective and found that for the pupils, the last term in the primary school was characterized by high anxiety, tinged with excitement and 'optimistic expectation'. The children in their study used words like 'being frightened', 'worried', 'nervous' and 'scared' to describe their feelings prior to transfer. These concerns in particular were related to bullying by older children, their new status and their separation from friends. Measor and Woods argued that what is at stake over transfer is questions about the children's identity, where the children shift from the 'cosy' world of the primary school to what they perceive as the large hostile world of the secondary school. They maintain that in making adjustments, the children evaluate themselves against others, particularly those within their friendship networks. Thus, making friends during the early weeks in their new school was very important.

There have very recently been studies which have focused on transfer and aspects of gender and identity within the process. Reay and Lucey's (2000) study of identities at transition explored how both the experience of anxiety and excitement that was evident in the children's accounts of transfer can contribute productively to the anticipation of 'future possibilities'. And working with the children who were going through the process of transfer, they found that:

> Despite the very great fears which children at times expressed in relation to the move from primary to secondary school and challenges which the new environment will present to them, there was much evidence to suggest that most are able to call on hopeful feelings that on some level, at least some of the time, that move will be a benign one, populated by people who will be willing and able to support them through changes. (Reay and Lucey, 2000, p. 203)

O'Brien's (2003) very recent study on transfer focused on girls' classes and feminine identities. O'Brien argued that although moving from one phase of schooling to the next was a highly significant step for all children, her research found that girls from a working-class background felt a greater sense of emotional pain and loss in leaving the familiar surroundings of their primary school and the sense of family and community that the primary school engendered. O'Brien suggests that working-class girls' identities are bound within experiences that make the dominant values and academic demands of the school system have less immediate relevance for their lives. She warns that as the working-class girls transfer, despite the excitement they express and opportunity they perceive the move will bring, the transition results in 'a series of exclusions that produces the first steps in "moving out" rather than "moving on"' (O'Brien, 2003, p. 265). Within this group of girls who are the focus of this chapter, Kate, after one term in her secondary school, was struggling with most aspects of her schooling and may well have 'moved out'. There was also resistance from some of the African Caribbean girls, to dominant views and constructions of femininity, but their acknowledgement that school was the way to gain credentials leading to greater opportunities ensured they 'moved on'.

THE PRIMARY SCHOOL AND LOOKING AHEAD

Through a detailed analysis of the girls talking about their perceptions and feelings of transferring to secondary school, it became clear, like the children in Measor and Woods (1984) and Reay and Lucey's (2000) studies, that the anticipated experience was painful, stressful and created feelings of anxiety, but this anticipated experience was also filled with excitement and expectancy. These conflicting emotions were articulated by several of the girls as Shumi, Isobel and Lisa's comments show:

I don't mind going to secondary school, but I don't want to actually start it. (Shumi)

Part of me wants to go but another part doesn't. (Isobel)
I have these different kind of times when I am nervous about it, I'm really like 'oh, it's going to be too hard, I'm going to have so much homework'. And then it's like 'oh, it's got to be so much fun. We'll have so much stuff to do'. (Lisa)

For all girls, the major differences they predicted as they moved from primary to secondary school were based on structural changes, for example, the size and layout of the buildings, the greater number of teachers and pupils and curriculum diversity.

It won't be the same as it is in primary school. It will be much bigger. And there will be a lot more things to do and it will be kind of scary – loads of people and different classes to go to. (Hafsha)
And it will be like moving around a lot like because we go to different teachers instead of sticking with one. (Lisa)

Hafsha and Lisa's comments suggest how the intimacy and homely environment of the primary school, and in particular the primary classroom, is in stark contrast with their expectations of secondary school. They already appear to conflate the perceived size of the school and the prospect of meeting different teachers with feelings of fear. However, they were also beginning to acknowledge and accept the impersonal, bureaucratic and regulatory ethos of the school. As Isobel predicted:

Bigger school, all together with children of all ages, stricter rules, loads more homework.

Important as these arrangements were to the girls, by far the greatest issue for them focused around friendship. At the end of the year, when the prospect of going to high school loomed with its highly organizational structures, many of the girls felt concern over what might happen to their friendship group. They felt certain that they would remain in contact with some if not all of their friends. Some of the girls felt that upheavals caused by the new organization would probably lead to a change in their social relationships. Adler and Adler (1998) argue that whilst in the primary school:

the intensity of the peer relationship is constructed around the restrictive and contained setting of the classroom base, the social system, which on the one hand may allow little opportunity for mobility and escape from unwanted clique attention, does, on the other hand, provide a great deal of security for its members. (Adler and Adler, 1998, p. 199)

As Lisa pointed out:

... here, in primary school, you can stay in the same class and all of your friends are in the same class as you. {Yeah} So basically you are always with them unless they are away.

The role of friendship in supporting one's own sense of identity, by reinforcing and reciprocating valued aspects of self alongside the offer of help and security in times of need and trouble, has a particular resonance at this time. The girls had earned respect, esteem and acceptance from their group at primary school and now these aspects may have to be fought for all over again. 'The prospect of marginality in their new school setting, placed the girls in a kind of limbo where understood referents used to identify themselves no longer applied' (Measor and Woods, 1984). The loss of existing friends and the ability to make new ones was a critical concern for all of the girls. Here Chloe, who was the only one from her school transferring to her particular high school, reflects on her feelings at the end of Year 6:

I was worried I wouldn't make new friends and that I would be the one person in the class who wouldn't be in a particular group. I was worried that everyone in the class would have a good friend already and that I didn't. I was worried I wouldn't find anyone I really liked and I'd have to pretend to be someone I wasn't ... to fit in.

Chloe's concern that she might have to pretend to be someone she wasn't in order 'to fit in', like the primary school friendships, highlights the importance of friends in making sense of situations and in establishing one's own identity. The loss of friends on transfer was clearly deeply disturbing for Chloe, for it threatens to dismantle 'the "props" of [*her*] support system' (Measor and Woods, 1984, p. 14).

Some of the girls strategically used this latter part of this final year in primary school to secure closer friendships and form new alliances with girls who had previously been part of another group within their class, but who were now going to go to the same secondary school. Furthermore, those girls who had been tolerated as part of their existing social network, but had been on the periphery of the group, were now legitimately eased out. These responses by the girls re-emphasize friendship as both practical and pragmatic. The culture of the girls' world: 'where pairs group up with other pairs, results in complex social relations. This complexity enables girls to construct new networks of potential friends, whilst breaking off with others' (Thorne, 1993, p. 94).

As Isobel, the group leader, responded when asked if she intended to stay in touch with her existing group of friends from primary school:

> *I don't know, I think I will stay in touch with Lisa. Not so much Shumi because we're really close friends, but we're not like, oh, phone each other up and give each other telephone numbers.*

The maintenance of existing friendships groups and the construction of new ones were clearly high on the girls' personal agendas. However the girls expressed differing levels of confidence in their ability to manage either the existing or the new. These differing levels of confidence reflected the girls' positioning within the hierarchical construction of their existing friendship group. Isobel, who was positioned as the group leader: *doesn't have to worry {she} gets friends easily.* Whereas Hafsha, who was to attend the same secondary school, expressed her anxiety that Isobel may leave her for new friends:

> *I don't know. I think she will make other friends but I don't think anymore that she'll leave me when we go to Dunwood Girls, because she has been my best friend, one of my best friends since I was little. So I don't think she would do that. I think I will be her friend all the way through school but I'll have other friends of mine. I don't know. Because*

*we might get other best friends, but if we, like, have been to the same
school all our lives then, umm, she is still going to be my best friend.*

Shumi expressed a level of confidence in making new friends which
served to mask her insecurity about moving into an environment,
which she perceived as threatening and potentially competitive:

*I think it is hard for people to try and get to know me really, because I
kind of, like, I make it hard for other people to ... I don't know. It's
just a natural thing like being aware that you have to get to know me
before I actually go 'yeah, I'll be your friend'.*

Shumi also drew upon 'contingency friendship' which, according to
Davies (1982), is a friendship that is called upon when it becomes
necessary to leave an existing friend because of inappropriate
behaviour, or in circumstances such as these, where children transfer
schools.

*I will make friends anyway for sure but, like, starting a new school is
something big and with a friend there it makes it easier. Like, in the
way that it's going to be easier to ... I'm gonna feel less scared around
teachers and everything or doing stuff, because my friend will be there.
And, like, if I have any problems and I don't make friends then I can
always stick to her and tell her about different stuff.*

The functional nature of friendship as identified by Davies (1982) is
very much in evidence in Shumi's discussions, for despite the
bravado of her initial response, she recognizes the support and
reassurance that contingency friends bring.

IMAGE AND STATUS

A concern with image and status among peers appeared to be
highlighted at this transitional phase, for the moving from the top
of one hierarchy to the bottom of another when transferring schools
provided another source of anxiety.

The girls' repositioning as the newest and youngest members of
the school community was anticipated as a source of potential

embarrassment and worry about being patronized and humiliated by older and bigger pupils:

> *Everyone says 'look at those sad Year 7's'.*
> *I won't be the biggest any more. I'll be like the smallest. And they probably will be, like, 'Oh, look at the new people, look at the new people'.* (Kate)

A further concern with image and status amongst peers became apparent at this transitional phase, and was articulated by Melody who felt grateful that her sister, a girl in Year 10, provided her with what she perceived as insider knowledge.

> *It was a real advantage having Katherine in the senior school, she made sure I fitted in and didn't look sad, 'cos everyone says 'sad Year 7's'. She told me what bag to get, it had to be a shoulder bag, not a rucksack, which colour socks ... black and the kind of shoes I should wear and that I should wear a baggy jumper, not a tight one and my skirt had to be above the knee. A lot of people didn't know this 'cos they didn't have a sister.*

The girls' anticipated feelings of humiliation because of their size, being the youngest, or their appearance has, according to Measor and Woods, been one of the reasons for the proliferation of myths and stories about prospective secondary schools. The passing down of stories and myths has been seen as one resource for helping them cope with the coming transfer (Measor and Woods, 1984, p. 16).

STORIES AND MYTHS

The girls in this study had constructed an institutionally defined image of what secondary school would be like; this construction was based on handed-down stories and popular myths from peers, such as terrifying teachers, huge daunting buildings and being bullied by older pupils.

> *They said if someone tells you that they are going to bully you or kill you, then you must go and tell the teacher.* (Heidi)

Heidi's response was unusual in so far as it referred to the physical aspects of bullying, which as Delamont's (1991) survey reported, tended to be found in stories told and reproduced by boys. However, stories about ghosts and the supernatural have been found to be fairly common among girls, and this was the case amongst the girls in this research.

> *I was told that there was a blue ghost in the school and that it was in the drama hut, and everybody who walked past it, including the teachers, got scared.* (Melody)
> *I heard that there was this ghost of this girl who had been killed in an accident at school, living under the stage and sometimes you could hear her crying.* (Lauren)

Delamont suggests that if the new school represents 'the topsy-turvy world that is coming, there may well be ghosts [and] ... staff may well be ogres' (Delamont, 1991, p. 252). She argues that stories and myths about strict teachers, bullies and ghosts serve to emphasize the status inversion, from being top of one tree to the bottom of the next, maintaining that myths about the sort of hazards new children think they will face from bigger and older pupils serves to humiliate them.

Measor and Woods suggest that 'the content of the myth involves the allocation of status and the legitimation of the power of a particular group or individual' (Measor and Woods, 1984, p. 26); for it is those who have power that usually tell myths. However, Reay and Lucey suggest that the myths and horror stories serve two purposes, one as a defensive strategy, for rather like fairy tales, these myths allow children to explore and examine their fears at a distance. Secondly, as a way of valorizing the child's sense of self-worth through their choice of school, for the choosing and being selected for a popular school acts as a defence against 'a deeper, more unconscious level of uncertainty that perhaps the school will not be good enough' (Reay and Lucey, 2000, p. 198).

The myths that had been passed down to the girls in this research were greeted with a degree of disbelief, but also with a degree of anxious anticipation.

CHOOSING SCHOOLS

In the last decade, the focus on primary/secondary transfer has shifted to a concern regarding school choice within an increasingly marketized education system (O'Brien, 2003). Research (Ball *et al.*, 1996; Reay and Ball, 1998) suggests that choosing a school and gaining a place at that school is circumscribed by social class as well as 'race' and gender, and that those with economic, cultural and other forms of capital (Reay, 1998) use them to secure the best schools for their children at secondary school transfer.

Whilst school choice was not a focus for this chapter, it is interesting to note that, of all the girls in the study, only two of them transferred to co-educational schools. Kenway and Bullen observe that gender is now a marketing feature of schools. They suggest that many girls' schools are putting themselves forward as specialists in girls' education, with some pursuing and imitating the aspects of the status of girls' schools in the private sector, or alternatively appealing to a feminist agenda where the aim of the girls' education is to fully equip the girls to confidently take their place in the world of work (Kenway and Bullen, 2001). Not all girls or their parents, however, chose an all girls school for the above reasons, some, for example, Laura and Sian, wanted to get away from boys who interrupted their games, chased them or were generally silly.

Laura: *Well, it'll be girls. I am going to a girls' school.*
RG: *Did you choose to go to that secondary school?*
Laura: *Yeah. And it's going to be weird only girls, um, I'm going to Foresters High Girls' School, an all girls school.*
RG: *Why did you choose that school?*
Laura: *'Cos I'm fed up with stupid boys always messing around and that.*

Whilst choice of school was significant to the girls, the data suggests that it was no more important than having friends.

I think it will be sad because I've been here for a long time. I'll, and I'll be moving away from my friends and stuff. And I've known them from when I was in reception. (Shumi)

Hafsha: *I don't know. Like we did an exam because we, I didn't know if I was going to go there, we just wanted to see if I was going to get in. But I really liked it because I did get in and I really liked it so . . . I don't know. I liked it more than the other schools. And my best friend was going there. So, or one of my best friends, yeah Isobel.*
RG: *And one of your best friends is going there. Was that an important factor or not?*
Hafsha: *Oh yeah! I wouldn't want to go to a school with no friends.*

In contrast, for some of the parents, having a sibling or relative in the school was seen as more important in the choice of schools for their daughters, as Jean describes:

Well, my mum and dad have always wanted me to go there because it's my nearest. It's like you can walk, you don't have to get a bus or the train or anything like that. And my brother goes there. And all my brother's friends go there and I know loads of people there. (Jean)

In the following extract, Heidi reflects her mother's concerns about being sent to a school not of her choosing.

RG: *Why, did you want to go there {Askey's Cross}?*
Heidi: *. . . my big brother, he's in Year 8 and he goes to Askey's which is quite close to us, my house, sorry. I really, I did like have a look around and I did have this test and I did really desperately want to get in. But they picked, well I suppose . . . I just didn't get in, didn't get picked. That was the main one that I really wanted to go to 'cos my brother was there already. And I do get on well with my brother and my mum wanted me to go there. So, but then as I just didn't get in I looked at loads of schools. That was the main one but, then I went to Foresters High. But my mum is quite scared 'cos it's a really big school and she doesn't want me to get lost or anything.*

What Heidi's experience shows is that the notion of parental choice can be an illusion, for in practice in many cases, it is the school that chooses the family rather than the family choosing the school. This adds to the complexity of the study, because school choice is exacerbated by the diversity of provision found in urban settings. The parents of the girls in this study are negotiating a minefield, for as noted earlier, the work of Ball *et al.* (1996), Reay and Ball (1998), and Reay (1998) show that through accruing economic, cultural and other forms of capital, that school choice becomes available to only some parents, usually at the expense of others.

INDUCTION

A consideration of the type of induction the girls received in preparing them for secondary school transfer revealed quite different levels of support; it also revealed scant attention being paid to the issue of peer relations or the importance of friendship within this process.

The girls' primary school had only informally talked about the process of transfer, for when asked: *in what ways has your primary school prepared you for going to secondary school?* neither Heidi nor Lisa could report on any significant interventions:

> *Umm, told you to look out for things ... umm, told you what it's going to be like there and uh ....* (Heidi)

Lisa simply responded by saying: *they haven't done anything.*

All the girls reported that they had visited their prospective secondary schools either on the school's open days or at an induction day, and at that time they had engaged in a variety of activities:

> *Well, it starts from 9.30 to 3.30 and you bring like pencils and rubbers and stuff. And you can try out the lunch and stuff, and meet all the teachers. And then at the end of the day you can buy like school stuff, like rulers and the jumpers and stuff.* (Shumi)
>
> *They gave us a form to fill out, if I play instruments ... stuff like that ... if I'm going to be school dinners.* (Laura)

They also reported that, in some cases, they had been asked to nominate a friend from their primary school to be in a class with them at their new school:

RG: *Do they ask you if you want to be in anybody's class particularly?*
Heidi: *Yeah.*
Hafsha: *Yeah .... er, no, I ... we don't say whose class we want to be in, just like who we want to be with and I said Isobel. And she said me ... well, she told me she did.*

However, for some of the girls, this question was not one that they could remember being addressed to them.

RG: *Did they ask you to say who your friends are or who you'd like to be in the same class with?*
Kate: *No, I don't ... umm, they didn't.*

The lack of serious concern about the girls' friendships lends support to the argument that the impersonal, bureaucratic imperatives of the school simply exacerbate the pain for vulnerable children already having to deal with a complex set of changes.

In exploring the girls' induction programme what did become evident was the headteachers' focus on issues concerning behaviour, curriculum matters and academic issues, which meant that little attention was paid to peer relations or the importance of friendship within the process. As noted above, only a few of the girls were asked directly about friendships, and the only other acknow-ledgement or concern with 'friendship' was when secondary liaison teachers consulted with their primary colleagues about which girls should or shouldn't be placed together in the same tutor groups at secondary school. The absence of any systematic and direct consultation with the girls in this study demonstrates the low priority given to this aspect of transfer.

The seeming lack of awareness of the importance of friendship was underlined at an induction evening at one of the secondary schools. Here, parents of prospective girl pupils were informed by the headteacher that the making and breaking of friendships of girls when they entered secondary school was an inevitable part of this stage of schooling, and therefore should not be seen as a cause of anxiety. This headteacher failed to acknowledge the importance that peer relationships has on girls when adjusting to a new environment. Rather, she adhered to an agenda, which continued to place a greater emphasis on the regulatory framework of the curriculum and the behaviour of pupils. Thus, the induction programmes, whilst seemingly useful in terms of providing information, did little or nothing at all to alleviate the girls' real concerns about their friends and other aspects of the informal culture of the school.

NEGOTIATING THE NEW ENVIRONMENT

The work of Furman (1989) and Cotterell (1996) suggests that the stress of transfer becomes more intense when pupils fail to relinquish their attachments to primary schools and furthermore that such pupils find it difficult to invest themselves emotionally in a group of new teachers or classmates. In the interviews conducted at the end of their first term in secondary school, most of the girls expressed a degree of relief in having survived this initial phase. However, the issues and concerns they expressed in primary school continued to be the basis through which they mediated their secondary school experience. Again, the curriculum did not feature in any discussion, but the social and environmental predominated:

I didn't really know anybody and I might not have been in the same class as Laura or Shumi, but it was great, they helped me and I also helped them. (Heidi)
I found that most of my friends from primary school were in my class, it made secondary school much better. (Melody)

Heidi and Melody's remarks point out that friendships during this first term were still organized around their primary school friends and how the functional aspects of friendship supports them in the negotiation of their new environment. Some girls continued to cling to girls who had either not been particularly close friends at primary school or had been in a parallel class.

I sat next to Rebecca on my first day at senior school, we were already kind of friends, not best or anything but we knew each other and we were nervous, but being with each other made us feel secure. (Tan)

Whereas Jeni chose Anna to sit with:

because she went to the same primary school as me but I didn't know her very well. (Jeni)

For Tan and Jeni the primary school connection provided a strong enough link to legitimate a relationship whose function was to provide social and emotional security in this seemingly 'big' and 'scary' environment. Whilst others, like Chloe, who had neither friends nor relatives attending her new school, sought out other girls who were in the same situation, quickly establishing new but tentative links:

Making friends was easier than I thought, because no one knew everyone, it wasn't seen as unusual to just go up and say 'hi, what school are you from?' ... and start a conversation from there. I had spoken to everyone by the end of the first week, I didn't have to pretend to be someone else because everyone was pretty much the same. I soon found my way around the school. (Chloe)

The speed with which Chloe made new friends provides further evidence of the pressing need for friendship at this critical point in the girls' schooling. A school can feel an unsafe place for those who are alone and the finding of a friend can reduce the chaos of the school (Shaw, 1996, cited in Gordon *et al.*, 2000). This was certainly the case for Chloe.

ONE YEAR ON

New friendships formed rapidly during the girls' first year at secondary school. As Year 8 commenced, some of the primary school friendships began to fracture and drift apart. New alliances emerged and adjustments and realignments took place. In the case of Isobel and Hafsha, the hierarchical nature of their friendship, which had been sustained during Year 7, was now challenged:

> *I mean, she still likes to think that we're best friends, but I think she knows that we're not really close anymore ... I think the people in our group, I think they find her quite annoying, and she used to be, like, really popular. And she's not popular anymore.* (Hafsha)

Whilst most of the girls were very positive about having made new friends, it was only Heidi who reported any personal bullying or harassment:

> *Well, the first time, I was in the dinner queue and these girls were in front of me. And they just looked behind and started sort of like looking me up and down and then sort of just fixed their eyes on my feet ... and then they turned round and they were laughing.* (Heidi)

Hierarchies and differences are often solidified at this early stage by marking out those who don't belong or are different (Gordon *et al.*, 2000). Heidi, in terms of her style, the way she wore her school uniform and other bodily signifiers, was different. At the end of Year 7 Heidi's appearance remained unaltered from her primary school days. She still wore two long plaits and dressed in an androgynous manner. Heidi may well have been picked out by *other* members of her class as not belonging, but through having a close circle of friends, consisting of Lauren, one of her friends from primary school, who was now a leader amongst her secondary school friendship group, Heidi's life was made more manageable.

One of the girls reported that she had not really made any new friends, nor had she maintained existing friendships from primary school. Kate, who had seemingly been a content, academically able and reasonably popular girl, although on the periphery of her friendship group at primary school, had found herself isolated, unhappy and disempowered by her new secondary school. She had felt unsupported by her teachers, who 'don't like me'. So acute was her loneliness, that she was ready to leave the school by the end of this first term. Kate's experience serves to underline the critical importance of making friends for enhancing self-esteem and confidence. Her experience also illustrates that, conversely, if you don't make friends, the potentially damaging effect on identity formation, confidence and achievement is immeasurable.

CONCLUSION

The dominant policy discourses relating to high school transfer have reflected current governmental concerns with raising academic standards and sustaining progress. They draw upon research evidence (Galton *et al.*, 2000), which suggests that pupils lose ground at the point of transfer:

> Pupils in secondary schools frequently see the years between national key stage tests and public examinations as somehow less important, and do not appreciate that working hard during these periods can have pay-offs. They can become preoccupied with friendships and gain a reputation for messing around; pupils who want to change from being a dosser to a worker find it extremely difficult to shake off their old image. Consequently, they may decide to give up rather than catch up.

Galton *et al.*'s observations epitomize the abrupt change from educating the whole child to schooling the individual to shape up to a preconceived set of regulatory and behavioural expectations. But, as this study shows, at the time of transfer from primary to secondary school, there is an intensified desire by all pupils to belong to, and be part of, a network of friends. Hargreaves *et al.* maintain that:

> Schools must recognise that the peer group is highly influential for young adolescents and that it can be, at one and the same time, both a major distraction and a powerful ally in the educational process. (Hargreaves *et al.*, 1996)

From the girls' responses, it became clear that the need for peer support and help became more acute with transition to secondary school. Choices of suitable allies as friends and being accepted as part of a group are critical for survival, and for a reduction in feelings of vulnerability. As the case of Kate above illustrates, non-acceptance and rejection by the group can result in long-term isolation and a heightening of a sense of anxiety. The emphasis on the structural arrangements of transfer, as currently advocated, is of little use to Kate; she is simply left to flounder on the margins. Kate's situation draws attention to the practices of teachers and school administrators and their distance from children's feelings and experiences of friendships, and in particular their anticipation or fear and loneliness in the transition stage. Schools and governments need to be more aware and value the pupils' concerns about social issues concerning transition, which, I would suggest, could ease the pathway. It would appear that, for this group of girls, the continuity and development of the curriculum is not as important as the continuity and development of peer group relations and friendships. The fear of being isolated or marginalized would seemingly override any other concerns. As Delamont observes:

> They fear the loss of friends made in the lower school and an absence of friendships in the new one. Peer groups or cliques are a major factor in adolescents' school life. (Delamont, 1991)

11 Developments in the Training of Teachers*

John Clay

THE CONTEXT

During the past two and half decades, the attention given to the education system by successive governments in Britain has been unremitting and relentless. The claimed postwar consensus that existed right to the end of the 1970s was abruptly ruptured by the introduction of the 1980 Education Act. This was designed primarily to reverse the comprehensive schools movement, which was seen as an egalitarian project that stifled competition and entrepreneurialism. The responsibility for the United Kingdom's slide downwards in the world economic league from its loftier position in the pre-war years was deemed to be caused by the lack of competitiveness of business and industry. However, the poor performance of British industry was blamed on the failure of the education system for not producing a suitably trained workforce and thus the system as a whole became the scapegoat. Poor teaching was deemed to be the reason for this crisis and teacher training institutions were held responsible for inculcating generations of teachers with 'woolly ideas' about equality and social justice at the expense of training teachers to teach the basic skills and to impart a fixed and immutable body of knowledge that was considered a part of the nation's cultural heritage.

---

* The views expressed in this chapter have been written in the author's capacity as a one-time member of the Hillcole Group.

Over an 18-year period of unbroken rule, the Conservatives successively restructured the public education system as part of the overall project to reform state welfarism and reduce public provision. The sea change brought about by the passing of the 1980 Education Act must be emphasized. This legislation introduced the 'Assisted Places Scheme' for pupils to transfer from state schools to the private sector on a subsidized basis; to a sector that was already paying less than its fair share of taxation through being granted charitable status. This was a direct shift of resources from the public to the private sector under the banner of 'parental choice'. The fact that this choice was largely limited to the already privileged middle classes did not go unnoticed and the courting of this fraction of the population has remained to this present day.

Along with this shift of focus and resources, the requirement for schools to publish their raw examination results; the right given to parents to appeal against the school allocated to their child by the Local Education Authority (LEA) and the right to send pupils across LEA boundaries, transformed parents from local tax payers with a stake in their community schools to that of consumers with a right to shop around for an education that had become a commodity. This change to public education that catered for 93 per cent of the school population was greatly accelerated by the introduction of the 1988 Education Reform Act that allowed grammar schools and schools with falling rolls to opt out of LEA control. The incentives to 'break free' from LEAs were considerable since it allowed these 'opted out', Grant Maintained schools to receive greatly enhanced funding directly from central government and administered through a non-elected quango. The 1988 Act also included proposals for open enrolment so that popular schools could increase their intakes and thus gain greater funds, which gave these schools a further edge when competing with the less popular schools. The publication of school examination results that started with the 1980 Act eventually resulted in a national league table of all secondary schools being published annually. Unsurprisingly, when the only indicator of performance measured was examination results, the top three hundred or so schools that consistently performed well were those in the long-established private sector and the increasingly more selective schools in the Grant Maintained sector that had benefited from the massive shift of resources over that period of time. The creation of City Technology Colleges with the grudging help of private finance from industry was also an attempt to weaken the ability of democratically accountable LEAs from rationalizing school provision and planning strategically for the medium and long terms. Seen in retrospect, the combined effects of the 1980 and 1988 Education Acts established the current system of educational provision as a commodity to be traded on the market as any other.

BUSINESS AS USUAL

The election of a Labour government in 1997 and the passing of new legislation brought to an end the most destructive aspects of the previous administration's policy. The Assisted Places Scheme was abolished and Grant Maintained Schools were returned to the LEA and reconstituted as Foundation schools, losing their enhanced funding but still retaining their right to select 10 per cent of their intake. The nursery voucher system was also discontinued. Nevertheless, in many other respects no attempt has been made to dismantle the disciplinary mechanism of the market. Every sector of the educational system, from schools to colleges and universities have been shaped and 'reformed' to the strictures of the market under the ubiquitous banner of 'choice', 'quality', 'standards' and 'efficiency'. In terms of organization, each school or institution within the education sector has adopted a style of management that is 'top-down' and hierarchical; a form of Taylorist management that has long been discarded by 'knowledge-based' organizations. This new but old style of management has nevertheless cloaked itself with the language of the market and this phenomenon of using jargon to conceal the realities and consequences as it affects people was coined 'obscuranto', by Frank Delaney, a BBC Radio presenter – denoting a language which stands in opposition to the term Esperanto that was designed as a language to transcend cultural and national barriers. Along with the jargon of the market, the predominant buzzword over the past decade has been the term 'globalization'. In the education policy arena according to Cole:

> 'Globalisation' has become one of the orthodoxies of the 1990s ... used ideologically to mystify the populace as a whole and to stifle action by the Left in particular ... in order to continue the Thatcherite project in Education. (1998, pp. 315–16)

'Globalization' is deemed to be an inevitable consequence of progress and that in order to be key players in the new world order we must embrace globalization uncritically and schools and other sites of educational provision must retool and refocus on producing a skilled workforce to sustain and operate successfully within a market economy. In this blueprint for modernization, the principle of a publicly funded education system accountable to the community it serves through locally elected representatives has been eroded even further. This 'democratic deficit' would appear to be of little concern to the current government. Bottery (1999) has argued that the organization and pursuance of an education system to meet purely economic goals:

> could well improve the international competitiveness of a nation state and its economic prosperity, but there are other effects which many, in the West at least, would see as heavy prices to be paid – an increased centralisation with a consequent decrease in individual autonomy, an increase in culture of purely rational-technical professionals and the dangers of a move towards an increasingly illiberal society. If individual choice is seen as an expensive luxury, it may well be sacrificed to national policy when the need arises. (p. 116)

I have argued elsewhere that education should promote a widespread participatory democracy and contribute to the rebuilding of a society where people will be knowledgeable, skilled, critical and confident – rather than passive, insecure, indifferent victims of economic necessity, which is what a market-led world will always produce for a large proportion of the population. We want to see people as agents of change rather than as mere objects of economic necessity (Benn and Chitty, 1997). The argument that increasing the skills base alone will somehow increase employability and employment which, in turn, will create wealth that can 'trickle down' to benefit those lower down the economic ladder would seem fanciful. In the aftermath of the closure of two hi-tech firms in the North of England, Frank Coffield, writing in *The Times Higher Education Supplement*, said:

> All the North's 16 year olds could have obtained five As in the GCSE exams, all its teachers could have MEds in school improvement, and all its directors and professors of education could have PhDs in robotic technology and still Siemens and Fujitsu would have closed ... the debate must move beyond the simplistic notion that raising standards in education will, of itself, create economic prosperity for all. Raising skill levels is not the key to the promised land; it is a necessary but not sufficient condition for such success ... over-concentration on raising skill levels puts the onus on education and takes the pressure off industry. (18 September 1998)

However, in attempting to flesh out the Third Way policy on education, the role of the market is deliberately played down and instead the emphasis is now put on the fostering of private/public partnership. The rhetoric of private/public 'partnership' conceals the true extent of the privatization of public provision. In the aftermath of Kings Manor School in Guildford being handed over to the private sector, lock, stock and barrel, Francis Beckett reminds us that:

> David Blunkett, the former council leader who once believed that local schools should be responsible to elected local authorities, is turning into the most centralising and most private sector friendly education secretary we have known. (*New Statesman*, 15 January 1999, p. 9)

TEACHER EDUCATION

The training of teachers within this market context involved, firstly, establishing a diversity of routes into teaching. Secondly, partnerships between institutions of teacher education and schools were put in place with schools given a leading role in the training and thirdly, establishing the Teacher Training Agency (TTA) in 1994 was intended to oversee not only the funding and management of teacher education but also to commission research to cement the imposed 'partnership' structures between Higher Education Institutions (HEIs) and schools through the commissioning of tightly specified classroom based research. The funding for initial teacher education was soon formulated to favour those institutions that were prepared to adhere strictly to the training model constructed and an inflexible Ofsted inspection framework used as the sole mechanism to ensure compliance. The result of such measures is that staff involved in initial teacher education have now become, probably, the most highly surveilled; subject to radical yet untested reforms imposed by central government on not only the curriculum of both schools and teacher education, but also on ways of transacting the teaching and learning. The pressure to conform to a model of 'good' practice as conceived from the Centre has become hegemonic. The new generation of teachers over the past decade has become increasingly efficient at delivering the curriculum and in preparing pupils to reach the 'standards' and meet the targets set. The imposition of a national curriculum for Initial Teacher Education (ITE) has narrowed the focus of the education and training even more and is 'technicist' and uncritical to produce technicians that can operate efficiently in the 'command classroom'.

Those involved in pre-service teacher education are subjected to the disciplinary controls of both the TTA and Ofsted. The implications for professionals at the receiving end of this are potentially very serious. Questioning and challenging the dominant orthodoxies can adversely affect career and/or academic advancement and, as a consequence, individuals involved become either compliant or move out of pre-service provision altogether. The new managerialist culture that is all-pervasive further corrodes the climate for promoting critical enquiry – where the debates and discussions on alternatives could be usefully explored. Pre-service teacher education programmes are increasingly staffed and led by managers who are considered to be solely focused on preparing future teachers who are 'Ofsted-proof'. This can have potentially serious consequences for recruitment practices of both student teachers and staff because only those who display unquestioning and conforming attitudes are likely to gain entry to the teacher education enterprise in the future. This could lead to an ironic situation where a diversity of providers will be involved in preparing a fairly uniform and homogeneous pool of future teachers.

A discernible fault line has appeared and we are beginning to witness staff solely engaged in pre-service education coalescing into a sub-set of 'trainers' distinct from those engaged in research and scholarship. The narrow technicist culture that is fostered by the funding and inspection regimes has contributed to the entrench- ment of that divide. A colleague with a co-ordinating role for ITE, when questioned about implementing a totally mechanistic form of an audit for demonstrating subject knowledge which involved testing and remedial instruction for its exemplification of a model of deficit pedagogy, replied triumphantly, 'I can't see what all the fuss is about; I'm glad I'm not an academic'. The term 'academic' was used in the perjorative sense of either a person divorced from reality or indeed a person who might possibly place too much emphasis on theory/research relating to the acquisition of the QTS credentials.

We would argue that within such a climate 'new regimes of truth' are emerging. They provide a rationalization and a justification for the behaviour and actions for those who have embraced the rhetoric of 'inclusivity' and empowerment, which carefully conceals the centralizing authoritarianism of the new politics. Drawing on Foucault, who characterized power as an integral component in the production of truth functioning independently:

Truth is a thing of the world; it is produced only by virtue of multiple forms of constraint and it induces the regular effects of power. Each society has a regime of truth, its 'general politics' of truth that is, the types of discourse, which it accepts, and makes function as true. (Foucault, 1980, p. 131)

What follows are two case studies employed to exemplify how new regimes of truth are constructed in teacher education and schools.

Case A

This is a tutor in an HEI with enormous experience of teaching both pre-service and CPD courses. This person has a strong interest in issues of equality and social justice and is committed to promoting critical enquiry. Seen as a 'problem' raising awkward questions in this climate of new managerialism and with an impending Ofsted looming in that area of teacher education, this tutor may have been seen as someone needing to be kept an eye on.

The process started with an official memorandum from the manager (defined in terms of heads of cost centres with responsibility for managing resources) early in the academic year reminding this tutor that following the annual appraisal, the targets discussed at the appraisal interview had not been translated into an action plan before the set deadline. This 'transgression' was translated subsequently into that of 'inability to meet deadlines'. A few weeks later another letter was sent 'requesting' this tutor to attend an official meeting to discuss specifically the:

- Delivery [sic] of modules
- Meeting deadlines
- Administrative duties

At the formal meeting that took place the tutor was told that some students had complained about a module that they were studying with this tutor. The evidence furnished for this inadequate delivery was centred on two letters written by a group of students (5 out of 28). One of the letters was sent in anonymously and was not dated. Furthermore, these letters had been given in to the programme leader on the fifth week of a fourteen-week module. An analysis of the letters reveals issues pertinent to this chapter.

The letter that was signed by five students highlighting their expectations of a module designed to prepare subject specialists to become curriculum co-ordinators in school cohered around the following sentence:

The whole class [sic] has the greatest admiration for our current lecturer's breadth of knowledge and expertise. However it is felt that X's approach is failing to deliver the intended purpose of the module which is to prepare students to be subject co-ordinators.

Wide knowledge and expertise seemed not to be an asset but almost detrimental to achieving a set of prescribed skills seen as synonymous with being a subject co-ordinator, a role seen as essentially about classroom practice. However, the sentiments expressed in this signed letter are elaborated in the second letter, which was anonymous.

My main concern is the title [of the assignment] *The Science Curriculum in the Year 2010. Considering this essay has to be handed in, I feel it is an inconsiderate choice. I do not have a clue as to how the curriculum is devised and do not know what it might be in a couple of years, let alone 2010. Books only speculate approaches to strategies nothing to fill 30 words let alone 3000 ... If I had known I would have to be psychic I would never had opted for such a poor thoughout* [sic] *subject study ... We come away with knowledge about debating social topics such as gender. I could have chosen a sociology degree. I would prefer to maintain an unknown status please.*

The letter was littered with spelling and grammatical errors. Considering the statutory requirements that students communicate effectively using standard English, both written and spoken, it is interesting that throughout the journey of this letter, no concern was raised as to how a student teacher could be embarking on the penultimate year of an Honours degree course with such a poor command of their native language. More importantly was the management's response in seizing this opportunity as further evidence to 'discipline' the tutor. The language of Ofsted and the TTA was invoked.

I accept how you believe that your approach is inclusive, but I did point out that in the current climate, it is essential that you are 'hitting the right button' in terms of internal and external quality assurance (including HEFCE, Ofsted and QAA).

The role of the teacher educators to challenge orthodoxies and to debate and speculate about alternatives has no place in pre-service teacher education. The power of these regulatory bodies to re-fashion and mould future teachers has become systemic.

Case B

This arose from a research project that a colleague was involved in and it is reported here to highlight the parallels that are occurring in the context of a school.

Susie, a primary teacher, is in her second year of teaching after completing a four-year degree at a prestigious university (her reasons for becoming a teacher).

Well I wanted to be a teacher since I was nine. And I think I have to say it was somebody who I thought the most appalling teacher. And I thought I'm going to be like her and not be like her – I'm going to be a teacher and not, not be like her, be nice and calm, not make any of my children cry and not shout at them. So, that's, that's an issue which brought me into it. Then as I became older and I went, and I had to choose a career I became very interested in environmental issues and thought well, the best place to get people to know about environmental issues is get them young.

Her 'ideals' have since been severely compromised. Her commit-ment to the teaching of environmental issues has been put 'on the back burner' because of other demands on curriculum time.

I think your priorities change. When you're in university, I guess you're quite idealistic but when you get into school the reality of it is so different ... you have to fit in with the priorities of the school. Now I'm not saying that if I had my way everybody would be recycling and we would all be you know, learning about the environment ... I realize some of my views did have to go on the back burner for the sake of SATs

*results and league tables which are the whole school's priority ... I'm
still proving myself as a competent and able teacher and still establishing
myself in school and within my career. And to do that I have to get you
know, English, Maths and Science and those have to be the things I have
to concentrate on for the moment.*

To achieve new goals that she sees as vitally important she now
justifies her pedagogy in the following terms:

*If you have to be incredibly strict and seemingly horrible and shout at
children then yes, do it. If you make the children cry then that's it, that's
what it takes. And in some way that does upset me because as I said
earlier, I came into teaching because I had a teacher who used to make
the children cry because she was so horrible. But you know, if you have to
do it – you have to do it.*

This disturbing shift so early on in her career lends weight to
another teacher's assertion that 'many of the current initiatives are
frightening people into situations and behaviour because of the way
success is currently judged and measured'.

Such compromises as described above are reinforced by the formal
and regimented organization that is found in Susie's classroom. She
justifies her classroom practice saying:

*... because of the changes in Government policy and Government's
priorities, like with the literacy and numeracy hour, we have to be like
that. We have to whole-class teach ... because we are junior teachers,
the way we all teach is quite similar because we all believe in similar
things and that kind of strengthens itself, that kind of reinforces itself so
because you believe it, you teach like that and because you see everybody
else teaching like that you believe that you're right.*

Susie's commitment to her newly constructed pedagogical practice
is bolstered by her belief that it is shared by the majority of her
colleagues. Such is the power of the governmental intervention into
not only curricula but also into the methods of transaction that this
alliance of classroom teachers feel sufficiently confident in sidelining
the headteacher's declared commitment to an Arts-led curriculum.
This group of teachers have consumed the whole rhetoric of raising

standards and that poor performance in the league tables is a personal failure on the part of the individual teacher. Furthermore, good SATs results are what education is all about.

Interestingly, as suggested above, the headteacher of this school feels he continuously has to defend the importance of maintaining a broad curriculum.

> *I've always wanted to defend a broad curriculum. When we set up the school, the initial governors and I wanted the arts and music to be a strength of the school and that's still an on-going battle because most of the staff will tell you they're committed in principle but in practice they are not. This is because they have to release children from maths, English and science. So there's a constant struggle. They are influenced by outside pressures and they throw it up in my face that there's so much pressure from the Government and the LEA but I remind them that I don't put any pressure on them. What I want to see is a broad curriculum where subjects are valued and children who aren't necessarily academic can get a lot from school. They worry about a lot of SATs results and things like that.*

The headteacher feels that his vision is being undermined and many staff in the school do not share his values. He is unable to persuade them that what is important in schooling is the broad canvas of leaning and not what is easily measured.

These two case studies illustrate that the macro-political agenda for education is being implemented at the micro-political level of the institution and a regime of compliance to the new orthodoxy has itself become another regime of truth about what makes a 'good' teacher.

WHAT CAN BE DONE?

Goodson (1999) argues for educational researchers to carve out a new role for themselves

> informed by collective memories of social justice ... [not] that I am talking about re-establishing some old master narrative of

social justice – more a set of voices and visions, a moving mosaic of intentions and plans. (p. 292)

This may be a touch romantic for we should keep in mind that young people embarking on a career in teaching will not have any idea of this 'golden past'. Nevertheless, his borrowing of Brienes' (1980) framework for contesting the given in terms of 'prefigurative' and 'strategic' politics is worth examining. Those of us involved in pre-service teacher education need to ensure that we do not evacuate the territory where student teachers meet future role models, namely the area of mentoring in schools. Here's an example of a prefigurative site that is currently dominated by a narrow culture of ensuring Ofsted compliance, and as a sweetener many HEIs make it 'worthwhile' by crediting this narrow training with Continuous Professional Development (CPD) credentials. As education researchers we have to accept the openings and opportunities afforded in this area to make the 'teacher as researcher' a truly empowering and transformational experience. We agree with Ivor Goodson when he says that:

First, education is far more than a practical matter. Practice constitutes a good deal more than the technical things teachers do in classrooms. Education is a personal as well as political matter ... To stay only with practice as a politically and socially determined form is inevitably to involve teachers in the implementation and acceptance of initiatives which are generated elsewhere. This would make collaboration and research into a form of political quietism. (*op. cit.*, p. 294)

Those of us in educational research, seeking to engage in influencing strategic politics at the macro-level (which we have considered in detail elsewhere), should not lose sight of these prefigurative sites of contestation and meaning making.

12 Rethinking the Future: the Commodification of Knowledge and the Grammar of Resistance

Mike Cole

INTRODUCTION

I first met Caroline Benn in 1989 at the inaugural meeting of the Hillcole Group of Radical Left Educators formed by Dave Hill and myself. Its remit was to respond in pamphlets and books to attacks on education from the Radical Right and to suggest Socialist alternatives. Since 1987, I had been under general attack from the right-wing educational establishment of the time. This included allegations of 'Marxist bias' in my teaching (the extent to which my work was perceived as a threat is evidenced by the fact that negative references to it are cited in *The Spectator* of 15 October 1988, in a pamphlet by the then influential Hillgate Group (1989, pp. 29–35) and in the first volume of Margaret Thatcher's memoirs (Thatcher, 1993, pp. 597–8).[1] Shortly after my first meeting with Caroline, I received a libel writ from a high-ranking Tory peer, who had recently made critical remarks about my work. Caroline hardly knew me then, but proceeded to devote a large part of her time, producing copious amounts of documented evidence, in helping me to defend myself. I was immediately struck by her unremitting and selfless dedication to the Socialist cause. We were to meet regularly after that as members of the Hillcole Group, where this selflessness was to make a lasting impact on the ethos of the group.

In September 1994, partly to spread Hillcole philosophy, and partly to commend our 1991 book *Changing the Future*, Caroline and I wrote an article for the magazine *Red Pepper* on the direction we believed education should take after the defeat of the Tories. We were incensed by what they were doing to education and wanted to intervene to suggest Socialist ways forward. We wrote:

> When the Tory nightmare finally ends, the temptation will be for government and society to do very little in education, on the grounds that a system battered by eight careless education acts and hundreds of incapacitating directives needs a long period to consolidate (Benn and Cole, 1994, p. 15).

We went on to argue that to do little would be as great a mistake as moving back to the old Left culture, which was often paternalistic and undemocratic. Our vision was of a *democratic* Socialist education system, controlled by and run for the people.

NEW LABOUR

Tony Blair had been elected Leader of the Labour Party a couple of months before our article was published. Just under three years later, he became Prime Minister, giving the Labour Party its biggest general election victory ever. In the intervening period, one debate among the Left had been whether Blair was hiding his true beliefs in order to secure victory, or whether he was, in fact, basically anti-Socialist. The debate continued right up to the second election victory in 2001, just after which Blair put his cards firmly on the table. Speaking to the Labour Party Conference in October, he said: 'The next stage for New Labour is not backwards. It is renewing ourselves again' (reported in the *Guardian*, 3 October, 2001). Any hopes that he was about to realign the Labour Party in the direction advocated by Caroline and myself were dashed when he went on to state:

> Just after the election, an old colleague of mine said: 'Come on Tony, now we've won again, can't we drop all this New Labour and do what we believe in?' I said: 'It's worse than you think. I really do believe in it.'

'Renewing ourselves again', rather than going 'backwards', meant, for Blair, continuing the modernization programme. 'Modernization', a key component in Blairite rhetoric, has become the conduit through which New Labour justifies *ideologically* the policy of continuing alignment to the needs of the global market (see Cole, 1998). Indeed, the words 'modernization', 'modernize' and 'modern', often used without reference to any specific practice or domain, occurred 176 times in a 2000 analysis of 53 of Blair's speeches (quoted in Finlayson, 2003, p. 66). What 'modernization' actually means is embracing global neo-liberal capitalism. Modernization means a final break with 'Old Labour' and an end to any speculation that, under Blair's leadership, we might see a re-commitment to social democratic, let alone Socialist, values as the guiding principles of the Labour Party.

What I think the Left failed to realize at the time of Blair's first election victory, however, was the *extent* to which New Labour would move the Labour Party to the Right; that New Labour would amount, in Dave Hill's words, to 'a determined Thatcherism, in its neo-conservative and, *in particular*, its dominant neo-liberal form' (see Hill, 1999, p. 28). The neo-liberalism of Blair has many dimensions, all of which relate to current trends in world capitalism. Dave Hill has identified five such trends:

1. The spread of capital(ism) both geographically, throughout the states of the world, and, within those states, sectorally. This embraces the 'businessification' of education, privatisation, deregulation of controls on profits, the introduction of business forms of management and intensification of labour.

2. The deepening of capitalist social relations with the 'commodification' of everyday life. This is carried out, in particular, through the media and educational state apparatuses, to recompose human personality.

3. The increasing use of repressive economic, legal, military and other state and multi-state apparatuses globally and within states. This is to ensure compliance and subordination to multinational capital and its state agents. The means include repressive state apparatuses such as the police, incarceration/

imprisonment, legal systems/laws, surveillance procedures, threat of and actual job dismissals. At the international level, it includes the enhanced UK 'neocon' project of militaristic imperialism, with its self-proclaimed right/*carte blanche* to attack any nation, such as Iraq, or group at any time in any place.

4. The increasing use of ideological state apparatuses in the media and education systems. This is in particular to both 'naturalise' and promote capital social and economic relations on the one hand, and to marginalise, demonise and punish resistant/anti-capitalist hegemonic oppositional ideologies, actions and activists on the other.

5. The increasing concentration of wealth and power (power to retain and increase that wealth) in the hands of the capitalist class. This embraces fiscal policy and (cutting back) social/ public welfare programmes and policies and opening to the market divisive marketised stratified programmes in pensions, healthcare, schooling and higher education. Such programmes increase hierarchies of provision, resulting in racialised and gendered social class inequalities. (Hill, 2004)

THE COMMODIFICATION OF KNOWLEDGE

In this chapter, I will concentrate on the second of these trends: 'the commodification of everyday life' and, in particular, the commodification of knowledge. The starting point for Marx in the three volumes of *Capital* is an analysis of commodities. In Chapter One of Volume One, Marx makes a distinction between 'use value' and 'exchange value'. Like every other commodity in capitalist society, knowledge has both a use value and an exchange value. What is significant about contemporary capitalist society is the extent to which, after it has been produced, knowledge is commodified and consumed in schools and universities like hamburgers (its exchange function both in schools and in the world of work has become hyper-dominant and its use value of benefit to capital).

In contemporary capitalism, relationships between workers and the state, and, indeed, workers and other workers, increasingly take on a commercial aspect. In general terms, the intense creative energy of the working-class is being channelled, for example, into pubs/alcohol and drugs, clubs, pop music, chat shows, football, soaps, play stations and videos (see Cole, 2004). Significantly, ITV, the commercial terrestrial channel aimed specifically at Britain's working-class, concerned about the general decline in news audiences, wants the news to concentrate more on 'leisure, consumer and showbusiness news' (Wells, 2001, p. 1).

Even allegations of child abuse are reduced to cash prizes and fun, as the following unsolicited email demonstrates:

Michael Jackson: Did he or didn't he?
Tell us what you think and enter to win a chance for $1000 Holiday Spending Cash!
It's quick. It's easy and it's fun. Join the InternetSurveyGroup today and begin winning cash and prizes just in time for the Holiday shopping season.
Membership is free and participation is voluntary.

With respect to the education system in Britain (as elsewhere), we have moved to a situation where everything is judged by the finished product or commodity. Success in schooling is judged by SATs and by league tables, rather than by the acquisition of knowledge, let alone emancipatory knowledge. As McMurtry has argued: 'the commodification of education rules out the very critical freedom and academic rigour which education requires to be more than indoctrination' (McMurtry, 1991, p. 215). With respect to commodification in universities, but equally prescient to the education system in general, the Campaign for the Future of Higher Education has recently pointed out that:

Students are neither customers nor clients; academics neither facilitators nor a pizza delivery service. Universities are not businesses, producing consumer goods. Knowledge and thought are not commodities, to be purchased as items of consumption, whether conspicuous or not, or consumed and therefore finished with, whether on the hoof as takeaway snacks or in more leisurely fashion. Education is not something which can be 'delivered', consumed and crossed off the list. Rather, it is a continuing and reflective process, an essential component of any worthwhile life – the very antithesis of a commodity.

As Dave Hill explains:

> Within universities and vocational further education, the language of education has been very widely replaced by the language of the market, where lecturers 'deliver the product', 'operationalise delivery' and 'facilitate clients' learning', within a regime of 'quality management and enhancement', where students have become 'customers' selecting 'modules' on a pick'n'mix basis, where 'skill development' at universities has surged in importance to the derogation of the development of critical thought. (Hill, 2004)

ALTERNATIVE EDUCATIONAL GOALS: REALLY USEFUL KNOWLEDGE

Things have not always been like this; nor do they need to be like this in the future. In order to move forward, it is sometimes useful to look to the past. In the rest of this chapter, therefore, I would like to address myself to the popular educational traditions in the period 1790–1848, a time when at least sections of the working-class were engaged in radical educational pursuits.

Drawing on four aspects of popular 'radical education', identified by Richard Johnson (1979), namely, *a critique of the existing system*; *alternative educational goals*; *education to change the world*; and *education for all*, and in the light of a dearth of *popular* radical thinking in Britain today, I argue that each of these has considerable relevance today.

Richard Johnson was referring to a period when knowledge was produced and exchanged, but, for these radicals, its 'use value' was to the working-class – this being its paramount purpose. I will deal with each in turn and indicate how each might inform a radical education for the twenty-first century. I would urge readers of this chapter to consider each with respect to *how reasonable they are as democratic principles* rather than to what extent they are realizable in the context of the current New Labour control of the education system.

CRITIQUE OF THE EXISTING SYSTEM

First, Radicals conducted a running critique of all forms of 'provided' education, which, in later phases of the period, involved a practical grasp and a theoretical understanding of cultural and ideological struggle in a more general sense (Johnson, 1979, p. 76). Schools and other educational institutions could be, sometimes have been and are, centres of critical debate, involving the local trade unions, teaching and non-teaching staff, parents/carers and pupils/students (relative to age). Discussion forums could include the effects on the community of New Labour policies. Questions about cultural and ideological struggle would arise naturally from such discussions. Such questions might include, for example, to what extent is New Labour's pledge to eliminate child poverty by 2010 on track or having an effect on the community; what are the effects of the privatization programmes; what are the reasons for and the effects of the imposition of Performance Related Pay; what is the nature of the Private Finance Initiative; what are the effects of league tables; to what extent are Blair's references to 'globalization', 'modernization' and 'renewal' ideological – to what extent do they occlude more than reveal?

Second, Radicals were involved in the development of alternative educational goals: this entailed notions of how 'educational utopias' could actually be achieved and a definition of 'really useful knowledge', incorporating a radical content – a sense of what it was really important to know. What knowledge is 'really useful' in the promotion of equality? The school curriculum has for too long been structured to exclude, repress and prevent certain issues being addressed. While clearly it is important for all to be literate and numerate, to what extent are working-class children denied access to a critical debate about areas of concern, such as British imperialism, its aftermath and continuing legacy, as well as the new twenty-first century American and British manifestations of global imperialism? What are the central equality issues that confront us? Elsewhere (see, for example: Cole, Hill and Shan, 1997; Hill and Cole, 1999) we and our co-authors have provided detailed practical advice on education for equality, with respect to issues of social class, 'race', gender, sexuality and disability with respect to each subject in the English and Welsh National Curriculum from age 5 to 16.

Prior to the ascendancy of the Radical Right in the 1980s, the dominant educational paradigm, the liberal progressive one, determined what happened in many, though not all, British primary schools and in some secondary schools. Debbie Epstein has offered a trenchant critique of what liberal progressivism often meant in practice, in the context of the real critical potential of primary age children. The 1967 Plowden Report's conceptualization of children as individuals rather than as members of groups (and the fact that social groups tended to be pathologized when they *were* mentioned) made it difficult to raise issues of power relations in primary schools. In addition, Plowden's deficit model of working-class children meant that efforts to promote equal opportunity focused on repairing the deficiencies of individual children rather than concentrating on structures and on curriculum (Epstein, 1993, p. 92).

The Plowden Report actually contains two contradictory views about the relationship between children and society. Society is treated *both* as something from which children must be protected *and* as an entity which they will enter at some future date, and for which they therefore need to be moulded. It is worth quoting Epstein at length:

> Both these views were aspects of Plowden discourse which diminished the likelihood that primary teachers working within their framework would try to consider and challenge social inequalities with the children they teach – for if the school is

regarded as a safe haven from the ills of society, why allow disruptive ideas about inequality to enter the classroom? Furthermore, while 'preparing' children to take their place in society (at some specified future date) might involve some ideas of liberal tolerance, it also carried the implicit assumption that the 'nature' of society is fixed and that we can predict what kind of society children should be prepared for. Again, there is no compelling logic which says that predictions about a future society will not involve recognition of a need to combat inequalities but the notion does preclude the idea that children should be involved, in the here and now, in deconstruction of dominant ideologies. (Epstein, 1993, pp. 92–3)

In place of the Plowden learning process set of perspectives, Debbie Epstein advocates a co-operative, democratic learning process, but in the mode of critical reflection, rather than Plowdenesque liberalism. It has been shown that children are aware of the feelings of others as early as their second year of life and *can* therefore 'decentre' and are thus amenable to understanding issues of equality. As their understanding increases, they become more independent in their handling of concepts. The implications for the possibilities for education to challenge all inequalities at a very early age are obvious. In Epstein's words: 'it is essential to view every school as a site of struggle, where the negotiations taking place can either strengthen or weaken possibilities for developing education for equality' (*ibid.*, p. 57). From an early age, children have the right to know what is really going on in the world. Young children do, of course, need to be protected, but they also have a right to be informed.

EDUCATION TO CHANGE THE WORLD

Third, radicalism incorporated an important internal debate about education as a political strategy or as a means of changing the world.

The pre-Thatcherite debates, about whether education is political or not, have not surprisingly subsided. Not only is education in Britain political (small 'p'), it is also quite clearly Party Political (large 'p'). Richard Hatcher has argued that three developments can help in this context of popular self-activity. First, information technology can allow the pupil much greater choice and undermine the role of the teacher as a gate-keeper of knowledge, and at the same time enhance the latter's role as *facilitator* of the learning process. Second, there must be an increase in the rights of pupils. Effective citizenship in a democracy must begin at school. Though welcome, the extent to which the new Citizenship component in the National Curriculum will promote equality is open to question. Third, the school's isolation must be challenged. We must take seriously the concept of a 'learning society' and open up all aspects of social, business and industrial life to educational enquiry (this makes an interesting counterpoint to the opening up of schools to business and industry, including business *values* – see Allen *et al.*, 1999; Rikowski, 2001; 2003). The combination of these three developments can place the classroom and the school at the centre of a complex learning network and help create a new popular culture about education.

Essential to a new popular education is the replacement of the attempted inculcation of 'facts' to be learnt and tested (where knowledge has been commodified, the extent to which facts have been learnt, is, as I have said, usually determined by the ticking of boxes), with a genuine dialogic education. Such a dialogic process needs to be differentiated from the postmodernist notion of multiple voices where 'anything goes' (for a critique, see, for example, Cole and Hill, 2002; for a more general critique of poststructuralism/postmodernism, see Cole, 2003). Rather, dialogic education is *empowerment* education. It is pupil/student-centred, but not permissive or self-centred. Like all education, dialogic education is not neutral, but aims to incorporate counter-hegemonic themes into the classroom.

This is not to say that schools should replace Capitalist propaganda with Socialist propaganda. Rather, it means that pupils be provided with alternative interpretations of why and how things happen and be constantly urged to ask whose history and literature is conventionally taught in schools and whose is left out; from whose point of view is the past and present examined? Empowerment education invites pupils/students to become thinking citizens but also to be change agents and social critics (Shor, 1992, pp. 15–16). Essential to dialogic education is critical thinking. Critical thinking needs imagination, where pupils/students and teachers practise anticipating a new social reality. Paulo Freire describes a conversation with a revolutionary in Bissau, in which she (the revolutionary) recounts a meeting with Amilcar Cabral. After an hour's discussion, evaluating the on-going liberation movement, Cabral closed his eyes and talked for thirty or forty minutes of his dream of what life should be like in Guinea-Bissau after independence. When challenged that this was a dream, Cabral opened his eyes, looked at the woman, smiled, and said, 'Yes, it is a dream, a possible dream ... How poor is the revolution that doesn't dream' (Freire and Shor, 1987, pp. 186–7).

Summing up the role of the Radical Left educator, engaged in a pedagogy of liberation to change the world, Freire concludes:

> This is imagination. This is the possibility to go beyond tomorrow without being naively idealistic. This is Utopianism as a dialectical relationship between denouncing the present and announcing the future. To anticipate tomorrow by dreaming today. The question is as Cabral said, Is the dream a possible one or not? If it is less possible, the question for us is how to make it more possible. (*Ibid.* p. 187)

EDUCATION FOR ALL

Finally, radical movements developed a vigorous and varied educational practice, which was concerned with informing mature understandings and on the education of all citizens as members of a more just social order. In this conception, no large distinction was made between the education of 'children' and 'adults' (in contrast to middle-class conceptions of childhood). Such an education should serve all citizens throughout their lives, should promote a democratically controlled and accountable education service at all levels and should apply the principles of equality and non-discrimination to all parts of the service.

It is time to move education away from the current destructive preoccupation with institutions as competitive private businesses divorced from localities and in pursuit of the commodification of knowledge and to encourage them to serve their own as well as the wider national and global communities as positive agents of development.

CONCLUSION

Education should not exist for the glorification of capital, of consumption, of commodification. Teachers at all levels of the education system need to foster critical reflection. This is not an easy task, bearing in mind the current successes of global capitalism, encapsulated in Hill's five trends outlined at the beginning of this chapter. Moreover, as he reminds us, the iron fist of repression is ever present in the velvet glove embrace of the ideological state apparatuses. But the system needs to be challenged. Such transformative action needs to be linked with a grammar of resistance, to link with and articulate life outside the classroom.

Along with McLaren (2000, p. 18) I argue for the necessity to 'transform schools into sites for social justice' in which teachers, other school workers and pupils/students agitate not only for changes within the classroom and within the institutional context of the school but also support a transformation in the objective conditions in which students and their parents labour. A revolutionary pedagogy entails the struggle for macroeconomic policies favouring full employment and guaranteed support in the public sector for state schools, global labour rights, sustainable development, environmental protections and the growth of movements for social and economic change. In other words, just as in the struggles of the period 1790–1848, we must reclaim *our* education.

If this all sounds implausibly idealistic, it might be worth considering again which is the more utopian: the continued survival of anarchic and destructive and anti-democratic world capitalism, or a democratic world, planned for need and not profit (see Meiksins Wood, 1995).

Whatever the twenty-first century has to offer, the choices will need to be debated:

> Each person and group should experience education as contributing to their own self-advancement, but at the same time our education should ensure that at least part of everyone's life activity is also designed to assist in securing the future of the planet we inherit ... Democracy is not possible unless there is a free debate about all the alternatives for running our social and economic system ... All societies will be struggling with the same issues in the 21st century. We can prepare by being better armed with war machinery or more competitive international monopolies ... Or we can wipe out poverty ... altogether. We can decide to approach the future by consciously putting our investment into a massive drive to encourage participation from everyone at every stage in life through training and education that will increase productive, social, cultural and environmental development in ways we have not yet begun to contemplate. (Benn and Chitty, 1997, pp. 94–5)

This was the conclusion to *Rethinking Education and Democracy: a Socialist Alternative for the Twenty-First Century*, a book co-written by Caroline and Clyde Chitty, along with other members of the Hillcole Group. In the six years that have passed, Blair, in cahoots with Bush, has moved Britain much further down the road determined by the diktats of American global imperialism. The point, however, is that this trajectory is not inevitable. Capitalism will always be vulnerable to working-class consciousness – it will always be under the threat of the working-class transcending itself from being merely a 'class-in-itself' to being also a 'class-for-itself', from objectively existing as an exploited class to being a class following its own objective interests and engaged in the struggle to replace Capitalism with Socialism. As Cleaver has put it: 'capital can never win, totally once and for all [since it has within its orbit] the continued existence of an alien subjectivity [the working-class] which constantly threatens to destroy it' (cited in Rikowski, 2001, p. 8).

We can tolerate the Blairite nightmare or we can rethink the future. In the words of Alex Callinicos (2000, p. 129), challenging the current climate requires courage, imagination and will-power inspired by the injustice that surrounds us. However, 'beneath the surface of our supposedly contented societies, these qualities are present in abundance. Once mobilised, they can turn the world upside down.'

It is the role of Radical Left educators, of which in life and death, Caroline is pre-eminent, to foster critical reflection; to facilitate this process.

NOTE

1 Margaret Thatcher states, in the context of a discussion on 'the need radically to improve teacher training' that she 'could barely believe the contents' of one of my courses at what was then Brighton Polytechnic that dealt with 'gender stereotypes' and 'anti-racist education' (Thatcher, 1993, p. 598). Unfortunately, the details of the course that had been sent to her by 'one concerned Tory supporter' contained a typing error. She cites the course, *Contexts for Learning*, as featuring a consideration of 'the debate between protagonists [sic] of education and those who advocate anti-racist education'. She comments that she felt 'that the "protagonists" of education had a better case'. In fact, the actual focus of that part of my course concerned with racism was 'the debate between the protagonists of *multicultural* education and those who advocate anti-racist education'.

13 Young People and Education: Processes of Inclusion and Exclusion*

Janet Holland

INTRODUCTION

The agenda of the New Right, with its emphasis on markets, 'choice' and division, has plunged deep into the heart of education in England and Wales. Caroline Benn's dream of equality and democracy through the vehicle of comprehensive education seems far from sight, although resistance to the steamroller of current education policy does remain. Recent versions of value added school performance league tables that put comprehensives in the top 75 per cent of places provide a boost for this position. While the ever more powerful media attack the government on every aspect of their policies, including education, they are attacking specific implementations from interested positions, rather than the principles which underlie the current agenda. The turmoil in education is taking place in a society that is said to be characterized by change and risk, where processes of individualization, detraditionalization and disembedding are stripping away traditional loyalties and supports. Individuals are left to make the best decisions they can on the best information they can get access to about all areas of their lives (Beck and Beck-Gernsheim, 2002; Lash and Urry, 1987;

* This chapter draws on the collective work of the Youth Values and Transitions team, who have undertaken a qualitative longitudinal study of young people over seven years funded by the ESRC on different programmes (L129251020, L134251008). The team is currently part of the *Families and Social Capital ESRC Research Group* at London South Bank University (www.lsbu.ac.uk/families). The team is: Tina Grigoriou, Sheila Henderson, Janet Holland, Sheena McGrellis, Sue Sharpe and Rachel Thomson.

Giddens, 1991). We can look on the broad level at education systems, and education policy, and see what impact these have on people in different locations in the society, based on class, 'race' and ethnicity, gender and other structural dimensions, and very many studies do this. But what about the experiences and understandings of those at the blunt end of education, those going through the process which will have a fundamental effect on the rest of their lives?

In this chapter I want to draw on a longitudinal, qualitative investigation of young people in five contrasting locations around the UK, to examine the complexity of youth transitions to adulthood in the context of issues of social inclusion and exclusion, and the role of education in these processes.

BACKGROUND

In the UK today, as in many western societies, the transition from youth to adulthood is becoming increasingly non-linear and complex. The traditional focus on the move from school to work in youth studies has been replaced by an exploration of the relationships between a series of transitional 'strands' – education, employment, training, housing, family, income, consumption and relationships (Coles, 1995). Rates of transition can be different along different strands, and people may be independent in some spheres of life and dependent in others (Jones and Bell, 2000). There is increasing interest in the diversity of experiences, the centrality of identity, and the interplay between individual agency, circumstance and social structure in the lives of young people.

The current government lays considerable emphasis on 'education, education, education', which is seen as a key to social mobility, individualized improvement in one's position in society. But despite government plans for 50 per cent of 18–30 year olds to enter higher education by the end of the decade, their inconsistent and contradictory education policies militate against any equalizing effects of these efforts. Some theorists argue that this will always be a lost cause:

But it is not sufficient to take as one's goal the true democratising of education. In the absence of a rational pedagogy doing everything required to neutralize the effect of the social factors of cultural inequality, methodologically and continuously, from kindergarten to university, the political project of giving everyone equal educational opportunity cannot overcome the real inequalities, even when it deploys every institutional and economic means. (Bourdieu, 1979, p. 76)

And it is clearly the case that the present government is not using every institutional and economic means to achieve this end, and the motivation for expansion of higher education has more to do with UK competitiveness in a global economy than a desire for equality. But the strength of individualism, and the rhetoric of individual responsibility and choice has its effects and people do make sense of social inequalities in terms of personal failings, an 'epistemological fallacy' in the words of Furlong and Cartmel (1997). As part of this effect, young people do appear to be optimistic about their chances, or feel that any shortfall in their progress is due to individual failure rather than looking for an explanation in the structure or workings of society. Evans *et al.* indicate that this is a particularly English approach, since in their study of the highly structured German system, young people could hold external factors responsible for failure, which allowed them to develop a positive sense of self and a belief in collective action (Evans *et al.*, 2003, p. 1).

As it happens, social and economic mobility in the UK fell significantly in the last decades of the twentieth century, and the expansion of further and higher education was partly responsible for this, since those who took advantage of it were from the middle classes. The expansion benefited the 'not-so-bright' middle-class rather than academically able working-class young people from disadvantaged backgrounds (Schoon *et al.*, 2001; Blanden, 2002).

Schoon *et al.* focused attention on individuals who 'succeed' against increasing odds, suggesting that:

adolescents from less privileged backgrounds are relying more on external sources of support and encouragement (such as parental commitment to education and the encouragement of teachers) than adolescents from privileged backgrounds who appear to depend more on their own individual resources (such as academic ability, positive motivation and belief in their own abilities). (*op. cit.*, 2001)

It would seem from this that individual resources such as determination and effort can be important for success, but they are clearly more important for the middle classes than the disadvantaged. Scott and Chaudhary report that in their study:

... sadly we uncovered many youngsters for whom school was associated with failure. Education is clearly something that matters enormously both to teenage children now and to their opportunities in later life. Yet, according to our research, young people have little idea as to how they can turn round failure at school. Moreover many young people seem to get into a negative loop of self fulfilling prophecy where perception of failure at school contributes to further failure. (Scott and Chaudhary, 2003, p. 47)

In our longitudinal qualitative study we were keen to keep in play both the variability and contingency of young people's individual biographical trajectories, and socially structured factors of class, locality, gender, 'race' and religion, which were related to the inequalities that they were experiencing. The short case studies provided in the chapter attempt to illustrate these multiple aspects of the young people's experience.

THE STUDY

The longitudinal qualitative study on which I draw here has been constructed from three studies. The first (1996–9) examined *Youth Values* through various methods with (1800) 11–18 year olds, located in five sites around the UK. The locations were an inner city site; a Home Counties commuter town; a deprived housing estate in the North-west; an isolated rural village; and contrasting communities within an Northern Irish city. The second, *Inventing Adulthoods* (1999–2002) took a sub-sample of 100 from this earlier sample and followed them through the transition to adulthood, collecting, comparing and interpreting their changing accounts of their experiences over time, through three repeat biographical interviews. The class distribution of the sample was broadly 43 per cent middle-class and 57 per cent working-class.[1] The current project, *Youth Transitions and Social Change* (2002–2006) continues this process of biographical interviews. At the fourth interview we have 70 young people still on board and they are now between 18 and 25. This unique study provides a fascinating insight into the experiences of young people in very varied social situations.

ACCESSING ADULTHOOD IN DIFFERENT AREAS OF LIFE

In the study we focused on particular areas of young people's lives, education, work, leisure and consumption, and the domestic, (which includes family, relationships and care). These areas overlap (leisure, for example, may be a part of relationships at school, college, work and home). But our main argument is that each of these areas provides the possibility for young people to access and to construct for themselves adult identities. It is through the experience of competence in particular areas, and the recognition of this competence by others, that young people make investments of time, energy and identity that have significance for their trajectories through life. For example, it is possible that young people who experience themselves as having little competence in education may invest more heavily in work, leisure and/or the domestic area. It is also the case that the degree and type of investment in particular types of adult identity is dependent on the young person's access to material, emotional, social and cultural resources.

Given the different strands and areas through which transitions are experienced, as suggested earlier, it is possible that independence in one area may be associated with dependence in another. For example competence as an autonomous consumer, or experience of long- or short-term sexual relationships could be associated with continuing to live at home in a condition of economic dependence. Young people may be motivated to invest in a particular area because they feel that their competence is recognized, but the choices they see as available to them are highly structured by gender, locality, ethnicity and social class. And importantly, the choices about investment in a particular area that they make have considerable consequences for subsequent processes of inclusion and exclusion. To illustrate these points I give some examples of experiences of education interrelated with work, and the meanings attached to these areas by the young people, from our first round of interviews.

Education
Educational achievement brings with it rewards of recognition, which encourage young people to invest more in this area in their construction of adulthood. Young people who invested heavily in education gave responses that indicated that their particular route could be seen as 'deferred youth'. This often involved a mature period of studiousness, being a sensible student – a 'grown up' period – while taking GCSEs and 'A' level examinations, followed by a youthful lifestyle while at university. This type of investment could lead them to a form of adulthood associated with professional work, and was often but not exclusively associated with a middle-class background in our sample (Thomson *et al.*, 2003).

Various patterns emerged for young people who failed to secure a sense of competence or recognition in education, and some of the case studies that follow illustrate these experiences. Possible trajectories might include pursuing an accelerated adulthood, with a traditional pattern of leaving school and entering work as soon as possible, or starting a steady relationship, and 'settling down'. In this case competence and recognition would be sought in the areas of work and domestic life. Another route might be to pursue an extended youth, with a desire to hold onto 'immature' ways, having fun in all the ways that teenagers are prone to, failing in education, and/or becoming a rebel. Another possibility was to struggle to maintain a connection with education, taking a series of vocational courses that might ultimately be considered to be leading nowhere, while also working in 'McJobs'. And finally they might make an investment in criminality, where the lifestyle and companions could offer competence and recognition (Thomson *et al.*, 2002).

Work

Work then was an attractive alternative source of competence and recognition for those who were unsuccessful in education. Like many young people in the UK, most in the study undertook high levels of part-time work, but it was those who were unable to find a sense of recognition in education who were more likely to prioritize the demands of work in the competition for their time and energy. The young people whose major investment was in education tended to take an instrumental approach to any part-time work that they undertook while at school: it was useful for financing a certain lifestyle; it could provide experience that would be valuable to them in their projected educational career, or perhaps further into the future in a professional career. For those who invested less in education, part-time work was more likely to be seen as providing personal affirmation in their role as worker. The money they earned also allowed some independence from their family, or in many cases helped them to contribute to the family finances. Many who took the work route on leaving school, however, regretted the choice when they saw themselves as left behind by those following the further and higher education track. They particularly feared being stuck in the Mc jobs that they had envisaged as an interim measure.

The following brief case studies illustrate some of the varied trajectories of the young people in the study, and the crucial role of education for social inclusion and exclusion.

MULTIPLE ROUTES TO INCLUSION AND EXCLUSION

The attractions of criminality
Hamad is perhaps the most literally excluded in our group of young people. He tells a story of being a 'naughty' boy at school, who

moves onto more serious trouble – a robbery for which he was caught – which leads to expulsion from school and a criminal career. He felt unable to fit in with available Asian identities:

> ... most Asian people you see, right, they're clever aren't they, but me, I'm different ... I'm different clever. Clever in my own way ... in this place [Pupil Referral Unit] there's no Asian kids.

We met him in the PRU, and he considered that he was receiving some useful advice on education and employment at this point, but it seemed to be too late, for his major recognition came from his gang and their activities and his investment was in the cultivation of a criminal identity. The gang were gradually becoming involved in more serious crimes, from tagging (graffiti spraying) cars and trains, to joyriding to hold-ups.

> When I got expelled I went back [to school] and it was like weird, yeah, I had all these little kids following me and that. And everyone knows your name.

This criminal identity, the respect of his fellow gang members and a gangster reputation with younger children were more empowering for Hamad than the pursuit of any particular education and employment transition, even were those types of opportunity available for him and he able to grasp them. In a focus group at the PRU we had, perhaps rather naively, asked a group of young men to respond to the statement 'A good education is the most important thing in life'. They strongly agreed with the statement and made a flood of comments about educational failure and exclusion. Considerable emotion was provoked and they endorsed a moral discourse of 'educational good' which they had been unable to access. Comments they made were 'get nowhere shit job', 'road sweeper', you need it but it teaches you nothing'. These responses indicate their level of awareness about the need and indeed the desire for 'a good education' and their acute feelings of failure and exclusion in the face of the education system as they experienced it.

When we last heard of Hamad he was serving a jail sentence.

A 'normal' middle-class trajectory

Edward describes himself as 'very middle-class' and illustrates a particular middle-class trajectory where the major investment is in education and the long-term plan is for a professional career. Throughout the years that we have been following him he did very well educationally, at school, and at university, and he received considerable recognition for his academic achievements. He had a great deal of support from his parents, both financial and in other ways. Although he manages his finances well, and chooses work that will forward his progress, his parents did plan to pay off his student debt. Edward's investment then was totally in education, for his gap year he chose work in an organization associated with the course he was to take at university, also providing excellent contacts for his future career. At our last meeting he was considering postgraduate work, probably abroad.

Although in general Edward's passage through life in these years of the study was smooth, predicated on a carefully planned route through education to a profession, he had suffered a period of unhappiness, toyed briefly with the idea of abandoning his route, and had some regrets about his relatively single-minded focus. He suspected that 'part of the reason for my unhappiness was that I was thinking too much about the future and not enough about now', commenting that 'you wait for things to happen and then you realize they're not quite as good, and you realize you've missed out on something in the meantime'.

Edward thought that his family background – they did many activities together – had affected his sociability, but he did in fact have a number of friends and contacts both social and in relation to work and education. He also accumulated contacts who would be useful to him: 'I know enough people that I can get a foot in the door' and felt he was in a better position than his contemporaries in his university in that regard. He sometimes felt, however, that life was both passing him by and becoming more complex:

> I do sometimes feel that I am getting older. I wonder where all the years have gone actually. I mean I can still remember being about eight years old and everything being so simple. Because

you didn't have homework, you didn't have to do anything at home, you didn't have all these worries. And it gets more and more complicated. And I'm beginning to suspect that each year it gets trickier than the year before.

The struggle for inclusion: hanging on in there

Monique illustrates the struggle to hang on in there, with a ragged route to social inclusion, which is still in progress. When we first met her she was 17 and living with her mother, her mother's boyfriend (with whom she did not get on) and her siblings in an inner-city location. While Monique recognized that education was important for her if she wished to achieve her long-term plan of being a social worker, she found this more difficult in practice, and located her feelings of competence in the home and family, taking considerable responsibility there. She drew strongly on her black culture in the construction of her identity.

Monique also valued independence, and had a Saturday job which helped her to contribute to the household, buy her own clothes, and finance her mobile phone. Throughout our contact she worked for however much time she could manage, to maintain her independence, sometimes to the detriment of whatever courses she was taking. She did fear that she might get stuck in one of these Mc jobs.

> Yeah. I need to get out of MacDs now. Everyone's like, 'where do you work, MacDonald's? STILL? You've been there three years.' 'Been there for about three years?' 'No only two, nearly two.'

She valued her extended family and the relationships within it, although during the course of the study she fell out with her mother. Unfortunately, too, her educational achievements did not match her ambitions. At our second interview she was on a Youth Entry to an HE course, having been able to take advantage of a government policy to assist the disadvantaged into HE. But at this stage Monique was not doing too well, and was in danger of being thrown out. Education was always ambiguous for Monique, who had difficulty committing to her courses despite the realization that she needed educational success to achieve her ambitions of a professional career. To us it always seemed in the balance whether she would hang on in there.

By the third interview Monique had become motivated once again, was enjoying her Youth Entry course, and was determined to go to university. Her long-term ambition was now to be an Education Welfare Officer. Subsequently she failed to get the marks required to get her into the university of her choice that would have taken her away from home as she wanted, but was accepted at another university to do a Social Policy course, and went into a hall of residence there. At our fourth interview Monique was following her university course, working long hours in a shop to support herself, and trying to have a social life.

> Interviewer: And how do you find juggling all the time, you know, with the uni, with working, with friends?
> Monique: Oh look at the bags, does it look like I've had any sleep recently? No sleep, no sleep, no sleep. Like I do get to sleep, but like I finish work at nine o'clock and my friends will – like not every day – but like my friends will come round for me half nine/ ten o'clock.

Monique is just hanging on in there, dependent on herself and her own efforts to make it, and like many of our young people is the first in her family to go to university. But her life is very complicated, and since she has no financial resources on which to draw, like many working-class students, she works long hours to support herself. We wait and watch.

You can make it if you really try
Sherleen is another young working-class black woman, an only child with a single-parent mother, who has the totally dedicated encouragement and support (including financial) of her extended family, or more particularly the women in her family and most particularly her mother ('my number one role model'), to make it through the educational route. She carries the weight of the family

desire for improvement and social mobility, but has taken it on as her own:

> I have the kind of drive where mum doesn't have to tell me. Even though my mum wants me to do better, and do kinds of things that she didn't get the opportunity to do, I want to do those things anyway.

She is one of our younger participants who we first interviewed aged 13 on the Youth Values study. She is ambitious and determined, and seeks a career in law, but she recognizes the pitfalls that lie in her route:

> I know I really do wanna be successful and I don't think I'll let anything hold me back, 'cause even one of my teachers, 'cause she's black and she said she used to be, what was it, accountant and she had a lot of racism, come into a lot of racism, and she said that she didn't let it hold her back basically, can't let anything hold me back right now, or in the future.
> I'm gonna have to try a bit harder than someone who lives in a posher area really, but I don't mind.

She recognizes the importance of education:

> I know I have to get a good education in order to be someone. I know it's not going to be easy, but I'm determined. I am determined to be something.

Her ability is recognized, she gains support in school for her ambitions, and is chosen for work experience placement in a barrister's chambers. She recognizes that she is in for a long haul to realize her ambitions, but she is not afraid of hard work. Only the financial side worries her,

> I think about money and stuff, where's it gonna come from, 'cause I know I'm gonna have to study, it's just the money side of it really.

In many cases in our study, young women need to sacrifice some of the pleasures (and pains) of youth in the shape of sexual relationships, if they want to pursue education and a potential career. Sherleen's mother advised this route when she was in school. But when Sherleen left for college to do A levels, she met a young man who fitted in with her plans, and her family has accepted him. He is taking the same academic subjects, and they work together, encourage each other and indeed compete with each other. But they are realistic about the future:

> ... he's going to university but not the same univer – well he's applied to some of the universities that I'm going to but he's, 'cos he's doing a different course, so it's like we've been looking at the best universities for our courses really, and just said if we end up going to the same one then that's fine, but if we don't then it's okay, so ... it's just been like that really. Even though everyone says, don't know how we're going to manage it because we're mostly joined at the hip.

Sherleen is on track to succeed.

The struggle for inclusion: education, education, education
The following cases from the most socially excluded site in our study, the deprived northern estate, demonstrate differences in response and experience between three young women of similar class and community location at a similar critical point in their individual trajectory, immediately after leaving school. The differences can be seen as emerging from influences at family, community and social levels, with complex interactions.

When we first interviewed the three young women in 1999 they were distinguished from the rest of this local sample by having professional ambitions, and seeing education as a route out of the estate. Each of the cases presents a different balance between individual and wider resources, illustrating the point made earlier that for young people from economically deprived backgrounds, individual resources of ability and ambition do not necessarily translate into success. Moreover, we show here that the 'costs' of social mobility and community oriented values, investments and identities may militate against social and geographical mobility.

For Valerie her family were a crucial resource, as a single child she gained a sense of autonomy and maturity from the relative privacy afforded to her. She also drew on her father's distinction from his surrounding culture through being knowledgeable, although this did tend to set her apart in the community. She presented herself as a confident, determined, independent young woman. She expressed a desire to leave the community of which she had negative views, and saw education as the way out, aiming initially to be a doctor. Over the interviews it became increasingly apparent that there was a mismatch between Valerie's aspirations and her capability. She disconnected from the negative social capital of her immediate environment by focusing on her own resources and fantasy life. But her case shows the contradiction between a narrative of social mobility that demands a rejection of a community of origin and an ability to access the resources that would have enabled her to make the journey. Valerie's ambitions were revised downwards.

Lauren was academically able, but she was also well integrated into her community of origin through work, friendships and boyfriends, and gained status from these investments. Her parents, particularly her mother, were key resources for her. At the first interview there was some conflict between her localized world view and competing forces that drew her towards a more individualized pathway of social mobility, but she had planned an A level course at college and had professional ambitions. Despite her academic ability, Lauren became stressed by her college course work, and her mother suggested that perhaps she was not a 'paperwork person'. She gave up the course and reoriented herself towards a more local future. Her integration within the community and family provided her with considerable social capital, but this form of social capital has value only within the locality, it is in tension with a more individualized project of social mobility.

Maureen too was academically able, but quieter and less self-confident and ambitious than the other two young women. Over the three interviews, however, the centrality of a quiet commitment to social mobility came increasingly to light, and by the third interview she was firmly set on course for university. Again the family was crucial as support. In this instance Maureen lived with her mother and boyfriend on a new housing development away from the most deprived part of the estate, but also had a room in her father's house. Maureen saw her two-site family as a positive resource and it seemed to enable her to situate herself (physically and in terms of horizons) outside the locality more easily than most. Her mother was a stable source of encouragement to follow an educational path out of the estate and all it stood for. Maureen herself saw her resources as her academic ability and organizational skills, and the practical and emotional support and advice provided by her family. She illustrates the necessity of getting out to get on for young people in areas of social exclusion, and also the need to defer active heterosexuality and womanhood until they would hold less of a threat to her future.

For each of these young women her family was a major resource and support, and for each to succeed meant they would need to leave the community within which they were embedded. For Valerie this became increasingly difficult, as she faltered in her pursuit of education, unable to access sufficient resources to push her out both geographically and socially. Lauren was perhaps the most academically competent of the three, but was also deeply involved in the community, with links at many levels. When she faltered in education, her mother stepped in to draw her back into the community, where she thought her daughter was better suited and would be happier. Maureen's determination emerged later than that of Sherleen, but with the support of her family she managed to withdraw from the community (going to a different college for A levels to that of those of her school friends who did manage to pursue A levels or GNVQ) and follow her plan to go to university. Maureen illustrates the necessity of getting out to get on for young people in areas of social exclusion.

CONCLUSION

The case studies presented here give some idea of the complex routes that young people now tread as they take on adulthood and adult roles and responsibilities. They demonstrate the variability and contingency of individual pathways alongside the inequalities generated by socially structured factors of class, locality, gender and 'race'. We have examined the situation from the young people's perspective, highlighting the importance of their access to resources, whether these are material, emotional, social or cultural and the different ways that these factors can have effects in individual lives. Young people take responsibility for their failures and their futures, and often strive against serious odds to manage their lives successfully through an education system that is increasingly divisive and destructive, and in a society that grows ever more polarized and precarious. We can only hope they act with a fair degree of good sense when they become the adults who are running the show.

NOTE

1   Class was assessed through a combination of parental occupation, education, housing status, newspapers read, and consisted of six categories, collapsed here into two (McGrellis *et al.*, 2000).

14 Why 'Improving Own Learning' is Important

Colin Waugh

At the time of writing (January 2004), the Key (formerly Core) Skills attached to FHE programmes are apparently being absorbed into Basic Skills provision. If so, this is the culmination of long-established trends.

The Major government decided that 16–19 year olds must study three Core Skills – Communication, IT and Application of Number – but that the other three such skills – Problem Solving, Working with Others and Improving Own Learning and Performance – should be non-mandatory. This decision, like Labour's failure to reverse it, hinders teachers from helping students develop capacities that are crucial for them as a group.

The three non-mandatory or 'additional' Key Skills should together constitute the core of programmes. A movement for this would automatically put on the agenda an oppositional view of how education should be conducted, in whose interests, to what ends.

Improving Own Learning involves skill but also knowledge and understanding, for example, the skill of putting items in order, the knowledge that books have indexes, the understanding that an action has causes and effects. It aims to help students develop a capacity to plan, monitor and evaluate their study activity and to change their approach accordingly, so that they become more proactive and more conscious of themselves, hence maximally independent of 'authorities'. Handled correctly, such material can transform teaching and learning. For example, when teachers encourage students to reflect on their own performance, dialogue can develop about the assumptions behind course content. Similarly, explaining how assessment criteria are applied can prompt students to think about who decides them and cause teachers to re-examine their practice.

The underlying rationale for prioritizing the 'additional' Key Skills is as follows. The history of working-class self education, grassroots politics and rank and file union activity shows that to be valid a working-class movement must be independent (as opposed, for example, to borrowing ideas, expertise or personnel from other classes), democratic (for example, organized from below as opposed to being ruled by a clique), and aimed at changing the 'world' (as opposed merely to bargaining within the existing order). However, class independence requires not that we just put a minus where those in power put a plus, but that we develop our own principles. Similarly, democracy is about minority rights as well as majority rule. And the world cannot be changed fundamentally by actions taken in isolation from principles and theory.

Building such a movement necessarily has an educational side, in that those involved seek both to develop their own capacity to think independently, organize democratically and act effectively, and to extend this to others. They may put on courses of their own, but should also try to utilize official provision, not least because if they do not, those in power will eventually use this provision against them. Both Key and Basic Skills are areas where this could happen.

Each 'additional' Key Skill runs parallel to one of the qualities a working-class movement needs: Problem Solving to changing the world, Working with Others to democracy, and Improving Own Learning and Performance to independence. These parallels exemplify Capitalism's tendency to create conditions for Socialism by developing in workers qualities they need to bring it into being. The 'additional' Core Skills first came onto the curricular agenda because employers lobbied for them when Kenneth Baker proposed a 'core' along with his 1988 Education Reform Act, and embody qualities which they wanted colleges to develop in their workforce.

However, there are also counter-tendencies. First, employers want these 'skills' in a limited form only. Thus, they want Working with Others to be about conformity to a group ethic imposed from above, Problem Solving to be about overcoming snags so things can continue as before, and Improving Own Learning and Performance to be about workers acting in their employer's interests without supervision. Secondly, other sections of the employing class – especially small employers in service 'industries' – have organized against those skills. Thirdly, some former practitioners – mainly managers in Basic Skills – have colluded with this. Lastly, we who should have promoted them have failed to do so.

The employers who call for these 'skills' are progressive by comparison with those who demand only spelling, adding up, etc., with academic and media commentators who on elitist grounds reject Key Skills altogether, with those left-wingers who dismiss such provision as means only to a compliant workforce, and with the official Basic Skills lobby's exclusive focus on literacy and numeracy. Such opposition has not prevented them being taught altogether, but rather has led in some college courses to them being 'mapped-on' to existing units without teaching to develop them, and in some private training to them being taught in a management-oriented fashion. As well as campaigning for colleges to provide them in full, we should organize ourselves to teach them anyway, through – and where necessary against the grain of – official structures. This would involve challenging the hidden curriculum.

The hidden curriculum is essentially the assumption that only 'academic' knowledge – the general knowledge possessed by traditional professionals – counts. This assumption, unquestioned in institutions like selecting universities or medical schools, dominates the whole system. But it dominates FE colleges and the recruiting/teaching universities in a different way from that in which it dominates, say, sixth form colleges. In FHE it has always been counterbalanced by the overt requirement of employers for skilled labour, such that it operates negatively and from outside – for example, through students perceiving themselves as 'not brainy', or through scarce resources. So here teachers have a better chance than elsewhere of holding it up to students' inspection.

To many working-class FHE students the hidden curriculum's restriction of their access to valid education is clear. However, this does not mean that they conceptualize it in a manner which allows them to fight for alternatives. On the contrary, in trying to counter it, one of our main problems is the tension generated when this instinct comes up against efforts to turn it into class consciousness. Further, the hidden curriculum is not a curriculum, in the sense of a race track leading somewhere, but rather a maze in which apparent exit routes are dead-ends. Moreover, it hides something from students, in that it stops them seeing possibilities. The walls of the maze are opaque, though covered with lifelike pictures.

Our alternative must be 'hidden' in one specific sense. Since we can build it, as distinct from campaign for it, only through what we do with students, we must introduce it through the present mandatory Key Skills or their Basic Skills successor. Nevertheless, this hidden curriculum of ours aims to bring about openness, by creating within official provision a space for dialogue between working-class teachers and working-class students. In short, we should try to build, by patient persuasion, from below, by the actions of practitioners and amongst students and potential students, their families and communities, a programme for turning FHE to their collective advantage.

In doing so we must challenge the separation of the 'additional' Key Skills from one another and from other course elements, working instead towards a single 'generic competence', taught, learnt and assessed via integration with specialist vocational and/or academic units. However, for now the view that all six 'skills' are in essence separate both from one another and from other course elements dominates more than ever. Why?

Teaching and learning are always underpinned by a theoretical framework, although those involved may not be aware of this and it may rest on assumptions surviving from an earlier period. For example, the dominant framework now, the subject-centred hidden curriculum, is in most sectors so deeply embedded as not to be recognized as such at all, and preserves within itself ways of organizing knowledge which reflect the period when the capitalist class recruited sections of the landed gentry – for example, Anglican clergy and Oxbridge dons – to help with its ideological self-formation. However, over the past thirty years, vocational FHE has consciously developed and implemented two frameworks of its own.

The first such framework was the version of Benjamin Bloom's taxonomy of educational objectives which the Technician Education Council (TEC) used to structure courses in the mid-1970s. Lecturers had in many cases to rewrite units in 'aims and objectives' – statements of what students would eventually be able to do. These objectives had to be 'behavioural' – to specify actions by which students would show whether they had learnt – and to correspond to the level of the course. For example, at each level only certain verbs could be used to describe behaviour. Objectives had to be classed as belonging to either the psycho-motor, cognitive or affective domain.

This framework was abandoned in 1983–4 when TEC merged with the Business Education Council to form BTEC (now part of Edexcel), a change which, reflecting the Thatcherites' expulsion of labour from industry, their destruction of apprenticeships, and their emphasis on financial services, went along with high youth unemployment and domination by the Manpower Services Commission. This then generated a framework of its own, derived from the thinking of Gilbert Jessup and Chris Hayes, which eventually provided a basis for National Vocational Qualifications (NVQs) and GNVQs. The NVQ framework centred on 'learning outcomes', and on 'competence', defined as the combination of knowledge, understanding and skill needed to perform a real-life role.

Despite their differences, both the TEC framework, because of its attention to cognition, and the NVQ one, because of its attention to 'understanding', assumed that students possessed a capacity to think, and a potential to develop it further, while the latter's definition of competence made an equation of 'knowledge' with academic or intellectual learning and 'skill' with vocational or manual – less easy than it would otherwise have been.

However, alongside these two frameworks, something else was developing. Starting with the general education servicing of vocational courses and in adult basic education, this 'something else' – Basic Skills – is now, with the decomprehensivization of schooling from 14, the separation of 'sixth form' provision from vocational FE for 16–19 year olds, the drive to extend level 2 and 3 qualifications to a wider range of adults, the tiered expansion of HE and moves to impose educational tests on citizenship applicants, in a stronger position than ever before.

Deriving partly from Basil Bernstein, who argued, from teaching Post Office messengers in an inner London college in the 1950s, that working-class speech rests on a 'restricted code', in contrast to the 'elaborated code' used by those he called 'middle-class', Basic Skills assumes that people who speak and write in non-standard ways lack a capacity for logical thought, and that therefore attempts to correct these other deficiencies neither can nor should have a cognitive dimension. At one level, Basic Skills was originally little more than a reaction of English or maths teachers to being expected to teach post compulsory students on non-academic courses, although it soon became an ideology justifying career development for some of these teachers. Rather than an independent framework, then, Basic Skills is the form which the hidden curriculum takes when it interfaces with employers' demands for technicians and semi-skilled workers.

Bernstein's position at London University Institute of Education allowed his assumptions to spread through the Inner London Education Authority, and, via its FE service, into FHE nationally. Here they fused with the tradition of adult literacy as charity work, flourishing especially when students' backgrounds included migration from areas where missionaries controlled schooling. Behind Bernstein also stood Sir Cyril Burt, with his 'experiments' in IQ, and behind them both Frederick Taylor, with his suggestion that the ideal industrial worker would be 'an intelligent gorilla'. Such standpoints were reflected also in behaviourist psychology, as it grew up in the USA and in 'common language' philosophy as exemplified by Gilbert Ryle and J. L. Austin.

Since the NVQ framework emerged in the late 1980s, official policy has repeatedly narrowed its (always limited) progressive potential in ways which strengthen Basic Skills. First, there was a decision to refer to the parts of Jessup's core as 'skills' rather than competences. Secondly, Jessup conceded that knowledge 'subsumes' understanding. Thirdly, the Major cabinet decided to make only three 'skills' mandatory. Next Dearing ruled that the term 'Core

Skills' be replaced by 'Key Skills'. Then New Labour opted to decouple Key Skills from vocational courses. And more recently Key Skills tests have been merged with Basic Skills ones at levels 1 and 2.

The issue is whether we are to have education that furthers the self-liberation of working-class people or not. Writers from whose work the outlines of such an education can be extrapolated include John Holt, who, in *How Children Fail*, addressed the question of what constitutes a 'good thinker'. Holt says:

> Intelligent children act as if they thought the universe made some sense. They check their answers and their thoughts against common sense ... It seems as if what we call intelligent children feel that the universe can be trusted even when it does not seem to make any sense, that even when you don't understand it you can be fairly sure that it is not going to play dirty tricks on you.

In contrast,

> The ones who get into trouble (i.e. in solving maths problems, etc., author's note) are the ones who see a problem as an order to start running at top speed from a given starting point, in an unknown direction, to an unknown destination. They dash after the answer before they have considered the problem.

He goes on:

> The poor thinker dashes madly after an answer; the good thinker takes his time and looks at the problem. Is the difference merely a matter of skill in thought, a technique which ... we might teach ... ? I'm afraid not. The good thinker can take his time because he can tolerate uncertainty, he can stand not knowing. The poor thinker can't stand not knowing; it drives him crazy.

On this view, then, the 'poor thinker' is someone who uncritically seizes whatever offers him or her the quickest way out of this situation, whereas the 'good thinker' is relaxed enough to weigh up several options. Holt adds: 'This panicky search for certainty, this inability to tolerate unanswered questions and unsolved problems, seems to lie at the heart of many problems of intelligence' (Holt, 1972, pp. 56–8).

If Holt is right, teachers' activities should be geared more than at present towards helping people to 'stand not knowing', as, for example, in some Art and Design courses where students are required to come up with at least three different approaches to a project rather than just develop their first idea. Accustoming students thus to 'thinking twice' necessarily makes them more conscious than hitherto of their own agency in the production of outcomes. Holt's argument therefore supports the claim that every working-class person should have the right to study Improving Own Learning. However, behind Holt's conclusion stands a philosophical debate about self-conscious thought, within which the key question is whether 'the universe' is such that, at least in principle, sense can be made of it by human beings.

In the later 1700s, Kant answered this question by saying that, while humans can know what 'the world' – or, in Holt's term, 'the universe' – looks like, its appearance, the universe as 'phenomenon', they cannot know what it is really like – the 'thing in itself' or, as he termed it, the 'noumenon'. A few years later, however, Hegel rejected this view, and later still (1844) Marx maintained that the dispute between these two positions was a 'purely scholastic' one, because whichever view you took, the reality was that technological development, and science linked to it, was reshaping the world or universe anyway.

What does 'the universe' or 'the world' mean (i.e. as an idea, not just as a term) in such discussions? Does it, for example, mean much the same as 'nature', and, if so, what does that mean? Is 'nature' that which would exist whether humans (and hence human consciousness) exist or not – for example, planetary bodies like the earth, which to us – though not necessarily to pre-Darwinian thinkers such as Kant or Hegel – existed before humans, and could exist if humans were obliterated? A problem with this is that there seems no reason to draw a line between at least the bodies of humans and those of other living things, and then between all these living bodies and the non-living material which composes both them and these geological entities. Given this, should we, then, count as 'nature' the totality of what exists that is other than (human) minds? But this too is subject to the objection that it is difficult to draw a line between minds and brains, leading to the further difficulty that there are animals other than humans which, whether or not they have minds, certainly have brains.

Perhaps, then, 'nature' includes everything except that which brains produce, namely thought? But there are problems with this too, one being that we may not wish to imply that thought exists independently of brains. We may, for example, regard this as leading to a religious view – to assuming an unembodied, pre-existing intelligence (in effect, God) – which we may reject for other reasons. Further, a brain that is dead and therefore cannot think still contains structures, for example, circuits, without which the person concerned could not, when alive, have thought.

Another problem is that thoughts are intertwined with sensations, with emotions arising from sensations, and with physical reflexes – i.e. a sharp line is, again, not easily drawn between thought and cerebral activity which appears inseparable from physical states, impulses, drives, etc. And a third problem is that, through planned activity, for example, the felling of a tree, thought shapes the 'world' or 'universe' as well as being shaped by it. And further, this shaping of the world commonly has its own influence on thought processes. For example, the thoughts people can have once they have invented, say, axes are different from those they could have before. The implement results in part from thought, but further thought results in part from the implement. Moreover, reshaping the world can be a means of working on the mind more directly, as, for example, in the case of plants grown to produce mind-altering drugs.

Given these problems, then, perhaps thought too is part of 'the universe'. But in this case the term 'universe' would merely serve to signify for us the totality of things when we wish to contrast this to particular things, everything as distinct from every thing. But must this 'universe', then, this everything, include everything that is thought or everything that can be thought, including things which can exist only in thought (for example, a Russian revolution that happens before the French one)? It seems that we need some way of abandoning a false distinction between thought and 'the universe', 'world', etc., while retaining the ability to distinguish between that which has (or can have) an objective existence and that which exists only subjectively.

There are several other ways of trying to deal with the problem of where to draw a line between thought and the world. One is that adopted by Marx and Engels, when they stressed the collective aspect of thought (in the sense of consciousness), by arguing, in effect, that thinking starts as a social product and is then introjected into individuals. In saying this they also took it that the central social activity is production, work in the broadest sense, and by this route they arrived at a labour theory of cognition – that thought in general arises mainly from the mental side of work. In Key Skills terms, then, they stressed Working with Others and Problem Solving, and linked them to explain the relation of thought to 'the world'. But this does not mean that they, as it were, regarded Improving Own Learning as unimportant.

The standpoint that sees thought as arising from the combination of work with society cannot on its own account for the fact that individuals by private thinking do come up with new ideas, new ways of seeing 'the world', new plans for acting upon it, etc. Thus although it seems more likely that, chronologically, individual thought developed from collective thought rather than the reverse, it has developed a dynamic of its own, such that the two interact. Collective thought is a necessary condition of private thought, but private thought has dimensions which cannot be reduced to introjected collective thought and which, unless we can find some other way of accounting for them, would again have to be explained in religious terms – for example, by the miraculous intervention of God in mental processes – a position which some philosophers before Kant took.

However, Hegel did arrive at a potential solution to this problem. He did so by arguing that the key difference between humans and other animals is not that humans think whereas other animals do not, but that only humans think about thinking. He explained this difference from a standpoint which is essentially religious, i.e. that there is an intelligence which creates the material world and comes to consciousness of itself through it; in other words, by saying that human minds are the means through which, in his terms, 'God' becomes conscious of himself. But his view could equally be justified on the basis of Darwinian evolution – that is, that there exists between humans and other animals a quantitative difference – the evolution in humans of a brain with a vastly greater memory capacity than the brains of other animals – and at a certain point this increase in quantity crosses a threshold and becomes a qualitative difference, namely the possession by humans of a capacity to think not only about other people's (and other animals') thinking but also about one's own thinking, and moreover, about thinking about thinking – as, for example, when we compare Hegel's explanation for this with a Darwinian one. The key distinction, then, is not between thought and the world, but, within thought, between thought that is conscious of itself and thought which is not. This position is the necessary complement to the approaches of Marx and Engels on the one hand and Darwin on the other, such that without it these approaches can easily be distorted into crude (i.e. pre-dialectical) materialism, which in turn is the complement of religion.

So the approaches to teaching and learning which are opposed to the Basic Skills approach stand on a firmer philosophical basis than it does. Reinforcing the lessons of working-class politics and curricular history, this philosophical standpoint implies that those who want Improving Own Learning to remain non-mandatory see the students from whose courses they thereby exclude it as not fully human. We who think otherwise must therefore try that much harder to put this 'Key Skill' – and with it the other two 'additional' ones – back into courses.

15 For Free Universities, Caroline Benn's Radical Alternative for Higher Education

Pat Ainley

Caroline saw very clearly that many of the problems in schools originated in higher education, particularly the intimate connection between the elite universities, the private schools and the exam boards that had historically dominated the whole system of academic selection in England. Her radical solution was 'to lay the great axe to the root of the tree', closing Oxford and Cambridge and turning them into adult residential colleges. Now that the Government wants to raise university fees towards full cost, how much can those who are opposed to what Charles Clarke, the present Minister of Education, proudly calls 'a basically free-market system' learn from Caroline's radical alternative? This chapter examines the situation facing higher education today in relation to further and adult education to ask what can be done by those who still maintain the ideal of free universities that will be 'free' in every sense of the word.

LAYING THE GREAT AXE TO THE ROOT OF THE TREE

Caroline proposed a deceptively simple policy for higher education. As part of a comprehensive reform opening free entry to universities to all living in their localities, she advocated converting Oxford and Cambridge into residential adult education colleges while national-izing their research capacities. This was not just for the benefit of adult returners to learning such as those she taught. It was because Caroline – unlike most academic education experts based in universities – saw that many of the problems facing schools and colleges originated in elite higher education.

The academic domination over the rest of education and training has become even more entrenched as a result of the deal between the Tory factions who agreed the 1988 Education Act. As intended, this has delivered selective schooling and preserved elite HE. The deal was completed by the 1992 Further and Higher Education Act which applied the same quasi-market principles to what became known as Lifelong Learning. Since then, the new settlement over compulsory (Foundation) and post-compulsory (Lifelong) Learning (i.e. Education and Training) has gone much further under successive New Labour governments than even Mrs Thatcher thought possible. This is part of New Labour's commitment to what has been called the post-welfare, 'new market-state' which they inherited from the Conservatives who introduced it and which they have developed and maintained much more ably than the failed attempt at its consolidation under John Major.

Now Blair's 'flagship bill' with its free-market principle of variable fees has survived the parliamentary horse-trading of 27 January 2004 despite – or because of – the insider wheeler-dealing by backbench Brownites of commitments not worth the paper they were not written on. Tory opposition to this Thatcherite legislation was entirely opportunistic and only the Lib-Dems emerged with principled support for funding HE from progressive taxation. The Higher Education Act will introduce what Charles Clarke called a 'fundamentally market-based system' (*Guardian*, 22 January 2003), 'a new watershed in public service delivery', as he added in the *Financial Times* the next day. This chapter briefly looks at the implications of this development and at progressive reactions to it to create, instead of education for sale, universities and colleges that are free in every best sense of the word.

TERTIARY TRIPARTISM

Under the new market-state, the relentlessly selective English education system against which Caroline fought has reconstituted itself at all levels of learning. In relation to schools, as Martin Allen argued in the November–December issue of *Post-16 Educator*, 'the qualification policy outlined in the 2002 Green Paper on 14–19 reform ... represents a further stage in the "tiering" of schools, with students following either academic, vocational or basic skills pathways'. Similarly with reference to Further Education, Paul Mackney, NATFHE's General Secretary, in his response to the Green Paper saw its proposals 'recreating 1944 at tertiary level with tertiary grammars (Sixth Form Colleges), technicals (Centres of Vocational Excellence), and moderns (General FE Colleges)'. While at the level of higher education, Charles Clarke crowned the Platonic associations of the Holy Trinity of Gold, Silver and Bronze with his vision of 'the great research universities, the outstanding teaching universities and those that make a dynamic, dramatic contribution to their regional and local economies' in reply to his first Parliamentary question as Secretary of State for Education reported in *The Times Higher Education Supplement* of 6 December 2002.

This then is an education system that at every level harks back to the lost postwar world of upper, middle and working classes. But this ordered social hierarchy has gone irretrievably because it no longer corresponds to the former division of knowledge and labour in employment between 'middle-class' non-manual managers or professionals and 'working-class' skilled or unskilled manual workers. With the collapse of heavy industry that clear social division has been eroded by the latest applications of new technology and the growth in services. In its place is a new division within the employed population between the respectable 'working-middle' and a new, casualized and under- or worthlessly qualified, so-called 'underclass'.

The simple solution offered by successive governments and their academic advisors is to end what they call the 'low skills equilibrium' by training the workforce to switch flexibly from one job to another as competitiveness dictates. But this is negated by the way employers use new information technology to remove routine tasks so that fewer workers are required in place of the less skilled they displace. Rather than re-, up- or multi-skilling the workforce, as the rhetoric of a 'Learning Society' pretends, there is a growing polarization of both skill and knowledge. At one end, 40 per cent of jobs in the labour market demand no qualifications at all. At the other, oversupply of qualified jobseekers forces employers to raise entry requirements to screen applicants. The result is rampant diploma devaluation with certification for all but the most casual employment. As a result, over one third of graduates, for example, enter occupations that do not require degrees for entry.

The raising of tuition fees towards their full cost would be predicted to choke off this oversupply. Its rationale though is the opposite – to reach the 2001 manifesto target of '50 per cent of young adults entering higher education by 2010', subsequently restated more cautiously by Margaret Hodge when HE Minister as '50 per cent of 18 to 30 year olds have the opportunity to experience higher education'. She thus wrote off not only *Half Our Future* not intended for HE but all those too old for HE at 30. Because they no longer count towards the target, adult access students are becoming a dying breed. Meanwhile, all 30+ except those on Basic Skills courses pay for their further and adult education. Given the debt aversion of younger students who can least afford it and are already struggling to complete their degree courses at local universities and colleges, this policy of introducing fees while aiming to widen participation of 18–30s would appear contradictory to say the least.

However, another government target for 28 per cent of 16–24 year-olds to be on Modern Apprenticeships by 2006 offers school-leavers a vocational alternative to paying fees for academic qualifications. Competence-based qualifications delivered in FE colleges will now culminate for those on this 'work-based route' in Foundation 'degrees'. As these two-year courses are administered by higher education institutions, those taking them can be recounted as HE students. At the same time, large parts of HE will effectively be turned into FE through converting academic to vocational courses. So both targets can be met! As FE is absorbed into HE, while large parts of HE actually become FE, Clarke's Holy Trinity will be between the Researching, Teaching and Training universities.

Yet the mass of students and trainees working their way through this mass certification system get less and less for more debt and more effort. While slaving at McJobs, they pay more for courses reduced towards 'bite-sized chunks'. These are combined with so-called 'personal and transferable skills for employability' (actually generic competences for flexible working across a variety of employments). So further and higher education students move from one module to another with no established peer groups and sensing that no one cares about them in increasingly chaotic and overcrowded organizations where they either sink or swim. They have little time and space for generalized reflection and negotiation of meaning with their teachers. Even on the most traditionally academic courses in elite universities which can be expected to raise their fees the highest, anecdotal evidence indicates students are churning out essays and other assignments as a mark of quality over competitors. But most students are well aware the required formats do not demonstrate real knowledge, or even thought, on their part but are a matter of acquired technique.

Similarly, several studies show teachers at all levels increasing their measurable performance while communicating less of their specialist expertise. In FE and HE, the battle to maintain standards is the more desperate as it is tied to lecturers' craft or subject identities. At the same time, unless standards are related to prospects for employment, they are rejected by necessarily instrumental students. Consequently, although more students and trainees go further and higher than ever before, at all levels they learn less of any real and direct meaning to them. They are habituated to this increasingly meaningless Lifelong Learning by a Foundation schooling that has produced the most examined and tested generation in history. As well as mass deskilling, this is therefore institutionalized stupefication on an unprecedented scale, 'the bamboozling of a generation' as Pierre Bourdieu once called it in France. It is time to wise up to it before abandoning what remains of the public service ethos of education to the market in fees.

LA TRAHISON DES CLERCS

Unfortunately the reaction of the mass of academics has been the opposite. The pass was already sold when New Labour not only abolished grants but introduced a £1000 up-front fee in 1997. Now, despite the opposition of their unions to fees, most teachers and researchers in HE have followed their vice chancellors in a Gadarene rush to raise fees towards the maximum allowed. Indeed, in the Russell group of elite universities, most of the so-called 'academic community' – always an illusory notion at the best of times – see in raising fees to full cost a way of continuing to live in the style to which they have become accustomed. Similar careerism is consolidating funding for research within the elite. Public-private collaborations and companies 'spun-off' from universities are likewise concentrated in the universities able to select their students by raising entry requirements. In the universities desperately recruiting students with lower academic qualifications there is more incentive if less possibility to move in the same direction. Meanwhile, illusions persist in the dwindling middle of teaching universities that they too can join the ranks of the researching universities.

Disunity is unsurprising since, although funded by the state since 1919, the elite universities and those modelled on them have always been closely connected to the private schools and took pride in their 'independence' from the state. By contrast, those HE institutions formerly under the control of Local Education Authorities share a public service ethos with the state schools, colleges and other parts of the former welfare state once directly under local democratic control. They also have most to lose from Clarke's 'free market solution' of fee-paying HE. Despite the pressures upon them, they are therefore better organized and less prone to illusions of professionality than their colleagues in elite, or would-be elite, HE. (Though arguably this has led their union, NATFHE, to join other staff unions in accepting a performance-related pay deal that is rightly opposed by AUT members in the pre-1992 universities.)

It is ironic that the unprecedented expansion of higher education with which so many professions – including teachers of all types –

sought to guarantee or to gain secure exclusive status has resulted in their actual proletarianization. Expansion is not only, or even mainly, a rearguard action by education professionals to preserve their depreciated status – depreciated along with the value of the educational credentials they supply. Even as their devalued currency inflates, educational credentials become more important, especially to parents seeking respectable 'working-middle' status for their children rather than see them fall into the uncertified 'underclass'. Credentialism also afflicts those clinging on or aspiring to security in shrinking core employment. Hence the growth in part-time, adult courses of continuing professional development, often run off-site and out of hours using distance and open learning. At the same time, the actual conditions of work in these 'professional' occupations become increasingly onerous and insecure.

Academics especially feel beset from all sides. They have sheltered not only behind professionalism but buttressed their claim to professional status by technicizing the academic form of generalized or what has been called 'Official Knowledge'. This is particularly the case in the arts and social sciences, which are most open to charges of vocational irrelevance from state and market. Instead of asserting this accusation as a virtue, many academics have taken a 'postmodern turn' into ideologies that deny students the possibility of even making sense of their experiences. At the same time, as an obscure academic discourse, varieties of postmodernism have complemented if not replaced the former orthodoxy of functionalism in social science, just as monetarism has replaced Keynesianism as the former paradigm in economics.

Instead of burying their heads in postmodern sand, academics should look beyond the boundaries of their sector to closely related FE to see the consequences of what is now hitting HE and schools. In FE the commodification of institutionalized learning and its semi-privatization have gone further than in any other sector of state education. Through their incorporation independent of LEAs in 1993 the FE colleges were semi-privatized and now, under the provisions of the 2001 Learning and Skills Act, are turned loose to compete as 'providers of learning and skills' with state-subsidized training for funding from monopsonic Learning and Skills Councils. More FE college closures and mergers are inevitable, together with more insecurity, contract and part-time working for lecturers and other staff.

Under the same pressures of competition for students and for research funding, these same processes will impact upon higher education, again with inevitable closures, mergers and redundancies. In the forgotten college sector of HE, colleges that do not attain university status will be especially vulnerable. So are new universities which lose out in the competition for students and research funds. Mergers in their cases may be accompanied by collapse into regional learning centres ranged around surviving management functions.

Academics are so confused by all this that in an instance of how far stupefication has gone some even accept the government's presentation of its policy as a progressive reform aimed at ending subsidies for wealthy students! The reality of course is that variable fees will only make transparent the link between the cultural capital enabling 'effortless achievement' in HE by those from privileged backgrounds and the real money capital of those who will soon be the only ones able to afford acquiring it in the private and 'better' state schools. This link will not be disguised by the proposed access regulator, widely known as 'OffToff'; nor by the encouragement of US-style bursaries that no English universities and colleges can afford.

Like the USA, however, only an Ivy League of the top colleges – or of their postgraduate schools – will be regarded as 'real education', although what they teach may well be increasingly academic and remote from reality. Mass universities for the many will thus be combined with elite universities for the few. In this worst of both worlds, academic competition shadows medieval pantouflage, entrenching the general rule that the older the institution, the younger, whiter and more conventionally middle-class are its students.

CORPORATE UNIVERSITIES IN THE NEW
MARKET-STATE

At the university which is one of the few exceptions to this general rule, the historian E. P. Thompson once asked, 'Is it inevitable that the university will be reduced to the function of providing with increasingly authoritarian efficiency, prepacked intellectual commodities to meet the requirements of management? Or can we, by our efforts, transform it into a centre of free discussion and action, tolerating and even encouraging "subversive" thought and activity, for a dynamic renewal of the whole society within which it operates?' In an article for *Red Pepper* in March 2001 Hugo Radice repeated these words from the Afterword to Thompson's 1971 *Warwick University Ltd* to show how little has changed in thirty years.

One thing that has not changed is the close link between universities, arms manufacturers and the military that occasioned Thompson's pamphlet. The Ministry of Defence continues to be a notorious tap for research funds, especially as their mismanagement is legendary. As a result, much of the growth of defence-related precision electronics in the 'golden triangle' of Oxford-Cambridge-London can be attributed to adjacent university research departments. This collaboration did not end with the Cold War for in the USA's 'new world order' the UK's support for the world's remaining superpower requires a permanent arms economy (estimated by CAFOD, the Catholic Relief Agency, at 20 per cent of UK export earnings).

Renewed globalization since 1989 has, however, seen re-regulation of the national economy to open it to trade in services along with capital investment from abroad. Under the General Agreement on Trade in Services private capital can invest in public sector institutions. This will take the present indebtedness of many universities and colleges to various banks and financial institutions much further. It will add to the burgeoning trade in overseas students and the export of education services abroad.

Research has also been globalized and so universities in the developed economies are shifting from being guardians of national knowledge to ancillaries in the production of knowledge for transnational corporations. As Jonathan Rutherford writes in the 2003 launch issue of his new journal *Mediactive*, 'In the past the intellectual commons was monopolised as a source of class cultural and political authority. Now, the threat comes from corporations driven by commercial gain.'

Thirty years ago in the old mixed economy, public services were clearly separate from the private sector. Today in a new 'mixed economy', private and state capital are mixed together as former services provided by the local or national state are sold off to private companies. Other public services are retained by the state but as semi-independent agencies to be run at a profit. The state also subsidizes private monopoly capital which dominates this new mixed economy instead of having to compromise with publicly owned industries and services as it did in the old mixed economy.

The introduction of a market in variable fees for HE takes further the Thatcherite model of independent schools and FE colleges competing for students with fees and/or vouchers. Only minor changes were necessary to produce such a result in HE as an elaborate hierarchy of universities already existed. The removal of the binary divide between universities and polytechnics in 1992 had completed this differentiated hierarchy at the same time as it removed the last vestige of local accountability and democratic control over HE.

If all Lifelong Learning is amalgamated under a Higher Education Funding Council merged with the Learning and Skills Council to bring together F&HE at regional level, a new binarism will predictably exclude the nationally or internationally 'excellent' research universities. They could privatize themselves out of the state system while being separately funded for their research not only by monopoly capitalist corporations but by the Department of Trade and Industry which already administers the research funding councils.

Competition for students, research funds, commercial sponsor-ships and consultancies exemplifies what has been called the 'new market-state'. Funded on the franchise or contract principle by quangos like HEFCE and the LSC, the privatization of the former-state sector in the 'new market-state' complements the state-subsidization of the private sector in the new mixed economy of state-subsidized private and semi-privatized state sectors.

Contracting and competition disorganizes dissent. The academic workforce is divided within itself and from students. It is confused about what is happening and faces the retirement of the welfare-state generation of teachers. The progressive gains that were possible under the welfare state to advance the public against the private sector are no longer possible under the new market-state. What is to be done?

FOR A FREE UNIVERSITY

The nature of the new market-state itself indicates the necessity of going beyond defensive sectoral opposition aimed at restoring the public services to their former bureaucrat-professional welfare-state forms. The redistributive element of public services should be taken as distinctive of their form of 'efficiency', not how efficiently they serve private monopoly capital.

The abolition of current up-front tuition fees of £1250 a year and the restoration of a means-tested grant, miserly though it is, are welcome. But these concessions to opponents of top-up fees, together with the Coalition of Modern Universities proposal to peg all fees at £3000, are not enough. Even if all universities charged this amount to a sustained number of students, Cambridge University Students Union calculate the annual deficit for the HE sector would remain around £2 billion. Other suggestions, such as a graduate tax, should also be rejected in favour of a return to progressive general taxation. The example of the fees-free zone of Scotland is a precedent to be built upon and links should be made with protests against neo-liberal reforms of education across Europe. As wide an alliance as possible is needed to advance public services and roll-back private provision.

This public sector alliance has to unite with the movement against US superpower imperialism and the economic globalization dominated by monopoly capitalist corporations that it supports.

While transnational capital has taken over many public services in the new market-state, a substantial public sphere remains. Alongside free trades unions, a free press, rights of assembly and demonstration and other essentials of democratic society, academic freedom must be preserved as part of this public sphere. It affords a space where matters of concern to the whole society can be explored free from the pressures of the new market-state. By contrast, most of what passes as public debate is conducted in the corporately owned mass media.

Freedom of discussion and inquiry must be preserved in higher education and extended to other sectors of education where they have been lost. The artificial distinction between the reproduction of knowledge in teaching and its production in research has to be abolished at all levels of learning. This is because, as Paolo Freire wrote in his last book, 'teaching is a creative act, a critical act, and not a mechanical one' (Treiver, 2003, p. 81). If teachers in mass HE are to engage with new generations of students to adapt tertiary level learning to them in the same way that comprehensive school teachers once struggled to open secondary schooling to the mass of the population, they will need to develop an alternative *Pedagogy of Hope*. This will be very different from the two sides of a coin currently on offer: on the one hand, academic transmission based upon narrow disciplinary cannons and, on the other, behaviourist competence-based training. As Freire indicates, negotiation of meaning is central to meaningful relations between teacher and taught. Teaching and learning are thus aligned with research.

Instead of separating teaching from research as is now proposed, investigation, experiment and debate by all students and as many other people as possible is vital when so many received ideas are today open to question. The space within education institutions to allow imagination free reign to develop from experience the new ideas necessary to comprehend and handle rapidly changing reality must be preserved and extended by making research and creation an integral part of the independent study of all students at all levels of learning.

In addition, valuing knowledge and skills other than, or as well as, the abstract and academic upsets the existing hierarchy between those who think and those who do. But this is happening spontaneously under the constant pressure of the potentiality of new communications and information technology. It was part of Caroline's originality and foresight that she recognized this potential for a transformation of work. As she wrote with Clyde Chitty, 'For the first time in almost two centuries there is the possibility of our society reshaping itself democratically because there is the possibility of reshaping work itself (Benn and Chitty, 1996, p. 379).'

The FE colleges once offered a second chance to those failed by academic schooling and supported the economy with the skills needed for working life. The polytechnics in turn represented an alternative relation of higher education to work. In the best cases they combined generalized knowledge with developing skill at work. The positive lessons of the polytechnic experiment in presenting an alternative to academic finishing-school elite HE should not be lost. For a renaissance of this radical alternative, universities free in every sense of the word need to be open as of right to all applicants at all levels of learning.

16 Arrivant Contemporaries: Caroline, her Arabian Brothers and the Pedagogy of Story

Chris Searle

Whenever I heard Caroline Benn speak publicly, she expressed a powerful awareness of, and commitment to, internationalism in all areas of political life, in particular education policy and practice. She fused this with a subliminal antiracism, a living principle she made clear on the last time I heard her speak, which was in April 1999 at the Goldsmiths College Conference to commemorate the twentieth anniversary of the death of East London teacher Blair Peach at the hands of Metropolitan Police officers in Southall in 1979, during a protest against a St George's Day march of the fascist National Front.

This commitment underlined all her relentless work in educational campaigning and scholarship, and her thirst for equity within the British education system through a national structure of comprehensive schools for all British children. As a child of an affluent family from Cincinnati, Ohio, with its long loyalty to the American Republican party and as a potential inheritor of its right-wing and frequently racist views, she had her own personal struggle of consciousness within her own family confines.

Thinking about this chapter, I have often wondered whether her own long campaign alongside teachers, trade unions, parents, progressive academics and activists was in any way connected to the fact that, like thousands of other men and women from all over the world where the British Empire had reached, she too was a postwar arrivant to Britain (see Benn, 1994). She first came in 1948, during the same year as the SS Empire Windrush docked in Tilbury, bringing the hopes of young men and women from throughout the Caribbean, making a signal for the multitudes who were to come after. Of course, Caroline De Camp was no typical arrivant. Prosperous and in a sense privileged, she came to study at Worcester College in Oxford (unlike the hundreds of other Oxford-bound migrants from the Caribbean who found jobs in the university city's Cowley automobile factory during the same postwar period (see, for example, Dash, 2002)), but it was to be her future pioneering and decades-lasting work and struggle for the educational advancement of the children of these and all other working-class families in Britain, which was to become the significant factor of Caroline's arrival. She returned to Cincinnati later in 1948 to continue her studies, and then returned to England permanently in July 1949, as the wife of Anthony Wedgwood-Benn, a young Left-Labour prospective parliamentarian who was to play a key role within the British Labour Party in anti-colonial struggles, notably in support of the independence movement of Arab peoples, during Algeria's war of independence, and in seeking to mobilize support within his party against the 1956 Suez invasion, a commitment fully shared by Caroline herself.

Among the thousands of men and women who came to Britain seeking work and a new life in the post-Windrush migrations were men from Yemen. They arrived from the early 1950s onwards, mainly single young men who looked towards gaining a wage which they could send back to their families in their homeland, creating a regular remittance which would begin to boost its national economy. They were Arabic-speaking, of Muslim faith, frequently from small, unelectrified mountain villages with peasant smallholdings, few schools and virtually no public health resources. Some had already had brief contact with British colonial authorities, having worked in the strategic naval port and dockyard of Aden, the gateway to Suez, or found passage as seamen on British merchant ships.

These young men, with no previous acquaintance with anything resembling heavy industry, arrived in the most unlikely of contexts – the industrial British cities of Cardiff, Birmingham, Liverpool and Sheffield, and, often within 24 hours, found regular work in factories and industrial plants. In Sheffield they walked into vacant jobs in the South Yorkshire steelworks, often filling vacancies which were filthy, dangerous and unwanted by native-born steelworkers, employment possibilities being so many that some were offered three or four jobs in one day. These young men found new workmates from a white, English-speaking, non-Islamic, working-class urban industrial culture. Sometimes these workmates were hostile; almost always communication and friendship were extremely difficult. The Yemenis had no experience of trade unions or the traditions of industrial struggle. They endured cold, damp, snowy winters in freezing and unheated terraced houses, some which they rented from rack-renting landlords, others which they sought to collectively buy for themselves, at great cost to themselves and their faraway families. The tasks of learning English were considerable. Their only classrooms were the steelworks. They learned a limited yet unique form of English based around the imperative mood, mainly because the version of the language they heard and copied was expressed in the giving and taking of shouted orders within the industrial din that surrounded them. One early arrivant Yemeni remembers the response when he enquired about classes to learn the language of their public and working existence:

When we first started work it was very hard to understand anything that anyone said. We spoke no English and our new workmates spoke no Arabic, except one or two and often they didn't work near us.

When I went to the Employment Office in Attercliffe, I asked the man there if we could go to English classes. 'We must learn English!' I tried to say to him. He looked at me hard and said: 'What? Listen to me! You are not here to go to classes. You're in England to work, only work.'

And that was what it was like. There were no English classes for us, we had to learn our new words in the foundries and rolling mills, and to try to understand what the gaffers shouted at us.

And it was very dangerous work too, and we couldn't read any of the safety notices or warnings they had in the steelworks when we first came. So there were some bad accidents because we couldn't read the instructions. It wouldn't be allowed now.

I remember in a rolling mill when a rod of steel went through a Yemeni's leg because he didn't know what to do. They took him to hospital and they cut off his leg. It was a very bad accident and he didn't work again in any steelworks.

For some of us, these classes that we have now, even though we are retired and old, are the first English classes we've ever had, and they're organized by our own community. The state gave us nothing, even though some of us have been in Sheffield and paid our taxes and rates for fifty years.*

It was against such educational rejection, for those men and the generations of their children and grandchildren who followed, that Caroline Benn campaigned. For learning English was just the beginning. For the Yemenis, although they could speak their Arabic with each other in their homes, cafés, mosques or nascent community organizations, English was the overwhelming tongue of their workplaces, streets, shops, the police, council and government offices, doctors' surgeries and solicitors. Time after time they were told that English was not for them or their arriving wives and children, just as some decades later and with some irony they were told categorically that Arabic could not be conceived as a part of the school curriculum, that for their children their mother tongue would best be allowed to atrophy and become extinct, all in the cause of 'integration' and the privilege of becoming 'truly English'.

What stands at the centre of this article is the testimony of arrivant Yemenis of Caroline's generation who, like her, struggled for betterment in their far adopted country, with some considerable long-term success. Even the class from which this collective witness has emerged is part of the fruit of that long struggle. They campaigned in different ways, in different places and for different specific goals, but both Caroline and these defiant and tenacious

---

* The quotations from Yemeni ex-steelworkers arose from recent classroom interactions with the author in the course of English classes organized through Sheffield's Yemeni Community Association.

Yemenis had an aim of a system of education that would bring equity and fulfilment for their children and grandchildren. Thus, it is without hesitation that I see my Yemeni students, now no longer young arrivant workers, but retired ex-steelworkers, many in their seventies, as Caroline's unacknowledged Arabian brothers, which is why I link their separate stories in a spirit of unity.

Furthermore, I believe that she would have approved of the classroom approach that I have sought to take with these veteran students who can look back to two worlds of lived experience: one of a Yemeni childhood in a small rural community, the other of adulthood within the working-class heart of a Yorkshire industrial city. It is out of these worlds that the stories germinate and learning grows. I call this technique 'the Pedagogy of Story', and although I have spent a teaching lifetime employing this pedagogy in teaching English in schools in many different places, from the Caribbean to East London, from Canada and Mozambique to Sheffield, it carries an even greater urgency and potential effectiveness when the lives that it embraces have such remarkable stories to tell – for this was a classroom method primarily dependent upon eliciting stories, creating narratives and then building discussion and debate around them for the purposes of the procreation of more. Perhaps one student would tell a childhood story set in a mid-twentieth-century village – perhaps about an authoritarian father or grandfather. This would certainly create argument, curiosity, humour, disagreement or indignation. All would be unbridled in the classroom. Then the accretions to the story would follow: counter-narrative or supportive tale-making, continuing from where the initial provocation concluded. Then very soon, through speech and confident self-assertion, these griots of migrant memory would create a many-textured collective story about remembered moments of Arabian boyhood, moving into tales of passage and arrival, of workdays and nights inside huge factories of steel, of deafening noise from giant mechanical hammers and close to blistering furnaces, giant rolling mills, towering indoor cranes and gantries and the endless intense heat, much, much hotter than the Arabian sun, of molten metal over their heads in giant containers and moving in channels close to their flesh. A life in steel, doing the work which native Englishmen had abandoned as too intolerable, too deadly, too much like a working life spent in hell. Yet such was the genesis of their stories, of the scaffolding of their proud and often defiant speech, and their future learning through it.

So many times while teaching these now elderly students, I marvel and ask myself: how could such young Muslim men, with hardly a word of English between them, move worlds in the way these Yemenis did, from their small-farming village life, to switch continents to become overnight a part of the British working-class, yet with no initial understanding of or preparation for that life, culture, institutions, language or tradition of that class, living in damp and crowded rooms surrounded on all sides by factories, forbidden pubs and strange, unwelcoming shops selling *haram* food they had never seen or tasted before, eating the staples of bread, butter and shared tins of tuna as their daily diet.

Indeed, this uncertainty about food – what was *haram*, what was *halal*, began on the very first day of the voyage from the homeland to this strange new country whose soldiers occupied your capital city:

When I came to England in 1956 I travelled on an Italian ship. We couldn't understand the menu in the ship's restaurant and we didn't want to eat any pork, so to make sure, all we ate were eggs. Every day, only eggs! Eggs for breakfast, eggs for lunch, eggs for dinner, eggs for supper too! Only eggs, eggs, eggs, all the way to Genoa. How I wished for a good lamb dinner, like I used to have in my home village!

There is a sense of universalism in these experiences of a culture of migration, a life-foundation known and shared by thousands of arrivant workers to Britain, throughout the decade of the 1950s. But the Yemenis were Arabs and this was also the era of a media-conducted and fermented racist campaign against the Arab peoples, stoked in the newspapers and public consciousness of Britain. For Egyptian Arabs had dared to take back their great strategic waterway, the Suez Canal, and their leader, the Pan-Arabist Gamal Abdul Nasser, had defied Britain, France and Israel and in July

1956 nationalized their greatest asset – whose southern guardian fortress was Aden, the colonized port of the southern Yemenis. The subsequent ineffectual 'invasion' of Egypt (code-named 'Operation Omelette') of early November 1956, so firmly opposed by Tony and Caroline Benn, was conducted in the white heat of anti-Arab racism and Islamophobia in the British press, and was certainly not the ideal historic period for Arab migrant workers to arrive in the heart of urban Britain (see Fullick and Powell, 1979). How did they live through it? How did they cope? Their varied and often contradictory adventures in dealing with their new English workmates and neighbours, sometimes hostile, sometimes hospitable and friendly, more times coldly indifferent, come out with verve and humour through the pedagogy of story, and are set down with detailed remembrance and wisdom. Take Saleh's first new hours of arrival, for instance:

When I arrived at Sheffield Station from London after I left the ship at Tilbury, I didn't know anyone and I didn't know where to go.

A taxi driver said: 'Try Attercliffe, I think there are some Arabs there', but I didn't understand him.

He took me to Attercliffe, and then to Darnall. He started to knock on the doors of the houses along one street to see if the people who lived there would rent me a room.

On the eleventh house where he knocked, a lady called Doreen opened the door. 'He can stay with me, he's welcome', I found out later she said when she saw me. So I moved into that house.

It was near the Brown Bailey steelworks. So later that first night I went there to ask for a job. And I got a job there in the middle of the night! When I came back to Doreen's house she was angry and worried because I didn't tell her where I went. She even slapped me because she was so upset and cared for me.

'Where did you go all night?' she shouted. 'I found a job', I shouted back happily in Arabic. I stayed for six months with Doreen; she always looked after me and even took care of my wages for me. She was a very honest woman.

Saleh's story provoked other memories of arrival, and English hosts very unlike Doreen:

An Englishman said to me and my friends, 'Listen to me! You give me £20 each, and I'll get you all good jobs' – for at that time for a few months it was hard to get work.

We thought that we could trust Englishmen so we all gave him the money. He took £20 from the five people in our house and went to many other houses where Yemenis lived in Attercliffe and they gave him £20 each too. So you can see what he took from us.

He gave us a name and address, then he disappeared and we heard nothing more from him. We went to look for him at the address that he gave us, but nobody knew him there. He took all our money and vanished.

In those days £20 was a lot of money, four weeks' wages! I had to borrow the money back from my father-in-law who was a merchant seaman. We had believed this man – we thought we could trust an Englishman! But he stole our money by his lies. It was a terrible lesson for us, as strangers to England. Up until now this man still owes me that £20, nearly fifty years later. He was a cheat and a swindler, and I still want my money back.

Time and again the theme of the Yemeni classroom narratives are defiance, resistance and a refusal to accept humiliation, starting from the outward voyage:

We travelled on a French ship, and the crew treated us badly as we were third class. We weren't allowed to come onto the deck and mix with the first class passengers who were enjoying themselves in the sun and swimming in the pool and having plenty to drink.

It was 1956 and just before the war over the Suez Canal. When we passed through Egypt the Egyptian immigration officers supported us and told the French crew to treat us better. But we were angry at them and decided to make a protest. So just before the ship reached Marseilles we started to throw a lot of the ship's furniture and bedsheets over the side and into the Mediterranean Sea.

They faced hostility and racism in the steelworks too, which was sometimes confronted by traditional responses more characteristic of village life than the ways of urban England. But, in the absence of official support, they sometimes proved just as effective:

> Every day when we arrived and clocked in, one of the white steelworkers said to my friend from my village, 'Hello black bastard!' He said this out loud every day for the first week. We asked him to stop, but he carried on saying it every morning, 'Hello black bastard!'
>
> So my friend and I went to the gaffer to complain about this daily insult. He said, 'Well that's what you are, a black bastard. It's true, isn't it?' And he did nothing to stop it.
>
> So my friend gave the worker a warning himself in the little English he had. 'I'll give you a week to stop. If you carry on with this insult after a week, then I will have to take action.' But every day he started with the same words. He did not stop.
>
> So after a week my friend was true to his word. He brought in a knife and cut the man who called him 'black bastard'. And he never called him that again.

Other Yemenis may have treated the same kind of hostility more light-heartedly, but they were determined that they would not let it pass:

> I worked with my cousin and two other Yemenis as crane drivers. I worked on a 12-hour shift from six o'clock in the morning to six o'clock in the evening, and I had to take a pot up in the crane to piss into, because we were up there so long. I used to throw the piss out of the crane cab down over the workers who didn't like us Arabs. We were high up above the factory floor, and there was a lot of smoke and it was very hot up there.

But the support of the union, when it at last emerged, created a sense of unity at the workplace which the Yemeni steelworkers had long yearned for:

There were a lot of us Yemenis working there, and we were friendly with the English steelworkers. We all talked, laughed and joked together. Then we went on strike together for better pay. The managers at first refused to recognize our union, and one manager maybe thought he could get at us Yemenis, and he came to my house when I was on strike to try to persuade me to come back to work. But we stayed out for another two weeks, and they raised our pay, and only then we came back.

From their own initial isolation and sense of siege at their workplace, the Yemenis gradually witnessed an increase in trade union participation and power, from which they, too, became the beneficiaries – even though, to many, it seemed a long time arriving:

When I arrived in 1956, I found that in our factory the union wasn't very strong, and the gaffers did almost what they wanted with us. They told us that we had to work on many jobs, one after the other, not just on one. When we finished work on one machine, they said that we must move on straight away to another job. They got a lot of work out of us all right, for the same low pay. If we refused to move on to the next job, they threatened to send us home or to sack us.

But later, the union got stronger and it said: 'One man, one job!' and it stopped the gaffers acting like dictators to us.

Sometimes they made us work for 16 hours at one time until we were nearly too tired to stand up. Then we had to go home to cook and sleep and then come back again for another double shift.

It was very hard work, and so hot too all the time. Hotter even than Aden! But after a time the union stopped all this pressure, and it became better for us.

The union may have had some impact at the workplace, but the Yemenis' survival and security in Sheffield East End neighbourhoods like Darnall, Attercliffe and Burngreave depended upon their willingness to throw their lives in with each other. Not only in daily living, friendship and the strength of families and community, but through a realization that any improvement in their lives would depend upon community consolidation and struggle. So in the early days a group of Yemeni steelworkers combined to buy a terraced house on Burngreave Road, the main artery passing through their suburbs. They made it a community centre, meeting place and essential social nucleus. It also became their own adult college, and now the classes to help build and develop their English are held four times a week in those same rooms, still owned by those prescient arrivant Arabs who understood very soon that it is only through recourse to community and the pooling of insight and brain power that a group of migrants in a strange and frequently angry land can grow, prosper and become a community in themselves.

In the preface to his autobiography, *Living to Tell the Tale*, published in this country in 2003, the Colombian novelist Gabriel García Márquez wrote: 'Life is not what one lived, but what one remembers and how one remembers it in order to recount it.' But living and the memory of living are not so ruptured in the exercise of the pedagogy of story. They feed off each other to give strength to both, life and memory, in order to add consciousness and understanding to the future in the present – which is education. This is as true for the 11-year-old boy or girl writing in truthful and imaginative reflection in their classroom about the street where they live and the other people who live there or the school where they go every day and its tensions, discoveries, friendships and aggressions. But five or six years of living memory is one resource for classroom learning with the development of literacy and the critical imagination. What if the resource were sixty or seventy years of remembering? How huge would such a classroom be, filled with the manifold narratives of its veteran students? What a foundation for the pedagogy of story, if effectively set in motion!

To speak the story in struggling English, the English of Sheffield steelworkers with its structural and figurative foundation in the Yemeni dialects of Arabic. To strive to write it down converted to Standard English, as that is the dialect we are seeking to learn. To read it closely with a copy for each one; to clarify and understand this language, always heard, but never spoken or studied. How reading provokes more discussion; sparks more stories about similar or related happenings; to be always moving forward in the grasp of new narrative and the great stirring of life, memory and experience.

These now-retired steelworkers, from what for decades for most Sheffielders was an invisible community, have many achievements stemming from their lives in Britain: most momentously their power of community organization, that at the present juncture owns four separate premises which house an economic and training project including several English and computer classes, a careers' project, which helps, in particular, elderly and disabled members of the community, a free lunch service, an advice centre, a family support unit, a thriving youth section and a long-standing community language school teaching Arabic, Yemeni history and culture to school-age students for four hours every Saturday and Sunday. There is also a vibrant student support project, in which Yemeni and other school students benefit directly from the teaching and mentoring power of young graduates, professionals and skilled workers from their own communities. The Yemeni Community Association has also fought many local campaigns, including a successful compensation claim for hundreds of ex-steelworkers still suffering from the lasting effects of industrial deafness.

All this too is part of the story of the arrivant pioneers who came in the 1950s and 60s. Many of their children have succeeded, often against the odds, and usually through the agency of local comprehensive schools for which Caroline fought so resolutely. The children of one steelworker and his remarkable wife, both from a small village in Shaib in the uplands north of Aden, have accomplished much, and they include a son who has a PhD from Sheffield University, a long-serving community leader and ex-Chair of Governors of a local comprehensive, and a UN consultant to the Arab nations. And a daughter who is a medical doctor, now working in a crucial area of cancer research.

These elderly Sheffield Arabs tell the truth of a story recounted by thousands of others of their generation, newcomers to Britain half a century ago and from the Caribbean, Africa and many parts of Asia, including the villages of Arabia. As they tell, memory sifts out the significant, the humorous, the insightful, the wise and the prophetic. Remembrance of one begets remembrance of the other, story nourishes story and the cooperative endeavour of the shared life is invoked time after time as voices speak and hands write, honestly, critically and proudly of living in and across two continents, two realities.

To consider Caroline Benn's own story in the context of these Yemeni lives is also deeply instructive: an affluent young American woman who arrives in postwar Britain to study at its most prestigious university finds the contours of her old mind revealed, her life transformed and re-dedicated to seeking a new educational dispensation for the mass of British working-class children within the struggle for an equitable and fulfilling school system – local, community-based and fully resourced comprehensive schools capable of motivating and stretching all young people to the full potential of their brainpower. There is a lifelong process and shift of class allegiance in her story of levelling from the other side of the line of class. Also a life which is another exemplar within the pedagogy of story, which is why I put the outline of her struggle next to those of some of her arrivant contemporaries, the Yemeni steelworkers of Sheffield, who, almost overnight, became an integral part of the British working-class. There is a powerful sharing here, if an unconscious one, across both time and place, which only a study and telling of the real history of peoples can unify.

17 Comprehensive Schooling and Educational Inequality: An International Perspective

Andy Green and Susanne Wiborg

Reducing educational inequality has been one of the organizing agendas of educational reform in the past half century and, until quite recently at least, probably the dominant force in the most developed countries. To this end, various forms of comprehensive – or non-selective – education have been developed in the compulsory school systems in different developed countries, so that now the vast majority are – at least formally – comprehensive. North America (the USA and Canada) has had common compulsory school systems for a long time; since the 1960s most of the current European Union states have followed suit, with only a handful (Austria, Belgium, Germany, Luxembourg and, arguably, the Netherlands) remaining predominantly selective in the lower secondary phase. The majority of developed East Asia states, including Japan, South Korea and Taiwan, also have comprehensive systems in the state sector.

This development of multiple forms of comprehensive schooling, alongside the few remaining selective systems, should, in theory, have provided ample opportunity for comparative study to analyse the genealogy and regional distribution of different models of compulsory schooling. Given the increasing availability of comparable international data, it should also have made possible comparative assessment of the validity of the claims that comprehensivization would lead to reduction in inequality of educational opportunity. However, until recently, comparative analysis has been surprisingly mute about the different forms of non-selective schooling and their effects on class reproduction.

This situation may now be changing. Two recent and ongoing international surveys by the OECD – The International Adult Literacy Survey (IALS) and the Programme for International Student Assessment (PISA) – provide much improved cross-national comparative data on learning outcomes and have already produced a groundswell of reassessment among policy-makers of the effects of different educational policies, particularly in relation to educational inequality. The surveys are important because they provide direct measures of skills among adults (IALS) and young people (the 15-year-olds surveyed by PISA) in literacy, numeracy and basic science (in the case of PISA) which are considerably more reliable than previously used proxy measures such as years of schooling, levels completed and qualifications attained. They allow better estimation of the effects of different school systems on educational inequality across countries. Taken together, the data show rather clear patterns of variation in levels of inequality across countries, which cluster both in terms of regions and system types.

THE DEBATE OVER COMPREHENSIVE SCHOOLS AND EDUCATIONAL INEQUALITY

International research has been unable to date to show conclusively that comprehensive reform does increase educational equality. In fact, most surveys until recently have shown relatively stable rates of educational inequality through the first six or seven decades of the twentieth century, including through the first years of comprehensive systems (Garnier and Raffalovitch, 1984; Handl, 1986; Featherman and Hauser, 1978; and Halsey, Heath and Ridge, 1980). Shavit and Blossfeld's classic 1983 study, *Persistent Inequality*, includes the findings from 13 separate country studies, seven of which are for western developed countries. Each of the studies analyses the impact of social origin (in terms of parental occupation and education) on both years of schooling and survival rates at key educational transition points – for successive cohorts between the early 1900s and 1960. The editorial conclusion is that 'despite the marked expansion of all educational systems under study, in most countries there was little change in socio-economic inequality of educational opportunity' (1983, p. 97). Only Sweden and the Netherlands showed a marked decline in the impact of social origin on educational attainment over the period.

The authors could find no evidence that major educational reforms made an impact on educational equality, even in Sweden where there were reductions in levels of inequality over time. Jan Jonsson, who was co-author of the Sweden study in the Shavit and Blossfeld collection, did re-examine his data for Sweden in a later publication (Jonsson, 1999) and, using more data points, was able to show a continuing decline in educational inequality through the first decade of comprehensivization in Sweden. School reforms, he says, were in part responsible for the reductions in inequality, which were not only across social classes but also in terms of regional differences and gender. However, Esping-Andersen (forthcoming), using different data, argues that diminishing educational inequality in Sweden has little to do with structural reforms in the school system. Following Bourdieu's thesis, he argues that a low level of cultural capital among parents plays the major part in lowering children's educational achievement through less cognitive stimulation in the early years; through failure to pass on the cultural codes which are valued in schools; through less parental ability to navigate school systems to the benefit of the child; and through making children more risk averse in relation to future educational decisions. Universal child care in Sweden, says Esping-Andersen, counteracts this by providing supplementary socialization in culturally mixed environments. Education systems, comprehensive or otherwise, he says, don't seem to make much difference.

PISA AND IALS

The PISA and IALS surveys tell a different story. They both show that levels of educational equality, measured in terms of the distribution of tested skills in areas such as literacy, numeracy and basic science, vary very substantially across countries both for adults and for young people. They also show that variations in skills inequality across countries follow distinctly regional patterns which can be related to, among other regional factors, the education system types which predominate in those regions.

The IALS study (OECD, 2000) gives clear evidence of regional variation. The Nordic countries, for instance, including Denmark, Finland, Norway and Sweden, were all among the most equal in their distributions of adult literacy while the English-speaking countries, including the USA and the UK, were usually among the most unequal (Green, 2003). However, although all the Nordic countries are notable for having almost entirely unstreamed comprehensive education in the compulsory years, by comparison with the rather incomplete and quite differentiated comprehensive school systems in English-speaking countries (with only 40 per cent in genuinely non-selective schools in England in recent estimates), the data tell us relatively little about the effects of different system characteristics.

A number of factors determine the distributions of skills within the adult population in addition to the effects of compulsory schooling. The distribution of skills among adult immigrants will have an effect as will the distribution of post-school learning. Distributions of adult skills are also affected by differences between cohorts receiving their compulsory education at different times and in different educational systems, so that systems which have undergone more rapid change will produce greater variation in levels of skill between different cohorts. (This may, for instance, partly explain why the UK comes out as the third most unequal of the countries since there may be large cohort differences between those who have and those who have not had the benefit of the massification of upper secondary education which came later than in many countries.) Using the figures for the whole adult sample will tell us relatively little about the effects of comprehensive schooling since a large proportion of the sample in each country were educated at a time when the school systems were selective.

One can look at the data across countries for particular age cohorts before and after comprehensive reforms and this shows that in most countries the distribution of prose literacy skills (as measured by the standard deviation) is more unequal for those aged

46–55 (schooled in the 1950s and early 60s) compared to those aged 26–35 (schooled in the 1980s) (Green, Preston and Sabates, 2003). This may reflect growing equality of educational outcomes in these countries. On the other hand, Sweden, Germany and Switzerland show more inequality among the younger age groups and Great Britain practically no difference. These results are mixed and in any case the procedure reduces the sample size rather substantially and therefore lowers reliability. The PISA data, however, based on tested skills of 15-year-olds, can give a much better guide to the effects of the school system.

The OECD PISA survey of skills in reading, numeracy and basic science of 15-year-olds in 32 countries provides the most recent evidence on how far different compulsory school systems generate equal or unequal outcomes in the performance of their students. The OECD provide the standard deviations for scores between the 5th and 95th percentiles for students tested in each country in each of three domains (OECD, 2001: table 2.3a, p. 253, for the combined reading literacy scale; table 3.1, p. 259, for the mathematical literacy scale; and table 3.3, p. 261, for the scientific literacy scale). The data show that countries do differ very substantially in how widely skills are distributed among 15-year-olds. For instance, students in Japan falling within the lowest sixth of international achievement are 42 points behind those who performed in the top sixth of international scores, while the gap between the same groups in Germany was 120 points (OECD, 2001, p. 189). There are also very regular patterns as regards the relative position of different countries on different measures of equality in education.

Taking a basic standard deviation measure of skills dispersal (averaging the standards deviations for the three tests conducted in reading, mathematical and scientific literacy), we find that the most unequal of the 23 advanced states in the sample are (in descending order) Belgium, Germany, New Zealand, the USA and Switzerland (with the UK coming close after). The most equal (in descending order) are Korea, Finland, Japan, Iceland, Canada and Ireland. Sweden is 10th most equal and Denmark 14th. It is notable that all the most equal education systems have comprehensive education systems at lower secondary level (see OECD, 2001, tables 2.3a–3.3). Among the least equal countries, three have selective secondary systems and two, the USA and New Zealand, have highly marketized comprehensive systems, where the emphasis on school choice substantially undermines principles of non-selectivity (Lauder *et al.*, 1999).

The alternative measure of inequality, based on the strength of social inheritance (in terms of parental wealth, occupation, education, and cultural capital combined) in determining educational outcomes, suggests a similar country patterning. The advanced states where social inheritance appears to have the greatest impact are: Germany, Switzerland, the UK, the USA, Belgium, France, Australia and New Zealand. The countries where the effect is least are: Korea, Japan, Iceland, Spain and Sweden. Denmark, Finland and Norway are again in the lower half but closer to the middle of the range (OECD, table 8.1). The country groupings are similar again. East Asian and Nordic states tend to predominate among the more education equal countries. Anglo-Saxon countries and countries in the region proximate to Germany tend to be most unequal. Among the unequal group, five of the ten systems are selective at secondary level, and four are highly marketized comprehensive systems. All the more equal countries have comprehensive systems

Breaking down the social inheritance syndrome into the separate effects of parental wealth and occupation also repeats the pattern. Parental wealth has the highest impact on the USA, Luxembourg, New Zealand, Portugal and Germany, and the lowest effect in the Netherlands, Japan, Finland, Italy, and Norway. Parental occupational status has the strongest effect in Germany, Switzerland, Luxembourg, Portugal, the UK and Belgium, and the lowest in Korea, Finland, Canada and Italy. The major changes to the pattern here are that Norway is closer to the more equal end of the spectrum in the parental wealth measure than in previous measures, and Portugal has found itself in the more unequal group of countries in both the above measures whereas on the previous measures they were closer to the middle. The regional clustering is still apparent.

Another interesting aspect of regional patterning becomes visible when we analyse the effect of school intake mix on variations in achievements between schools. According to the OECD analysis, school status, measured in terms of the average level of parents' occupational level, wealth and 'cultural capital', has a major impact on the performance of individual students internationally – more even than the effects of the individual students' own background characteristics in many countries (OECD, 2001, p. 210). However, school intake mix has a much larger impact on the differences in outcomes between schools in the English-speaking countries than elsewhere. For the OECD countries taken together school status explains 34 per cent of the variance in average outcomes (on combined literacy measures) between schools, whereas in the English-speaking countries its impact is much higher: explaining 64 per cent of the between-school variance in Australia; 59 per cent in Ireland; 70 per cent in New Zealand; 61 per cent in the USA; and 61 per cent in the UK (OECD, 2001, p. 197). In Japan and Korea the impact of school status on differences in school outcomes is much lower (explaining 11 and 17 per cent of between-school variance respectively). Intake effects are also moderately low in Scandinavian countries, except in Sweden where the differences in outcomes between school are very low in any case.

The conclusion drawn by the OECD is that greater social segregation in school intakes increases educational inequality whereas increasing the heterogeneity of intakes, and narrowing the gaps between schools, reduces it (OECD, 2000, p. 201). The Nordic and East Asian countries would appear to have considerably less segregation in school intakes than most of the English-speaking countries (except Canada) and the effect of intake differences on inequalities between schools is much lower. Since 36 per cent of the total variation in student performance is attributable to the variation between schools, this leads to substantially less overall inequality in outcomes.

The regional clustering is not, of course, perfect, but the patterns above suggest strong regional/historical affinities in terms of levels of educational equality. The Nordic and East Asian countries form two rather well delineated regional groups with relatively low levels of inequality. The English-speaking countries, excepting Southern Ireland and Canada, form another with higher levels of inequality.

A third group with rather high levels of inequality include some German-speaking countries and other multilingual countries which are geographically close to Germany and may be expected to share certain influences, although the Netherlands is not in this group. A fourth group includes France and the Mediterranean states which appear to occupy an intermediate position relative to other countries in terms of levels of inequality. Clearly each group of countries have a number of socio-political characteristics in common, which may in part explain the commonalities in levels of educational equality. However, education system characteristics are also regionally patterned and it would be hard not to conclude that these may also play a part.

How can we explain the marked regional differences in inequality of outcomes with reference to the common regional characteristics of education systems? The positive cases of East Asia and the Nordic states offer a good place to start.

COMPREHENSIVE SCHOOLING IN EAST ASIA

Japan has long been known to produce rather equal outcomes in education. Studies by Merry White (1987) and Ronald Dore and Mari Sako (1989) both emphasize the success of Japanese schools in encouraging the majority of children to achieve and the relatively low variation in performance outcomes between children. William Cummings, whose research focused mainly on primary schools in Japan in the 1960s, entitled his major study *Education and Equality in Japan* and claimed that 'Japan's distribution of cognitive skills is probably more equal than in any other contemporary society' (1980, p. 6). Even official studies for the UK Government, which are not usually noted for their strong endorsements of international reports, also frequently note this characteristic. The DFE report *Teaching and Learning in Japanese Elementary Schools* (DFE/Scottish Office, 1992, p. 19) concluded that: 'A pervasive and powerful assumption of Japanese elementary education is that virtually all children are capable of learning and understanding the content prescribed in the Course of Study, provided they work hard enough and receive adequate support from their families, peers and teachers' (although it should be noted that some Japanese scholars maintain that up to a third of Japanese children are unable to keep up with the class by the last years of primary education: see Ichikawa, 1989).

This common perception of high average standards and relative equality of outcomes has been repeatedly confirmed by International Evaluation of Educational Achievement (IEA) surveys. In the IEA survey of science attainment in 19 countries (Coomber and Reeves, 1973) Japanese children at 11 and 14 years achieved the highest average scores with among the lowest levels of variation between individuals. A second science survey conducted in the mid-1980s found Japanese 14-year-olds still had the second highest average scores with the lowest levels of variation between schools (IEA, 1988). Attainment spread is greater at the higher grades in Japan, as one would expect, but the evidence does confirm the frequent observations of outsiders that compared with many other countries, Japan does achieve relatively equal outcomes in the compulsory years of education (Ichikawa, 1989).[1]

The achievement of relative equality within Japanese schooling is the result of a host of quite specific social and educational factors, some of which go back to the early modernization period, but most of which are specifically postwar phenomena.

Learning in Japan has always carried high social esteem, partly because of the value placed upon it within the Confucian tradition and partly because of the relative absence of public socializing agencies other than the school. Education was quite widespread in pre-industrial Tokugawa Japan; the school was both a repository of Confucian learning and a place for the education and socialization of children, thus combining two functions which in most western societies were divided between the school and the Church (Dore, 1997, 1982; Passim, 1965). Economic and social modernization after the Meiji Restoration in 1868 gave schools further prominence. They were to become the essential vehicles of ideological unification and modernization in a concerted process of state-led nation-building engineered by the Meiji reformers. At the same time, they were called upon to generate the knowledge and skills that were vital for Japan's nascent industrialization process.

Like all subsequent late-developing countries, Japan was particularly dependent on education for economic growth since this rested precisely on the ability to learn from other countries (Dore, 1997). From its inception in 1872, the public education system was thus already conceived as a key institution for the attainment of national goals in citizen and human capital formation (Green, 1997, 1999). This alone would have guaranteed its strong emphasis on universality and inclusiveness, as demonstrated by the rapid achievement of full enrolment in elementary schools by 1910 and the relatively socially mixed nature of their intakes (Dore, 1997; Passim, 1965). However, other historical social factors to do with class formation have also combined to emphasize equality in Japanese education.

Modernization virtually eliminated the old elites in Japanese society, as it did not in countries like Germany and Britain, and postwar Japan has emerged as one of the less class-divided of advanced societies: for all its vertical divisions of gender and sector, the Japanese labour market has a narrower distribution of income than in any other of the developed economies (although this is now widening) (Perkin, 1996). Nation-building, the lack of old elites and non-educational vehicles of social mobility, and relative economic and cultural homogeneity have thus all combined historically to produce an environment favouring educational equality.

However, it is only in the period since World War II that an education system has emerged with specific institutional characteristics favouring equality. Most important of these has been the creation of the 6-3-3 public system of elementary, secondary and high schools first proposed by the American occupying powers after the war and readily accepted then by a Japanese population eager to embrace a new democracy in education. Envisaged as a fully comprehensive system, and strongly supported as such by the influential teacher union *Nikkyoso*, this was never fully realized at the upper end since the postwar high schools rapidly became both selective and specialized under the pressure of increasing demand. Nevertheless, public elementary and lower secondary schools remained both non-selective and neighbourhood-based, providing relative equality of access to children from all social groups.

Other institutional factors have been important in fostering equal opportunities in education. Centralized control has been used to equalize funding between schools, just as frequent rotation of teachers and heads between schools has worked to ensure consistency in the other key area of resourcing.[2] Mixed ability classes throughout the compulsory years and automatic promotion between grades have promoted uniformity of school experiences and standards for each age cohort of children (Ichikawa, 1989). This uniformity has been further reinforced through central control over curricula, assessment methods and textbooks, all of which are tightly prescribed by the Ministry of Education through its detailed Course of Study for each year of schooling and which teachers tend to follow quite closely.

Lastly, but not least, there has been a strong equalizing force from the prevailing view in Japan that achievement is largely the product of effort rather than innate ability (Takeuchi, 1991). This belief is widely held by teachers in public schools (White, 1987) and appears also to leave its mark on children. A review of research by Susan Holloway (1988) on concepts of ability and effort among school children strongly suggests that Japanese children are much more likely than their American counterparts to ascribe both their successes and failures to levels of effort rather than ability. Not only have Japanese children traditionally been encouraged to believe that they can all do well if they try hard enough, but they have also been encouraged to help each other in the process, with the faster ones commonly helping the slower ones in group tasks which are subsequently assessed on group rather than individual performance (White, 1987).

Although there are less data in English on equality of outcomes in Taiwan and South Korea, except the PISA data already noted for the latter, it would not be at all surprising if these two countries showed similar properties in this regard to those of Japan. South Korea and Taiwan both experienced long periods of Japanese occupation when their school systems were substantially re-moulded after the Japanese pattern. After independence, school reforms were highly influenced by the US model, as was the case in Japan until the mid-1950s, and they also, particularly in the case of

South Korea, followed Japan as a model for educational reform (Brown, Green and Lauder, 2001). The other two of the four tigers in East Asia, Singapore and Hong Kong, were much more influenced by their British colonial legacy and share more features educationally with the UK than with Japan, and so, not surprisingly, do not exhibit the same patterns as the other two in relation to structures designed to equalize outcomes. Japan, South Korea and Taiwan all developed a 6-3-3 school system for primary, lower secondary and high school education, following the American model. They also adopted a system of unstreamed neighbourhood comprehensive schools in lower secondary education in the state sector, although a much more stratified system of private evening crammer schools (Juku in Japan) exists alongside this in Japan and Korea. These shared characteristics no doubt go some way to explaining the similarly high levels of educational equality in Japan, South Korea and Taiwan (although we have only the near universalization of upper secondary education to go on here), but there are also other important social and cultural characteristics, which cannot be explored here, which may also help to explain the obvious educational affinities.

In any case it would seem that there are sufficient commonalities in the histories and structures of the educational system in these three East Asian states to justify a claim that they do to some extent represent a dominant East Asian model, from which Singapore and Hong Kong inevitably diverge, and that this model is exceptionally favourable towards educational equality. Current reforms in all the states may be undermining this model (Green, 1997) but they had not gone so far in the years covered by the PISA surveys in the mid-1990s to undermine the equality effect visible in the data in that study.

THE NORDIC MODEL

The Nordic states in some ways offer an even more convincing case of a regional model of compulsory schooling which favours egalitarian outcomes. All the Nordic states, including Denmark,

Finland, Norway, Sweden, and even Iceland, share the same basic institutional structure. This comprises nine or ten years learning in the primary/lower secondary phases of compulsory education in mixed ability classes in all-through non-selective comprehensive schools. The selective private sector is also relatively weak in each country, unlike in East Asia, with in Denmark, for instance, 89 per cent of children in state schools. The 'private' schools here, as elsewhere in Scandinavia, are, in any case, largely state funded (80–85 per cent in Denmark) – and therefore also largely controlled by the state (see Winther-Jensen, Larsen and Wiborg, forthcoming). High schools are differentiated in most Nordic states – Sweden being the exception with its integrated academic/vocational Gymnasieskola – but upper secondary education has near universal enrolments in all of these countries. School choice has been introduced in Denmark and Sweden but its salience at the secondary level is limited since most children stay in their initial primary school through the secondary level and its impact has mainly been limited to the major urban areas. Measures to increase private schools have not substantially enlarged that sector in any of the countries (OECD, 1994; Green, Wolf and Leney, 1999).

The Nordic states all then share an exceptionally egalitarian structure of schooling with all kinds of selection delayed until the upper secondary phase. It cannot be a coincidence that all these countries on which we have data are also all alike in the relatively low levels of inequality in their educational outcomes. Other societal factors will also contribute to this common regional phenomenon, but the chances are they are working through education in having their effects

Why has this very particular common regional pattern emerged in the Nordic states? A number of preconditions existed in the nineteenth century which helped in the early introduction of linear educational ladders, as opposed to the parallel education systems that persisted often until the mid-twentieth century in other European states such as the UK, France and Germany. The Scandinavian states shared a common Lutheran religious heritage which was favourable to the establishment of universal literacy and they were also early to introduce state regulation of education in the early part of the nineteenth century, thus creating the basis for later systematic reforms (Skovgaard-Petersen, 1976; Sjöstrand, 1965; Dokka, 1967). However, there were other countries in Europe, such as the German states, which shared a dominant Protestant heritage and which also developed early state education systems but they were much slower than the Scandinavian states to begin to unravel their elitist parallel systems of elementary and secondary education for different groups.

The Scandinavian states had three distinct advantages. Firstly, when state systems of education first developed it was within political systems which had already evolved substantial elements of popular democracy due to long-standing historical traditions (Boli, 1989). Secondly, their class systems were distinctively favourable to populist politics since they combined relatively weak landowner and bourgeois classes with a strong class of independent peasant farmers who were able to form alliances with the smaller nascent working-classes of the industrial areas (Isling, 1984; Esping-Andersen, 1985). Thirdly, populations in these largely agrarian societies were relatively dispersed which provided pragmatic arguments for common schooling.

The combination of these factors allowed the early evolution of consolidated single education ladders in Denmark, Norway and Sweden. The relative numerical weakness and hence political weakness of the landowner and bourgeois classes meant that social representation in the traditional Latin school was rather less skewed towards the higher classes than in many other countries, thus making it easier to combine these schools with the primary schools. In addition, the relative political weakness of the upper classes in the lobbies for the Latin schools meant that it was much harder for them to defend their elite status than it was in other countries. The strong independent peasant interests were thus the major force in propelling the liberal parties in the latter decades of the nineteenth century progressively to transfer the lower secondary classes from the elite Latin schools to new middle schools which then provided a single educational ladder from the primary schools through to the upper secondary schools. This happened first in Norway (1869) and somewhat later in Denmark (1903) and Sweden (1905) which, unlike Norway, had bicameral parliaments which allowed the landowner interests to block reforms in the upper house for some time.

The second major wave of refom occurred under social democratic governments in all these countries and dates largely from after World War II. As Esping-Andersen (1985) argues, the social democratic parties have been exceptionally influential in the Nordic states since the 1930s. This was due partly to their powerful organizational apparatuses and partly to their ability to weld political alliances between the industrial working-class, the small farmers and sections of the middle classes. It has been these social democratic parties, often in coalition with liberal allies, which have pushed through the particularly radical comprehensivization of school systems during the middle decades of the twentieth century. Norway abolished its middle schools in 1936, progressively integrating them with the primary schools to create a nine year all-through comprehensive school by 1969. Denmark abolished its middle schools in 1958 and by 1975 had completed its own nine year comprehensive school. Sweden introduced its nine year comprehensive system in 1962, after extensive trials during the 1950s, and then after 1969 started to integrate its high schools as well. All three countries progressively eliminated streaming and setting in all subjects so that the comprehensive schools are now almost entirely mixed ability.

The Nordic model of compulsory schooling shares with the East Asian model the key equality-favouring characteristics of mixed ability comprehensive schools, but it has, in addition, the integration of primary and lower secondary education into one school. This may make it even more favourable to reducing equality in that it eliminates school choice at lower secondary phase entry except in the unusual cases of school switchers. Moreover, unlike the East Asian model, it also has an almost all-encompassing state sector so that this model applies almost universally throughout compulsory schooling. The Scandinavian states, and the Nordic states more generally (the non-Scandinavian Nordic states having similar structural characteristics to the others, although we have not shown this here) have adapted a peculiarly radical form of comprehensive schooling which may go some way to explaining why they have relatively equal outcomes in the IALS and PISA studies.

THE LESS EGALITARIAN SYSTEMS

The less egalitarian systems, according to our outcomes data, include the countries in German speaking regions, some of the Anglophone countries and the Mediterranean states. How can we explain their relative low performance in inequality reduction?

The Model in the Germanic region
The 'Germanic' model is perhaps the best place to start, since the countries included in this set all share very similar institutional structures in their education systems and since they are notably similar in their rather high levels of educational inequality among 15-year-olds.

Austria, Belgium, Germany, Luxembourg, Switzerland (and, arguably, the Netherlands) are the only states in Europe to retain selective secondary school systems and these are based largely on the German model where children are tracked at the age of 11 or 12 into different types of school for different ability levels. Parents do have a choice, officially, as to where children go during the end-of-primary level orientation phase, but children will be re-allocated to other schools over time if their performance does not conform to the academic standard of the school chosen, so the system is effectively allocating by ability to different school types. In Germany the proportions in each type of school changes over time, but in the late 1980s in the FRG 25 per cent of 14-year-olds were in lower-level *Hauptschule* (taking grades 5–9/10) as against 55 per cent in the academic or more vocationally oriented higher schools, the *Gynmasien* (grades 5–13) and the *Realschulen* (grades 5–10 or 7–10) (Leschinsky and Mayer, 1999, p. 24). There are also some nominally comprehensive schools coexisting with the selective system in some Länder, but only 9 per cent of children in the 7th grade in the unified FRG were in these schools in 1997/8. The new

Länder have dumped the old GDR comprehensive model (with the comprehensive *Polytechnische Oberschule*) and adopted the FRG's traditional selective system, although in some cases rolling up the *Hauptschule* and *Realschule* into a single institution (in Saxony, Thuringia, Saxony Anhalt). Germany thus retains a selective system in all states, except, arguably, in Berlin, where the comprehensive *Gesamtschulen* do now predominate. The other states named above have similar systems.

Why Germany, and these other geographically and culturally proximate states, alone in all of Europe, retained a selective system, and despite various attempts to reform it in Germany in the 1970s, has continued to be something of a mystery to educational research. It is certainly the case that most of the countries concerned are constrained in their reform efforts by being federal systems, that is to say where the individual regions substantially control school education and find it difficult to agree state-wide reform. However, regional control is much weaker in the states outside Germany and this does not seem to provide a satisfactory answer. Comparative logic would suggest that the reasons will lie in the examination of those distinctive societal characteristics which these countries have in common.

Germany, Austria, Belgium, Switzerland and the Netherlands all retain strong apprenticeship systems as well as selective school systems. It seems likely that these distinctive facts are connected and that the reasons for the two overlap. Apprentice systems have traditionally provided acceptable progression routes and employment opportunities for graduates of the least favoured schools, the *Hauptschulen*, in ways that post-school provision in countries without strong apprenticeship systems have generally not (Green, Wolf and Leney, 1999). This may well explain why the pressure for eliminating the low status schools, not least from among middle-class parents whose children were consigned to them, has not reached the levels in these countries it did in other countries where governments were forced to concede that selection by ability at the end of primary schooling was socially unacceptable. We therefore need to identify what common conditions in these states have led to the retention both of selective schools and strong apprentice systems.

Various factors have no doubt contributed. Firstly, most of the countries which still practise selection have been influenced by German language and culture, not least the traditions of cultural particularism and differentiation associated with ethno-cultural German models of citizenship (Brubaker, 1992; McLean, 1990). This encourages differentiated forms of schooling. However, at the same time, the neo-corporatist states like Austria, Germany and Switzerland have retained strong craft traditions, have high levels of unionization, and manifestly robust traditions of social partnership which have enabled the extension of the privileged status of skilled workers widely thoughout the workforce, thus underpinning notions of 'equality of productive capacity' (Streeck, 1997) and working in favour of income equalization. This relative professional egalitarianism of the skilled has served to legitimate a school system which differentiates young people into different tracks leading, usually, to different occupational destinations, but where each track retains its own identity, status and social value (OSA, 1994; Streeck, 1987; Brown, 1997). In other countries, with more universalist cultural traditions, and with weaker craft traditions and weaker occupational identities for manual and junior white collar workers, such legitimacy for selective organization has not been sustainable, and comprehensive reforms have followed.

The survival of strong apprenticeship systems also depends on more specific characteristics of labour market organization and regulation associated with social partnership. Germany, and to a lesser extent the other countries, have strong occupational labour markets and a degree of labour market co-ordination which allows companies to provide apprentice training without excessive cost, still allowing mobility between firms (Marsden and Ryan, 1995). Sectoral agreements on pay in skilled jobs reduce the danger of poaching and, therefore, increase the incentive for employers to invest in training (CEDEFOP, 1987; Brown, Green and Lauder, 2001).[3] Social partnership in labour market relationships, within a strong framework of central government regulation, have thus proven indispensable to the survival of strong apprenticeship systems and no countries without these have retained them, although many, like the UK, have tried.

These shared regional characteristics in the German-speaking area no doubt provide a large part of the explanation for the survival of the selective secondary systems and the apprenticeships systems with which they articulate. The selective education systems must surely contribute substantially to the high levels of variations in outcomes among 15-year-old children observed in the PISA study. However, paradoxically, the apprenticeship system, which may be seen to legitimate the school system producing this inequality, probably also contributes to a mitigation of its effects in later life. Germany is both one of the most unequal in its outcomes at 15 years, according to PISA, and one of the most equal in adult skills, according to IALS. The early universalization of upper secondary education through the apprenticeship system may have an effect here in reducing inter-cohort differences. However, it is also likely that the further three to four years of education that lower-achieving young people from the *Hauptschulen* receive within the dual system, espcially in compulsory Maths and German lessons in the *Berufsschule*, substantially improve their basic skills so that the skills gaps between German adults are not as great as they would otherwise have been.

The Mediterranean states
Despite their widely shared Napoleonic legacies of centralized control and curricular encyclopedism (McLean, 1990), the educational systems in France and the Mediterranean states are clearly too various to be considered as a single model. It should not surprise therefore that their outcomes on the PISA inequality measures are fairly diverse. However, for the most part they do seem to occupy intermediate positions which may relate to certain common school system features.

The Mediterranean states have all adopted comprehensive lower secondary school systems during the past forty years, although some, like Greece and Spain, only relatively recently, and they all have institutionally differentiated upper secondary systems. In the lower secondary schools these countries are distinguished by their use of grade repeating, whereby students falling too far behind the average level for their class are obliged to stay down and repeat a year. This is generally defended on the grounds that, unlike streaming, it reinforces the same norms for all students, allowing lower achievers more time to meet the standards set for all. Whether it has this – potentially equalizing – effect on outcomes or, alternatively, simply labels children and reinforces failure, is hotly debated. However, it is also the case that most Mediterranean states have retained some forms of setting in core subject areas.

In France, for instance, streaming has been progressively eliminated officially since the 1978 Haby reforms. However, school heads still have sufficient latitude to organize some classes according to ability and research indicates that some 40 per cent of schools do this in order to make classes more homogeneous and easier to teach. Research by Duru-Bellat and Mingat (1999) suggests that the gain to lower achieving pupils from learning in mixed ability classes in France is stronger than the loss to the more able pupils. Although they may have relatively little to lose from mixed classes, it is the middle-class parents who are more likely to push for ability grouping. In addition to the continuation of setting, France, and some of the other southern European states, have also experienced the introduction of some moderate school choice policies. In France, these are carefully controlled so that the area committees which review school choices made by parents are bound to reject these choices where they would detract from the overall provision of schooling, as where exit from a particular school is damaging its quality (OECD, 1994; Green, Wolf and Leney, 1999). However, research by Trancart (1993, cited by Duru-Bellat and Mingat, 1999, p. 99) does suggest that even this limited introduction of school choice has already widened disparities between schools in terms of intakes and average achievement levels.

The Mediterranean states do not have a single model of comprehensive schooling and one would not expect them to perform as a group in terms of level of equality of outcomes. However, as comprehensive systems with substantial elements of internal differentiation – through grade repeating and setting – one would expect them to achieve only middling levels of equality, and considerably less than the levels achieved in the East Asian and

Nordic systems and this is in fact where most of them fall in terms of the PISA data.

The English-speaking systems
The systems in the English-speaking countries are again too diverse to classify into a single model, even in the most general terms. However, there are clear similarities in the systems of those states which have the more unequal outcomes – that is to say of the USA, the UK, New Zealand. These countries all have nominally comprehensive school systems, but comprehensivization has been radically incomplete in certain ways and it is now being substantially undermined by streaming, setting and school choice and diversification policies (Whitty, Power and Halpin, 1998). Equality within comprehensive schooling in the USA was always substantially undermined by the continued existence of a large private school sector and by the huge disparities between states and even education districts in curricula, school structures and levels of school finance (Carnoy, 1993; Winkler, 1993). Not only has there never been a national comprehensive curriculum in the USA, there has never been a national structure of comprehensive schools either.

The same can be said of the UK, which now has four different education systems in its constituent countries. Even in England and Wales there was never a single national model of comprehensive schooling. Circular 10/65 had requested LEAs to develop comprehensive systems but, according to the typically voluntaristic mode of educational legislation prior to 1988, they were free to choose different models and they did so, with the majority opting for a combination of 11–16 and 11–18 comprehensive schools. This left a major inequality between schools containing sixth forms and those without, as the sixth form became the main signifier of superior quality. Additional differentiation occurred in those areas which kept some of their grammar schools. Arguably, Britain did not complete its comprehensive reforms until 1988 when there appeared the first national curriculum and when the single lower secondary exam, GCSE, was beginning to be operationalized. However, by that time in the UK, as in the USA, a new movement towards introducing market competition into the school systems was about to undercut the comprehensive nature of the school system in new ways.

School diversification and school choice policies in New Zealand, the UK and the USA have now substantially undermined the comprehensive principle of non-selection. Many comprehensive schools in these countries now legally or illicitly select their intakes and national policies actively encourage greater differentiation between schools. On one estimate only 40 per cent of children in England and Wales go to genuinely non-selective schools. New Zealand's schools have gone in the same direction (Lauder *et al.*, 1999). Given their incomplete original comprehensivization, and the subsequent undermining of comprehensive education through the introduction of quasi-markets in education, it is therefore not surprising that the education systems in these countries, despite being nominally comprehensive, show high levels of inequality in outcomes in the PISA study, and also wide distribution of skills among adults in the IALS study.

CONCLUSIONS

We have not sought to conduct rigorous statistical tests here on which factors are most responsible for equalizing educational opportunities across the countries, although this might well be done. However, comparative logic would suggest that where there are relevant common characteristics shared by the country systems which demonstrate egalitarian outcomes and which are absent in those systems which do not, we may be able to identify the key mechanisms. The problem with this approach, as always, is that there may be many characteristics which are present in the 'positive' cases and absent in the 'negative' cases, including some which we have not observed (Ragin, 1981). However, in the analysis above we can see a number of contenders.

It might plausibly be argued that it is economic equality (low income differentials) which provides the best explanatory variable. Certainly, the countries in the sample above with higher levels of educational equality are also countries with lower levels of income inequality (as standard gini measures of inequality show – see Green, Preston and Sabates, 2003), and this may provide part of the explanation for greater educational equality. However, the correlation does not invariably hold. Germany, for instance, is one of the most income equal countries in Europe (Perkin, 1996) but is not so equal educationally. If we concede that there is a connection in most cases – and research has repeatedly shown that income distribution and skills distribution are highly correlated across countries (Nickell and Layard, 1998; Green, Preston and Sabates, 2003b) – then this does not rule out an education effect since income effects are likely, in part at least, to be working through education structures. Countries with very unequal incomes are likely to generate divided education systems as those with more purchasing power lobby for the opportunity to buy better schooling, as with private schools or school choice.

In a similar vein we might argue that it is countries with high levels of social cohesion which are more likely to generate educational equality. Since social solidarity is a central motif of social democratic government, particularly in Scandinavia, this argument fits well with the outcomes in the Nordic cases. It might also be said to fit well in Japan whose cultural traditions place a high premium on the group or collectivity, the *iemoto* (family-like) grouping being a basic organizational principle (Perkin, 1996). However, the argument fits a lot less well in cases like South Korea, which has only recently matured into a democratic system and which has had years of rather intense class conflict since de-colonization. Again, if social cohesion and social solidarity is an explanatory factor in some of the cases it no doubt works through education. Research, again, shows a high correlation across countries between aggregate levels of social cohesion (measured by a combined factor for crime, trust and civil cooperation) and levels of educational equality (Green, Preston and Sabates, 2003b). It is very likely that solidaristic ideologies are a necessary precondition for achieving egalitarian educational reforms.

In terms of education system factors, what the more equal countries have in common, which is absent in the less equal countries, are the structures and processes typically associated with radical versions of comprehensive education: non-selective schools, mixed ability classes, late subject specialization and measures to equalize resources between schools. That these features should work towards lowering educational inequality should be no mystery. The great French sociologist Raymond Boudon gave the most cogent explanation of this some thirty years ago in his famous 'positional theory' of social reproduction in schooling (Boudon, 1974).

Inequalities in educational achievement by different social groups arise partly because of the unequal learning advantages given to children from different social backgrounds. This is the standard argument of Bourdieu and cultural capital theory. Children from families with higher levels of education and more cultural capital have acquired more of the cultural 'habitus' and language codes required in the school system to get on. They are likely to have more confidence and higher aspirations and have the assistance of their parents in knowing how to navigate the system. However, school structures also make a difference.

Children from less affluent families not only tend to have less of the advantages from their families that make it easier for them to achieve, they are also more likely to make educational choices that will make achieving less likely. Where they are positioned in the social structure affects the logic of their choices (both rational and otherwise) and they are more likely to make less academically aspiring choices than middle-class childen of similar ability. Middle-class children may have more to lose in pursuing non-academic routes which are likely to lead to downward mobility than working-class children for whom choosing a non-academic route will very likely lead to social class maintenance. Regardless of cognitive ability, children from less well endowed backgrounds will perceive greater positional risks in choosing long academic routes not only because of fear of failing, but also from concern that success may entail costs. These may include deferring earning and building debt and, also, ultimately, the emotional strains of cultural dislocation as academic success brings mobility from their class of origin. Duru-Bellat and Mingat's analysis of streaming at the end of lower secondary in 1990 in France, for instance, well illustrates how this works. Looking at transition to different types of lycée they show that while 25 per cent of the social class differences in transitions to high or low streams could be attributed to ability, a further 25 per cent derived from the choices made by parents and their childen which are unrelated to achievement (Duru-Bellat and Mingat, 1999).

Education systems are not neutral in terms of these social class effects arising from positional choices. As Boudon (1974) rightly argues, systems which provide more and earlier 'branching points' provide more opportunity for social class differences to assert themselves through the early educational career choices made by students which will affect their later achievement. The East Asian and Nordic countries in this study which demonstrate lower levels of inequality have systems which minimize all the significant branching points. They limit choice between schools (the Nordics having no choices at all at lower secondary phase entry, except for school switchers), minimize the difference between classes and have no separate tracks at all before the end of compulsory schooling. Less branching, less inequality.

Limiting choice in education is clearly not a very fashionable position in this day and age. However, the research still seems to suggest that it is the most effective way of reducing inequality. PISA has provided the most powerful evidence of this to date. As the surveys are repeated over the years, allowing more rigorous testing over time, they may well lead to a major scholarly reassessment of the impact of comprehensivization on educational inequality, giving more credence to the claims of its advocates. If research does finally return this verdict it would be highly ironic at a time when comprehensive systems are being systematically dismantled in many countries. But it would hardly be the first time that such wisdom comes only with hindsight. As Hegel once said: The Owl of Minerva only flies at dusk.

NOTES

1   The evidence from the recent Third International Maths and Science Study (TIMSS) is less clear-cut but awaits full analysis.

2   Head teachers tend to be moved around every three to five years: interview at National Institute for Education Research, Tokyo.

3   Ryan also argues that larger German firms offer better prospects of promotion for skilled workers than UK firms, although this may now be changing (see Brown, 1997).

Postscript: An Obituary of
Caroline Benn*

Brian Simon

I first met Caroline at a small party for London teachers and others.
We found ourselves sitting together talking animatedly about the
move to comprehensive education. I had no idea who she was, but
discovered shortly after. This must have been in 1964/5. But I was
already deeply struck by her knowledge of the situation and her
close involvement.

Caroline was the driving force behind the Comprehensive Schools
Committee, set up at that time. Assuming the modest office of
'Information Officer', she set about monitoring closely every aspect
of the movement. Under her guidance CSC quickly became a very
effective pressure group. Indeed there is no doubt that Caroline
knew a great deal more about what was happening on the ground
(which was crucial) than anyone else, the DES included.

When the publishers McGraw Hill asked me for a book on the
entire movement, having checked with Caroline, I agreed provided
they would accept a joint production. This they did. So *Half-way
There* ('Report on the British Comprehensive Reform') was born.

Caroline was a superb collaborator. She put everything into our
work, largely designing the crucial questionnaire, tracking all
recent developments, keeping in close touch with key schools,
teachers and local authority officials. Further, she bore the brunt of

* We are proud to publish as a postscript to this book an obituary of Caroline written by the late
Brian Simon at the beginning of 2001 and which appeared in the *2001 Hungarian Yearbook –
International Labour Movement* and (in a shortened version) in *Forum*, Volume 43, Number 1,
Spring 2001.

the writing and data analysis – of the 21 chapters she wrote 12, myself 7, while 2 were joint productions. For the second (Penguin) edition (1972) which greatly extended the first (things were happening so quickly), Caroline wrote a new chapter (on developments in 1970/71) and two follow-up sample surveys were carried through (on grouping procedures and sixth form size and growth). Though most of the book was written by one or other, we were able to confirm in the Preface that we were both 'in full agreement on all opinions expressed and all recommendations made throughout the book'. The two editions sold some 20,000 copies. A remarkable response rate of over 80 per cent to our main questionnaire was achieved. The book presented a dynamic analysis of every aspect of the comprehensive school movement at that point in time. It was well received and very widely reviewed in both the national and local press.

After publication of the second edition in 1972, Caroline devoted herself to strengthening the transition to comprehensive education which, in spite of Margaret Thatcher's work as Secretary of State for Education (1970/74), took off now with extraordinary rapidity, fuelled by what had become a popular mass movement from below. Intelligence as to what was happening was crucial. To provide this effectively, annual surveys were published by CSC together with other publications on the topic. Annual conferences were run by CSC in collaboration with the educational journal *Forum*. As fiscal and political crises hit education in the early mid-seventies, strong bastions of support for comprehensive education were constructed throughout the country.

It was an astonishing achievement, on Caroline's part, to repeat the whole project thirty years later with Clyde Chitty, who had helped with the original book. *Thirty Years On* stands as a massive, and worthy, memorial to Caroline's indispensable role in the crucially important move to comprehensive secondary education from the 1960s on, involving a seismic change in the whole structure of education. Those who oppose that move today display only a surprising (or is it a considered?) ignorance of its true significance.

Caroline was also so cheerful and optimistic, being driven by a real faith in comprehensive education as *the* means of realizing human potential. While working on *Half-way There* she was nurturing her own family of four, caring for an exceptionally busy husband and running her house with informal affection and a warm hospitality for all. Completed chapters would appear from nowhere – if sometimes a little illegible, each was a completed scholarly study. She was absolutely remarkable, and above all such fun to be with. I was very privileged to work so closely with her over the four years or so that it took to produce the two editions of *Half-way There* and later, when she continued to contribute her lively articles for *Forum*.

I have a file of perhaps a hundred letters received from Caroline, dating from September 1972 just as the Penguin edition of our book was published, to one written with difficulty just a week before she died on 22 November 2000, aged 74. These, often hurriedly written, refer to her many activities over the last three decades of the century. During this period, apart from producing *Thirty Years On*, Caroline taught regularly at a college of further education in London – mostly adults. It would be good to know more of this activity which was also focused on developing a comprehensive policy for post-16 education, an area that still greatly needs transformation. She also acted for many years as a governor of her local inner-city comprehensive which was by no means an elite school (as hostile critics asserted), and one which had plenty of problems to contend with. Caroline remained supremely loyal to this School, serving as Chair of the Governors for many years – a very responsible and time-consuming position; in this case, a labour of love. Other concerns during this period were with developing an effective and workable policy for bringing independent schools within an integrated state system of education – crucial if the country was ever to develop a truly national system, but still (2001) evaded by Labour (and of course Tory) governments, and a penetrating and detailed analysis of so-called 'Gifted and Talented' students and how they should be catered for within comprehensive schools.

In the 1980s Caroline, who was very knowledgeable about the history of the Labour Movement in Britain, turned her attention, again with her abundant energy, to writing a biography of Keir

Hardie, the accepted 'founder' of the Labour Party. The result was a major study, and recognised as such by Labour historians, of Hardie's many dramatic activities through the 1880s and 90s to his death in 1915. To this study Caroline brought her own experience as wife of a leading Labour politician to throw light on Hardie's family relations, his relations with his wife and other women and the problems he and his family faced on account of his active work for the cause of Socialism. This was published in 1992. The book is certainly a *tour de force* and will remain the authoritative study for very many years. How Caroline managed so many diverse activities at the same time must be something of a mystery. The partial answer is tenacity and passion.

Caroline Benn was elected President of the Socialist Education Association a few years ago. Her attendance, in a wheelchair, at the Association's last annual conference in the summer of 2000 was reported. An extremely popular President, everybody knew by that time that she was suffering from cancer and probably had not long to live. Nevertheless she maintained her activity and the sharpness of her analysis. In November 2000 I wrote her a letter telling her of a highly critical article I had written for *Forum* on Tony Blair's educational policy, particularly the plan for a two-tier 'comprehensive' system embodying specialist schools. Her response was immediate and characteristic, in a letter written just a week before she died. This was sharply critical of New Labour's policies, typically coming straight to the point. In her words, talk about 'modernization' and 'reform' conceals what Blair really wants to say: 'abolition'. All this is very difficult to accept. But Labour's MPs and others are still dedicated to the comprehensive principle, though there is a point beyond which they will not go, as Blair knows. Caroline looked forward to seeing the article: 'I may not be able to move a single muscle below the waist but I can still move the arms to pick up a book.'

On Tuesday 6 March 2001 a Memorial Service was held for Caroline at St Margaret's Church, Westminster (the parliamentary church). The Church was packed, mostly by London educators – teachers, administrators, academics and others. There was music and hymns and four short addresses by Stephen and Melissa, two of

Caroline and Tony's children, by Tony himself and by her close friend and collaborator over many years, Clyde Chitty, joint author of *Thirty Years On*. Clyde appropriately quoted Roy Hattersley, 'if Labour had taken Caroline's advice our secondary schools would be a great deal better than they are today'. Yet her influence *was* enormous, Clyde insisted, and although comprehensive education has lost one of its greatest champions, the values she lived for will never die. There are very many who will agree with Clyde's diagnosis and fight to transform these values into reality.

References

INTRODUCTION

Benn, C. (1992) *Keir Hardie*, London: Hutchinson.

Benn, C. and Chitty, C. (1996) *Thirty Years On: Is Comprehensive Education Alive and Well or Struggling to Survive?*, 1st edn, London: David Fulton; (1997) 2nd edn, Harmondsworth: Penguin Books.

Benn, C. and Simon, B. (1970) *Half Way There: Report on the British Comprehensive School Reform*, 1st edn, London: McGraw-Hill; (1972) 2nd edn, Harmondsworth: Penguin.

Brighouse, T. (2003) 'Comprehensive schools then, now and in the future: is it time to draw a line in the sand and create a new ideal?', *Forum*, Vol. 45, No. 1, Spring, pp. 3–11.

DfES (Department for Education and Skills) (2004) *Five Year Strategy for Children and Learners*, Cmnd 6272, London: HMSO.

Newsam, P. (2003) 'Diversity and admissions to English secondary schools', *Forum*, Vol. 45, No. 1, Spring, pp. 17–18.

ON DREAMS AND DILEMMAS, CLASS AND CITIES

Brighouse, T. (2003) 'Comprehensive schools then, now and in the future: is it time to draw a line in the sand and create a new ideal?', *Forum*, Vol. 45, No. 1, Spring, pp. 3–11.

Sennett, R. (1970) *The Uses of Disorder: Personal Identity and City Life*, New York and London: W.W. Norton.

IN PRAISE OF SIXTIES IDEALISM

Benn, C. (2001) 'A credible alternative: some tasks for the future', *Education and Social Justice*, Vol. 3, No. 2, Spring, pp. 2–5.

Maclure, S. (1970) *One Hundred Years of London Education, 1870–1970*, London: Allen Lane, The Penguin Press.

COMPREHENSIVE SUCCESS

Aaronovitch, D. (2003) 'The real class issue', *Observer*, 12 October.

Adonis, A. and Pollard, S. (1997) *A Class Act: The Myth of Britain's Classless Society*, London: Hamish Hamilton.

Ball, S. J. (2003) *Class Strategies and the Education Market*, London: Routledge.

Benn, T. (1994) *Years of Hope: Diaries, Papers and Letters, 1940–1962*, London: Hutchinson.

Benn, C. and Chitty, C. (1996) *Thirty Years On: Is Comprehensive Education Alive and Well or Struggling to Survive?*, London: David Fulton.

Blair, T. (1998) 'Forging an inclusive society', *The Times Educational Supplement*, 11 September.

Blair, T. (1999) Speech to the Labour Party Conference, Bournemouth, October.

Bradley, J. and Taylor, J. (2002) *The Report Card on Competition in Schools*, London: Adam Smith Institute.

DfEE (Department for Education and Employment) (1999) *Excellence in Cities*, London: HMSO.

DfEE (Department for Education and Employment) (2001) *Schools: Building on Success: Raising Standards, Promoting Diversity, Achieving Results*, Cmnd 5050, London: HMSO.

DfES (Department for Education and Skills) (2003) *A New Specialist System: Transforming Secondary Education*, London: HMSO.

Gallagher, T. and Smith, S. (2002) 'The effects of selective education in Northern Ireland', *Education Review*, Vol. 15, pp. 74–81.

Garrett, A. (2002) 'Top dollar to be top of the class', *The Observer*, 21 September.

Gillborn, D. and Youdell, D. (2000) *Rationing Education: Policy, Practice, Reform and Equity*, Buckingham: Open University Press.

Goldthorpe, A. (1997) 'Problems of meritocracy', in Halsey, A. H., Lauder, H., Brown, P. and Wells, A. S. (eds) *Education, Culture, Economy and Society*, Oxford: Oxford University Press.

Hattersley, R. (2004) 'Wrong division', *Education Guardian*, 3 February.

Jesson, D. (2001) 'Selective systems of education: blueprint for lower standards?', *Education Review*, Vol. 15, pp. 8–14.

Jesson, D., Taylor, C. and Ware, J. (2003) *Educational Outcomes and Value-Added by Specialist Schools*, London: the Specialist School Trust.

Miliband, D. (2003) 'Class haunts the classroom', *The Guardian*, 18 September.

Ministry of Education (1963) *Higher Education: A Report of the Committee Appointed by the Prime Minister under the Chairmanship of Lord Robbins, 1961–63*, Cmnd 2154, London: HMSO.

OECD (2002) Programme for International Student Assessment (the PISA Study), Paris: Organisation for Economic Co-Operation and Development.

Ong, A. (2003) 'Higher learning: educational availability and flexible citizenship in a global space', in Banks, J. A. (ed.) *Diversity and Citizenship Education*, San Francisco: Jossey-Bass.

Pollard, S. (2001) 'Selection is back', *Education Guardian*, 5 September.

Pring, R. and Walford, G. (eds) (1997) *Affirming the Comprehensive Ideal*, London: Falmer Press.

Reay, D. (1998) *Class Work*, London: UCL Press.

Reiffers Report (1996) *Accomplishing Europe Through Education and Training*, Brussels: European Commission.

Schagen, I. and Schagen, S. (2003) 'Analysis of national value-added data sets to assess the impact of selection on pupil performance', *British Educational Research Journal*, Vol. 29, pp. 561–82.

Smith, D. J. and Tomlinson, S. (1989) *The School Effect: A Study of Multiracial Comprehensives*, London: Policy Studies Institute.

Tomlinson, S. (1997) 'Sociological perspectives on failing schools', *International Studies in the Sociology of Education*, Vol. 7, pp. 81–98.

West, A. and Hinds, A. (2003) *Secondary Schools Admissions in England: Exploring the Extent of Overt and Covert Selection*, Research and Information on State Education, London School of Economics.

Young, M. (1958) *The Rise of the Meritocracy 1870–2033*, Hermondsworth: Penguin.

Young, M. (2001) 'Down with the meritocracy', *The Guardian*, 29 June.

EUGENIC THEORIES AND CONCEPTS OF ABILITY

Benn, C. (1982a) 'The myth of giftedness (part 1)', *Forum*, Vol. 24, No. 2, Spring, pp. 50–53.

Benn, C. (1982b) 'The myth of giftedness (part 2)', *Forum*, Vol. 24, No. 3, Summer, pp. 78–84.

Blishen, E. (1969) *This Right Soft Lot*, London: Thames and Hudson.

Brown, I. (1988) 'Who were the Eugenicists? A study of the formation of an early twentieth-century pressure group', *History of Education*, Vol. 17, No. 4, pp. 295–307.

Burt, C. (1909) 'Experimental tests of general intelligence', *British Journal of Psychology*, Vol. 3, pp. 94–177.

Burt, C. (ed.) (1933) *How the Mind Works*, London: Allen and Unwin.

Burt, C. (1950) 'Testing intelligence', *The Listener*, 16 November.

Burt, C. (1969) 'The mental differences between children', in Cox, C. B. and Dyson, A. E. (eds) *Black Paper Two: The Crisis in Education*, London: Critical Quarterly Society, pp. 16–25.

Carey, J. (1992) *The Intellectuals and the Masses: Pride and Prejudice among the Literary Intelligentsia, 1880–1939*, London: Faber and Faber.

Denham, A. and Garnett, M. (2001) *Keith Joseph*, Chesham: Acumen Publishing.

Galton, F. (1869) *Hereditary Genius*, London: Macmillan.

Galton, F. (1883) *Inquiries into Human Faculty*, London: Dent.

Gardner, H. (1983) *Frames of Mind*, London: Heinemann.

Hearnshaw, L. (1979) *Cyril Burt – Psychologist*, London: Hodder and Stoughton.

Heim, A. (1954) *The Appraisal of Intelligence*, London: Methuen.

Herrnstein, R. J. and Murray, C. (1994) *The Bell Curve: Intelligence and Class Structure in American Life*, New York: Free Press Paperbacks.

Hobsbawm, E. (1975) *The Age of Capital, 1848–1875*, London: Weidenfeld and Nicolson.

Jensen, A. R. (1969) 'How much can we boost IQ and scholastic achievement?', *Harvard Educational Review*, Vol. 39, No. 1, pp. 1–123.

Kamin, L. J. (1974) *The Science and Politics of IQ*, New York: John Wiley and Sons.

King, D. (1999) *In the Name of Liberalism: Illiberal Social Policy in the United States and Britain*, Oxford: Oxford University Press.

Lawler, J. M. (1978) *IQ, Heritability and Racism: A Marxist Critique of Jensenism*, London: Lawrence and Wishart.

Lowe, R. (1980) 'Eugenics and education: a note on the origins of the intelligence testing movement in England', *Educational Studies*, Vol. 6, No. 1, pp. 1–8.

Ministry of Education (1963) *Half Our Future* (The Newsom Report), London: HMSO.

Nietzsche, F. (1883–5) *Also Sprach Zarathustra*, translated and with an introduction by R. J. Hollingdale (1961), Harmondsworth: Penguin Books.

Norton, B. (1981) 'Psychologists and class', in Webster, C. (ed.) *Biology, Medicine and Society, 1840–1940*, Cambridge: Cambridge University Press, pp. 289–314.

Pedley, R. (1963) *The Comprehensive School*, Harmondsworth: Penguin Books.

Simon, B. (1953) *Intelligence Testing and the Comprehensive School*, London: Lawrence and Wishart.

Simon, B. (1955) *The Common Secondary School*, London: Lawrence and Wishart.

Simon, B. (1971) *Intelligence, Psychology and Education: A Marxist Critique*, London: Lawrence and Wishart.

Simon, B. (1974) *The Politics of Educational Reform, 1920–1940*, London: Lawrence and Wishart.

White, J. (1998) *Do Howard Gardner's Multiple Intelligences Add Up?*, Perspectives on Education Policy No. 3, London: Institute of Education, University of London.

Wooldridge, A. (1994) *Measuring the Mind: Education and Psychology in England, c.1860–1990*, Cambridge: Cambridge University Press.

Yeats, W. B. (1939) *On the Boiler*, republished in Larrissy, B. (1997) *W. B. Yeats: A Critical Edition of the Major Works*, Oxford: Oxford University Press, pp. 389–96.

DEVELOPING COMPREHENSIVE EDUCATION IN A NEW CLIMATE

BBC News Online (2004) 'Specialist schools now a majority', 29 January.

Benn, C. and Chitty, C. (1996) *Thirty Years On: Is Comprehensive Education Alive and Well or Struggling to Survive?*, 1st edn, London: David Fulton.

Brighouse, T. (2003) 'Comprehensive schools then, now and in the future – is it time to draw a line in the sand and create a new ideal?' *Forum*, Vol. 45, No. 1, Spring, pp. 3–11.

Crook, D., Power, S. and Whitty, G. (1999) *The Grammar School Question*, University of London, Institute of Education.

Daunt, P. E. (1975) *Comprehensive Values*, London: Heinemann.

[DfES] (Department for Education and Skills) (2001) *Schools: Achieving Success*, Cmnd 5230 London: HMSO.

[DfES] (Department for Education and Skills) (2004) 'Over 50% of secondary schools now part of the specialist network – Miliband', DfES press release, 29 January.

Edwards, T. and Tomlinson, S. (2002) *Selection Isn't Working*, London: The Catalyst Forum.

Edwards, T. *et al.* (1989) *The State and Private Education: An Evaluation of the Assisted Places Scheme*, Basingstoke: Falmer Press.

Gewirtz, S., Ball, S. J. and Bowe, R. (1995) *Markets, Choice and Equity in Education*, Buckingham: Open University Press.

254 REFERENCES

Giddens, A. (1998) *The Third Way: The Renewal of Social Democracy*, Cambridge: Polity Press.

Goldstein, H. (2004) 'Value added – a commentary on the KS1-KS2, KS2-KS3 league tables December 2003 and KS3-KS4 January 2004', mimeo, University of London, Institute of Education.

Gorard, S. and Taylor, C. (2001) *Specialist Schools in England: Track Record and Future Prospects*, Occasional Paper 44, School of Social Sciences, Cardiff University.

Hargreaves, D. (1982) *The Challenge for the Comprehensive School*, London: Routledge.

Hutton, W. (1996) *The State We're In*, London: Vintage Books.

Hutton, W. (2001) 'Cohesive future depends on comprehensives', *Times Educational Supplement*, 16 February.

Hutton, W. (2004) 'Comprehensively great', *The Observer*, 18 January.

Imison, T. (1999) 'A new way to be divisive?', *The Times Educational Supplement*, 1 January.

Jackson, B. (1976) 'Sniped at now from all sides', *The Times Educational Supplement*, 3 December.

Jesson, D. (2000) 'The comparative evaluation of GCSE value-added performance by type of school and LEA', mimeo, York, University of York.

Jesson, D. and Taylor, C. (2001) *Educational Outcomes and Value Added Analysis of Specialist Schools for the Year 2000*, London: Technology Colleges Trust.

Kerckhoff, A., Fogelman, K., Crook, D. and Reeder, D. (1996) *Going Comprehensive in England and Wales*, London: Woburn Press.

Maden, M. (ed.) (2002) *Success Against the Odds Five Years On*, London: RoutledgeFalmer.

Mansell, W. and Wright, G. (2004) 'A comprehensive win', *The Times Educational Supplement*, 16 January.

Morris, E. (2001) 'We need your help to make a difference', *Education Review*, Vol. 15, No. 1, p. 4.

Newsam, P. (2003) 'Diversity and admissions to English secondary schools', *Forum*, Vol. 45, No. 1, Spring, pp. 17–18.

O'Leary, J. (1997) 'Private schools boost bright pupils' chances', *The Times*, 22 September.

Penlington, G. (2001) 'Specialist spin that works', *The Times Educational Supplement*, 10 August.

Power, S., Edwards, T., Whitty, G. and Wigfall, V. (2003) *Education and the Middle Class*, Maidenhead: Open Books.

Riddell, R. (2003) *Schools for our Cities: Urban Learning in the 21st Century*, Stoke-on-Trent: Trentham Books.

Sammons, P., Power, S., Elliott, K., Robertson, P., Campbell, C. and Whitty, G. (2003) *Key Findings from the National Evaluation of the New Community Schools Pilot Programme in Scotland*, Edinburgh: Scottish Executive Education Department.

Schagen, I. and Goldstein, H. (2002) 'Do specialist schools add value? Some methodological problems', *Research Intelligence*, 80, pp. 12–15.

Schagen, I. and Schagen, S. (2003) 'Analysis of National Value-added Datasets to Assess the Impact of Selection on Pupil Performance', *British Educational Research Journal*, Vol. 29, No. 4, pp. 561–82.

Smith, N. (2004) 'Specialists' delight as they trounce rest', *The Times Educational Supplement*, 16 January.

Taylor, C. (2001) 'Specialist schools – the real facts behind their success', *Technology Colleges Trust News*, 18.

West, A., Noden, P., Kleinman, M. and Whitehead, C. (2000) *Examining the Impact of the Specialist Schools Programme*, London: Department for Education and Employment.

Young, M. (1999) 'Some reflections on the concepts of social exclusion and inclusion: beyond the third way', in Hayton, A. (ed.) *Tackling Disaffection and Social Exclusion*, London: Kogan Page.

THE PROCESS CURRICULUM

DES (Department of Education and Science) (1977) *Education in Schools: A Consultative Document*, London: HMSO.

DES (Department of Education and Science) (1977) *Curriculum 11–16* (Red Book 1), London: HMSO.

DES (Department of Education and Science) (1978) *Primary Education in England*, London: HMSO.

Desforges, C. (2003) *The Impact of Parental Involvement on Pupil Achievement*, London: DfES.

Mitchell, C. and Sackney, L. (2000) *Profound Improvement: Building Capacity for a Learning Community*, Netherlands: Swets and Zeitlinger.

Norwegian Ministry of Education (1994) *Core Curriculum for Primary and Secondary Schools*.

Rudduck, J. and Flutter, J. (2004) *How to Improve Your School*, London: Continuum.

Sayers, Dorothy L. (1948) *The Lost Tools of Learning*, London: Methuen.

Schools Council (1975) *Working Paper 53: The Whole Curriculum 13–16*, London: Methuen.

Schools Council (1981) *Working Paper 70: The Practical Curriculum*, London: Methuen.

Schools Council (1983) *Working Paper 75: Primary Practice*, London: Methuen.

Warnock, M. (1978) *Meeting Special Needs*, London: DES/HMSO.

THE IMPORTANCE OF FRIENDSHIP DURING PRIMARY TO SECONDARY SCHOOL TRANSFER

Adler, A. and Adler, P. (1998) *Peer Power: Preadolescent Culture and Identity*, New Brunswick: Rutgers University Press.

Ball, S. J., Bowe, R. and Gewirtz, S. (1996) 'School choice, social class and distinction: the realisation of social advantage in education', *Journal of Education Policy*, Vol. 11, No. 1, pp. 89–112.

Cotterell, J. (1996) *Social Networks and Social Influences in Adolescence*, London: Routledge.

Davies, B. (1982) *Life in the Classroom*, London: Routledge and Kegan Paul.

Delamont, S. (1991) 'The hit list and other horror stories: sex roles and school transfer', *Sociological Review*, 39, pp. 238–59.

Furman, W. (1989) 'The development of children's social networks', in Belle, D. (eds), *Children's Networks and Social Supports*, New York: Wiley.

Galton, M., Morrison, I. and Pell, T. (2000) *International Journal of Educational Research*, 33, pp. 341–63.

George, R. and Pratt, S. (2004) 'Transferring friendship: girls' and boys' friendships in the transition from primary to secondary school', *Children & Society* (forthcoming).

Gordon, T., Holland, J. and Lahelma, E. (2000) *Making Spaces: Citizenship and Difference in Schools*, Basingstoke: MacMillan Press Ltd.

Hargreaves, A. and Galton, M. (eds) (in press) *Moving from the Primary Classroom: 20 Years On*, London: Routledge.

Hargreaves, A., Earl, L. and Ryan, J. (1996) *Schooling for Change: Reinventing Education for Early Adolescence*, London: Falmer Press.

Kenway, J. and Bullen, E. (2001) *Consuming Children*, Buckingham: Open University Press.

Measor, L. and Woods, P. (1984) *Changing Schools: Pupil Perspectives on Transfer to a Comprehensive*, Buckingham: Open University Press.

O'Brien, M. (2003) 'Girls and transistion to second-level schooling in Ireland: "moving on" and "moving out"', *Gender and Education*, Vol. 15, No. 3, pp. 249–66.

Reay, D. (1998) *Class Work: Mothers' Involvement in their Children's Schooling*, London: UCL Press.

Reay, D. and Ball, S. J. (1998) ' "Spoilt for choice": the working classes and education markets', *Oxford Review of Education*, Vol. 23, No. 1, pp. 89–101.

Reay, D. and Lucey, H. (2000) 'Children, school choice and social differences', *Educational Studies*, Vol. 26, No. 1, pp. 83–100.

Shaw, J. (1996) *Education, Gender and Anxiety*, London: Taylor and Francis.

Thorne, B. (1993) *Gender Play: Girls and Boys in School*, Buckingham: Open University Press.

DEVELOPMENTS IN THE TRAINING OF TEACHERS

Beckett, F. (1999) 'Blunkett accepts school for profit', *New Statesman*, 15 January.

Benn, C. and Chitty, C. (eds) (1997) *Rethinking Education and Democracy: A Socialist Alternative for the Twenty-first Century*, London: Tufnell Press.

Bottery, M. (1999) 'Education under the new modernisers: an agenda for centralisation, illiberalism and inequality', *Cambridge Journal for Education*, Vol. 29, No. 1, pp. 103–18.

Brienes, W. (1980) 'The New Left and Michele's "iron law" social problems', *Community and Organisations*, 27, pp. 419–29.

Cole, M. (1998) 'Globalisation, modernisation and competitiveness: a critique of the New Labour project in education', *International Studies in the Sociology of Education*, Vol. 8, No. 3, pp. 315–32.

(DES) (Department for Education and Science) (1980) Education Act, London: HMSO.

(DES) Department for Education and Science (1988) Education Act, Department for Education/Welsh Office.

Foucault, M. (1980) *Power/Knowledge: Selected Interviews and Other Writings, 1972–1977*, New York and London: Harvester Wheatsheaf.

Goodson, I. (1999) 'The educational researcher as a public intellectual', *British Educational Research Journal*, Vol. 25, No. 3, pp. 277–97.

RETHINKING THE FUTURE

Allen, M., Benn, C., Chitty, C., Cole, M., Hatcher, R., Hirtt, N. and Rikowski, G. (1999) *Business, Business, Business: New Labour's Education Policy*, London: Tufnell Press.

Benn, C. and Chitty, C. (eds) (1997) *Rethinking Education and Democracy: A Socialist Alternative for the Twenty-first Century*, London: Tufnell Press.

Benn, C. and Cole, M. (1994) 'Lessons for the 21st century', *Red Pepper*, 4, p. 15.

Callinicos, A. (2000) *Equality*, Oxford: Polity.

Chitty, C. (ed.) (1991) *Changing the Future: Redprint for Education*, London: Tufnell Press.

Cole, M. (1998) 'Globalisation, modernisation and competitiveness: a critique of the New Labour project in education', *International Studies in Sociology of Education*, 8, pp. 315–32.

Cole, M. (2003) 'Might it be in the practice that it fails to succeed? A Marxist critique of claims for postmodernism and poststructuralism as forces for social change and social justice', *British Journal of Sociology of Education*, Vol. 24, No. 4, pp. 487–500.

Cole, M. (2004) 'New Labour, globalisation and social justice: the role of education', in McLaren, P., Sunker, H. and Fischman, G. (eds) *Critical Theories, Radical Pedagogies and Global Conflicts*, Lanham, Maryland: Rowman and Littlefield.

Cole, M. and Hill, D. (2002) ' "Resistance postmodernism" – progressive politics or Radical Left posturing', in Hill, D., McLaren, P., Cole, M. and Rikowksi, G. (eds) *Marxism Against Postmodernism in Educational Theory*, Lanham, MD: Lexington Books.

Cole, M., Hill, D. and Shan, S. (eds) (1997) *Promoting Equality in Primary Schools*, London: Cassell.

Epstein, D. (1993) *Changing Classroom Cultures: Anti-racism, Politics and Schools*, Stoke-on-Trent: Trentham Books.

Finlayson, A. (2003) *Making Sense of New Labour*, London: Lawrence and Wishart.

Freire, P. and Shor, I. (1987) *A Pedagogy for Liberation: Dialogues on Transforming Education*, Basingstoke: Macmillan Education.

Hill, D. (1999) *New Labour and Education: Policy, Ideology and the Third Way*, London: Tufnell Press.

Hill, D. (2004) 'Books, banks and bullets: controlling our mind – the global project of imperialistic and militaristic neo-liberalism and its effect on education policy', *Policy Futures in Education*, Vol. 2, No. 3 (forthcoming).

Hill, D. and Cole, M. (eds) (1999) *Promoting Equality in Secondary Schools*, London: Cassell.

Hillgate Group (1989) *Learning to Teach*, London: Claridge Press, in association with the Educational Research Centre.

Johnson, R. (1979) 'Really useful knowledge: radical education and working-class culture, 1790–1848', in Critcher, J. C. and Johnson, R. (eds), *Working Class Culture: Studies in History and Theory*, London: Hutchinson, pp. 75–102.

McLaren, P. (2000) *Che Guevara, Paulo Freire, and the Pedagogy of Revolution*, Lanham, Maryland: Rowman and Littlefield.

McMurtry, J. (1991) 'Education and the market model', *Journal of the Philosophy of Education*, 25, pp. 209–17.

Meiksins Wood, E. (1995) *Democracy Against Capitalism*, Cambridge: Cambridge University Press.

Rikowski, G. (2001) *The Battle in Seattle: Its Significance for Education*, London: Tufnell Press.

Rikowski, G. (2003) 'The business takeover of schools', *Mediactive: Ideas, Knowledge, Culture*, 1, pp. 91–108.

Shor, I. (1992) *Empowering Education: Critical Teaching for Social Change*, Chicago: University of Chicago Press.

Thatcher, M. (1993) *The Downing Street Years*, London: HarperCollins.

Wells, M. (2001) 'ITN cuts jobs and shifts towards lifestyle news', *The Guardian*, 22 November.

YOUNG PEOPLE AND EDUCATION

Beck, U. and Beck-Gernsheim, E. (2002) *Individualization*, London: Sage.

Blanden, J. (2002) 'Mobility has fallen', *CentrePiece*, Vol. 7, No. 2, pp. 8–13.

Bourdieu, P. (1979) *The Inheritors: French Students and Their Relation to Culture*, Chicago: University of Chicago Press.

Chisholm, L. and Hurrelman, K. (1996) 'Adolescence in modern Europe: pluralized transitions patterns and their implications for personal social risks', *Journal of Adolescence*, 18, pp. 128–58.

Coles, B. (1995) *Youth and Social Policy: Youth Citizenship and Young Careers*, London: UCL Press.

Evans, K., Rudd, P., Behrens, M., Kaluza, J. and Woolley, C. (2003) *Taking Control: Young Adults Talking about the Future in*

Education, Training and Work, Leicester: National Youth Agency with the Youth, Citizenship and Social Change ESRC Research Programme.

Furlong, A. and Cartmel, F. (1997) *Young People and Social Change*, Buckingham: Open University Press.

Giddens, A. (1991) *Modernity and Self Identity: Self and Society in the Late Modern Age*, Cambridge: Polity.

Jones, G. and Bell, R. (2000) *Balancing Acts: Youth, Parenting and Public Policy*, York: York Publishing Services for Joseph Rowntree Foundation.

Lash, S. and Urry, J. (1987) *The End of Organised Capitalism*, Cambridge: Polity.

McGrellis, S., Henderson, S., Holland, J., Sharpe, S. and Thomson, R. (2000) *Through the Moral Maze: A Quantitative Study of Young People's Values*, London: Tufnell Press.

Schoon, I., McCulloch, A., Joshi, H., Wiggins, D and Bynner, J. (2001) 'Transitions from school to work in a changing social context', *Young*, 9, pp. 4–22.

Scott, J. and Chaudhary, C. (2003) *Beating the Odds: Youth and Family Disadvantage*, Leicester: National Youth Agency with the Youth, Citizenship and Social Change ESRC Research Programme.

Thomson, R., Bell, R., Holland, J., Henderson, S., McGrellis, S. and Sharpe, S. (2002) 'Critical moments: choice, chance and opportunity in young people's narratives of transition, *Sociology*, Vol. 36, No. 2, pp. 335–54.

Thomson, R., Henderson, S. and Holland, J. (2003) 'Making the most of what you've got? Resources, values and inequalities in young people's transitions to adulthood', *Educational Review*, Vol. 55, No. 1, pp. 33–46.

WHY 'IMPROVING OWN LEARNING' IS IMPORTANT

Holt, J. (1972) *How Children Fail*, Harmondsworth: Penguin Books.

FOR FREE UNIVERSITIES, CAROLINE BENN'S RADICAL ALTERNATIVE FOR HIGHER EDUCATION

Benn, C. and Chitty, C. (1996) *Thirty Years On: Is Comprehensive Education Alive and Well or Struggling to Survive?*, 1st edn, London: David Fulton.
Paolo Freire (2003) *Pedagogy of Hope, Reliving 'Pedagogy of the Oppressed'*, London: Continuum.

ARRIVANT CONTEMPORARIES

Benn, T. (1994) *Years of Hope: Diaries, Papers and Letters 1940–1962*, ed. Ruth Winshore, London: Hutchinson.
Dash, P. (2002) *Foreday Morning*, London: BlackAmber Books.
Fullick, R. and Powell, G. (1979) *Suez: the Double War*, London: Hamish Hamilton.

COMPREHENSIVE SCHOOLING AND EDUCATIONAL INEQUALITY

Boli, J. (1989) *New Citizens for a New Society: The Institutional Origins of Mass Schooling in Sweden*, Oxford: Pergamon.
Boudon, R. (1974) *Education, Opportunity and Social Inequality*, London: Wiley-Interscience.
Brown, A. (1997) 'Becoming skilled during a time of transition: observations from Europe', monograph, Guilford, University of Surry, Department of Educational Studies.
Brown, P., Green, A. and Lauder, H. (2001) *High Skills: Globalization, Competitiveness and Skills Formation*, Oxford: Oxford University Press.
Brubaker, R. (1992) *Citizenship and Nationhood in France and Germany*, Cambridge, MA: Harvard University Press.
Carnoy, M. (1993) 'School improvement: is privatization the answer', in J. Hannaway and M. Carnoy (eds) *Decentralization and School Improvement*, San Francisco: Jossey-Bass.

CEDEFOP (1987) *The Role of the Social Partners in Vocational Training and Further Training in the Federal Republic of Germany*, Berlin: CEDEFOP.

Coomber, L. and Reeves, J. (1973) *Science Education in Nineteen Countries: An Empirical Study*, New York: Wiley.

Cummings, W. K. (1980) *Education and Equality in Japan*, Princeton, NJ: Princeton University Press.

Department for Education/Scottish Office (1992) *Teaching and Learning in Japanese Elementary Schools*, London: HMSO.

Dokka, H.-J. (1967), *Fra allmueskole til folkeskole*, Bergen: Universitetsforlaget.

Dore, R. (1997) *The Diploma Disease: Education, Qualification and Development*, 2nd ed., London: Institute of Education.

Dore, R. (1982) *Education in Tokugawa Japan*, London, Athlone.

Dore, R. and Sako, M. (1989) *How the Japanese Learn to Work*, London: Routledge.

Duru-Bellat, M. and Mingat, A. (1999) 'How do junior secondary schools operate? Academic achievement, grading and streaming of students', in A. Leschinsky and K. Mayer (eds) *The Comprehensive School Experiment Revisited: Evidence from Western Europe*, Berlin: Peter Lang.

Esping-Andersen, G. (1985) *Politics against Market*, Princeton, NJ: Princeton University Press.

Esping-Andersen, G. 'Unequal Opportunities and Social Inheritance', in M. Corak (ed.) (forthcoming) *The Dynamics of Intergenerational Income Mobility*, Cambridge: Cambridge University Press.

Featherman, D. L. and Hauser, R. M. (1978) 'Design for a replicate study of social mobility in the United States', in K. Land and S. Spilerman (eds) *Social Indicator Models*, New York: Russell Sage Foundation.

Garnier, M. and Raffalovitch, L. E. (1984) 'The evolution of equality of educational opportunity in France', *Sociology of Education*, Vol. 57, No. 1, pp. 1–11.

Green, A. (1997) 'Educational achievement in centralized and decentralized systems: a comparative analysis', in A. H. Halsey, H. Lauder, P. Brown and A. S. Wells (eds), *Education: Culture,*

Economy and Society, Oxford: Oxford University Press, pp. 283–99.

Green, A. (1997) *Education, Globalisation and the Nation State*, London: Macmillan.

Green, A. (1999) 'East Asian skills formation systems and the challenge of globalization', *Journal of Education and Work*, Vol. 21, No. 3, pp. 253–79.

Green, A. (2000) 'Converging paths or ships passing in the night? An "English" critique Japanese School Reform', *Journal of Comparative Education*, Vol. 36, No. 4.

Green, A., Preston, J. and Sabates, R. (2003a) Education, equality and Social Cohesion: a distributional approach, *Working Paper No. 7 Wider Benefits of Learning Centre*, Institute of Education.

Green, A., Preston, J. and Sabates, R. (2003b) 'Education, equality and social Cohesion: a distributional approach', *Compare*, pp. 451–68.

Green, A., Wolf, A. and Leney, T. (1999) *Convergences and Divergences in European Education and Training Systems*, Bedford Way Papers, London, Institute of Education.

Halsey, A. H., Heath, A. and Ridge, J. M. (1980) *Origins and Destinations*, Oxford: Clarendon Press.

Handl, J. (1986) 'Sex and class specific inequalities in educational opportunity in Western Germany, 1950–1982,' unpublished.

HMI (Her Majesty's Inspectorate) (1991) *Aspects of Upper Secondary and Higher Education in Japan*, London: HMSO.

Holloway, S. D. (1988) 'Concepts of ability and effort in Japan and the United States', *Review of Educational Research*, Vol. 58, No. 3, pp. 327–45.

Husen, T. (1998) *International Study of Achievement in Maths: A Comparison of Twelve Countries*, Vol. 2, International Association of Evaluation in Educational Achievement.

Ichikawa, S. (1989) 'Japanese education in American eyes: a response to William K. Cummings', *Comparative Education*, Vol. 25, No. 3, pp. 303–307.

International Association of Evaluation of Educational Achievement (IEA) (1988) *Science Achievement in Seventeen Countries*, London: Pergamon Press.

Isling, Å. (1984) *Kampen för och mot en demokratisk skola 1*, Stockholm: Sober Förlags AB.

Jonsson, J. (1999) 'Dismantling the class society through education reform? The success and failure of Swedish school politics', in Leschinsky, A. and Mayer, K. (eds) *The Comprehensive School Experiment Revisited: Evidence from Western Europe*, Berlin: Peter Lang.

Lauder, H., Hughes, D. and Watson, S. (1999) *Trading in Futures: Why Markets in Education Don't Work*, Buckingham: Open University Press.

Leschinsky, A. and Mayer, K. (eds) (1999) *The Comprehensive School Experiment Revisited: Evidence from Western Europe*, Berlin: Peter Lang.

Marsden, D. and Ryan, P. (1995) 'Work, labour markets and vocational preparation: Anglo-German comparisons of training in intermediate skills', in L. Bash and A. Green (eds), *World Yearbook of Education: Youth, Education and Work*, London: Kogan Page, pp. 67–79.

McLean, M. (1990) *Britain and a Single Market Europe*, London: Kogan Page.

Nickell, S. and Layard, R. (1998) *Institutions and Economic Performance*, LSE Discussion Paper, London: LSE.

OECD (1994) *School: A Matter of Choice*, Paris: OECD.

OECD (2000) *Literacy in the Information Age*, Paris: OECD.

OECD (2001) *Knowledge and Skills for Life: First Results from PISA 2000*, Paris: OECD.

OSA (Organisante voor Stratyegisch Arbeidsmarktonderzoek) (1994) *Structure of Vocational Education and Training and the Match between Education and Work: An International Comparison*, Synthesis report by J. Gordon, J.-P. Jallard and D. Parkes, Paris: European Institute of Education and Social Policy.

Passim, H. (1965) *Society and Education in Japan*, New York: Teachers' College Press.

Perkin, H. (1996) *The Third Revolution: Professional Ethics in the Modern World*, London: Routledge.

Ragin, C. (1981) 'Comparative sociology and the comparative method', *International Journal of Comparative Sociology*, XX11, 1–2, pp. 102–17.

Shavit, Y. and Blossfeld, H. P. (1983) *Persistent Inequality: Changing Educational Attainment in Thirteen Countries*, Boulder: Westview Press.

Sjöstrand, W. (1965), *Pedagogikens Historia 3:2*, Lund: CWK Gleerups Förlag.

Skovgaard-Petersen, V. (1976), *Dannelse og demokratic*, Gyldendals pædagogiske bibliotek, Kbh.

Streeck, W. (1987) 'Skills and the limits of neo-liberalism: the enterprise of the future as a place of learning', *Work, Employment and Society*, Vol. 3, No. 1, pp. 89–104.

Streeck, W. (1997) 'German capitalism: does it exist? Can it survive?', *New Political Economy*, 2(2), pp. 237–56.

Takeuchi, T. (1991) 'Myth and reality in the Japanese educational selection system', *Comparative Education*, Vol. 27, No. 1, pp. 101–12.

White, M. (1987) *The Japanese Educational Challenge*, London: Macmillan.

Whitty, G., Power, S. and Halpin, G. (1998) *Devolution and Choice in Education: The School, the State and the Market*, Buckingham: Open University Press.

Winkler, D. (1993) 'Fiscal decentralization and accountability: experience in four countries', in J. Hannaway and M. Carnoy (eds) *Decentralization and School Improvement*, San Francisco: Jossey-Bass.

Winther-Jenson, T., Larsen, J. and Wiborg, S. (forthcoming) 'Education and social integration: a comparative study of the comprehensive school system in Scandinavia', in Mattheou, M. (ed.) *Comparative Study of Education Problems and Policies in the World*.

Index